Dietrich Fischer-Dieskau

Robert Schumann
Words and Music

Dietrich Fischer-Dieskau

Robert Schumann
Words and Music

The Vocal Compositions

Translated by Reinhard G. Pauly

AMADEUS PRESS
Reinhard G. Pauly, Ph.D., General Editor
Portland, Oregon

For Jörg Demus

Cordial thanks are extended to
Frau Ulla Küster for her valuable assistance
in the completion of this book

© 1981 as
Robert Schumann: Wort und Musik—Das Vokalwerk
by Deutsche Verlags-Anstalt GmbH,
Stuttgart

Translation © 1988 by Amadeus Press
All rights reserved

ISBN 0-931340-06-3
Printed in Singapore

AMADEUS PRESS
9999 S.W. Wilshire
Portland, Oregon 97225

Library of Congress Cataloging-in-Publication Data

Fischer-Dieskau, Dietrich, 1925-
   Robert Schumann, words and music.

   Translation of: Robert Schumann, Wort und Musik.
   Bibliography: p.
   Includes index.
   1. Schumann, Robert, 1810-1856. Vocal music.
2. Vocal music--History and criticism.   I. Title.
ML410.S4F613 1988   784.3'0092'4   88-10411
ISBN 0-931340-06-3

Contents

Chapter 1

Robert Schumann is among those figures in cultural history who seem to elude objective assessment. Historical and cultural fashions have distorted his picture thanks to emotional or nationalistic prejudices, and even more importantly these prejudices have led to underestimating his role in musical and cultural history. It is to Schumann's credit that in the many years since his death no fitting historical niche has been defined to memorialize his massive and lasting contribution to the arts. Thus, it is not surprising that in spite of his ample legacy of diaries and writings, even the most recent studies of 19th Century musical esthetics (including the key question of program music) have ignored Schumann's decisive influence. Such a failure to come to grips with his place makes it all the more necessary to give close consideration to the questions Schumann posed and to the answers he put forward, all of which can only be found by careful interpretation and evaluation of his music.

The extraordinary complexity of Schumann's work can be confusing, which in turn creates special challenges for both interpreters and listeners. We encounter in his work echoes of the past and premonitions of the future; the familiar and the exotic; the simple style of folk song and complicated counterpoint; miniatures juxtaposed with larger forms. In order to understand the essence of his art, we can quite reasonably turn to the central role E.T.A. Hoffmann's musical esthetics had upon Schumann's views. The figure of "Kapellmeister Kreisler" depicted in the small volume *Lichte Stunden eines wahnsinnigen Musikers (The Lucid Hours of an Insane Musician)* haunts not only Schumann's piano work "Kreisleriana." Yet, Schumann's music was to an even greater degree influenced by Jean Paul, whom the young Schumann revered as his literary idol.

The poetic posture and elements which Schumann found in the writings of Jean Paul inspired him to seek an analogous poetic statement in music. While Schumann's music arises from the wellspring of lyrical emotion, he does not allow it to take the form of random melodic outpourings but rather shapes it in the context of the poetic model derived from Paul. Schumann carefully structured and organized his musical expression to give a concrete and comprehensible form to the stuff of human emotions, in all its nuances. To do so he employed carefully thought out and well defined guidelines to mold both the form and content of his composition into what he referred to as the "poetic state."

Romanticism, as Schumann viewed it, was defined by and the equivalent of this poetic state. Thus the creative objective of music was to lead the listener to a heightened esthetic experience. The musical means for invoking this heightened awareness depended upon stimulating the listener's imagination so as to move him or her away from the mundane domain of reality and allow him to "float"—to use one of Schumann's favorite terms.

However, Schumann's esthetic objective was not satisfied by such dreamy esthetic experiences, as has often been assumed. As he matured artistically he was increasingly driven to develop more precise and concise musical means to define the esthetic sensibilities he wished to evoke. He believed that a composition possessed "true musical character" only "when the sentiment was clearly expressed, so clearly in fact, that no other interpretation was possible."

In articulating his esthetic views, Hoffmann had assigned purely instrumental music to a loftier esthetic position than vocal music—indeed, that instrumental music represented an "elevated style." He insisted that music was only compromised by words and so absolute music was better suited to express the limitless yearning of the human soul while at the same time it provided a purer and more complete, hence independent musical form. Hoffmann's view that instrumental music was "true" music was closely tied to his esthetic ideal of the sublime in art.

However, Schumann shared with many of his contemporaries of the pre-1848 period the view which saw the word as the new, redemptive power in the renewal of art. This posture reinforced Schumann's growing sensibility of and sensitivity to the hidden interactions between word and tone which in part explains his early hypersensitive behavior. His highly charged perceptions led not only to the enormous influence which Jean Paul's writings had upon him, but also to his haunting and obsessive vision of having a double. This sense of a divided nature not only informs Schubert's late *Heine-Lied,* but might well be considered, as some have done, the lifelong division between Schumann's literary and musical natures. Jean Paul, who shared this sense of a dual consciousness, yearned for the integrated existence of the simple folk, hoping to realize his childhood dream of again becoming and remaining whole.

Here we are reminded of the archetype found in the early self-portrait of Courbet entitled "The Man Mad With Fear." The obvious discontinuity between the figure and the wild chaotic landscape symbolized for an entire generation the personal romantic urge to escape the strictures of 19th Century society and to realize a new, integrated, and more harmonious ideal. The hidden forces which compel the anguished figure into the abyss were replete with allegorical significance; we are reminded of Schumann's life-long fear of heights and of falling. Both the painter Courbet and the composer Schumann drew inspiration from the same literary sources: Goethe's *Werther* and *Faust,* as well as Byron's *Manfred.* The themes which appeared virtually simultaneously in Courbet's

Gustave Courbet, "The Man Mad With Fear"

painting of 1843 and Schumann's *Heine* Cycles of 1840, were later explored and espoused by the intelligentsia in the latter half of the century under the slogan, "Without Morals or Religion," and mark the death of Romantic illusion. In a letter to his patron, Bruyas, Courbet inveighed against the vanity and triviality of society and identified this shallowness as both the cause of his persistent melancholy, as well as a stimulus for his attacks upon the Philistines. Schumann's musical journal published in Leipzig reflects the same concerns which remained a leitmotif of his approach to life and art.

This shared vision marked a radical movement away from received views of the role of art and the meaning of life. The aim was to do away with the conventional, the customary, and the comfortable in order to discover or recover an integrated sense of life. This new view, styled Realism, can be seen as the successor to the Enlightenment of the 18th Century and the revolutionary epoch of the early 19th Century. Realism turned against everything metaphysical, seeking to find the meaning of life in social ethics, not in religious morality. But, the reader must surely ask, do not music historians clearly place Schumann among the Romantics? Undoubtedly the greater part of his artistic output is rightfully placed in the context of Romanticism. But Schumann took up the challenge of moving European cultural values in the direction of Realism. He did so in ways quite characteristic of the man: by opposing the conventional spirit of his time with a kind of passive resistance in making his musical statements.

However, Schumann the writer was more direct and openly radical. His reviews in the *Neue Zeitschrift für Musik* quite clearly and vigorously attacked the "Philistine" values he saw as the mark of his time. His contempt for operatic practices was only marginally less vitrolic. In his polemics he derided Meyerbeer and the Italian Style, employing such scathing phrases as "vulgarity," "distortion," "affectedness," "immorality," and "non-music." His German nationalism also occasionally surfaces and unhappily leads him at times to lose his objectivity. With righteous zeal he derided Bellini's operas, *La Sonnambula* and *Norma,* as the "most tedious things on earth." In his judgment, the first two chords of Beethoven's *Eroica* symphony reflected more *melos* than "ten melodies by Bellini."

Schubert reacted to the anti-German views of his teacher Salieri by concentrating on the German *Klavierlied.* Similarly Schumann juxtaposed his *Lieder* with Italian song remarking, "In order to defeat foreign sing-song and to support and revive our people's love of music which expresses natural, deep and clear emotion in an artistic way, our good German *Lied* must be cultivated and protected." Until he was ready to include traditional German elements in his own composition, however, his musical protest was typically masked by a variety of devices which often even obscured the distinctions between musical genres. Thus a brief glance at the title of a piece is often insufficient to classify it as an instrumental or a vocal work. The interchangeability of the "sung" and "unsung" word (as well as the indeterminacy of his writing) has often been regarded as characteristic of Schumann's music and indeed of Romanticism in general with its fondness for mystification. In view of this it would be quite wrong to label the instrumental music of the period as "program music," as Mendelssohn made perfectly clear when he explained that his "Songs Without Words" expressed thoughts too specific to be contained in words.

The connection between poetry and music in Schumann's compositions only seems to be more obvious than in those by Mendelssohn, whom, incidentally, Schumann viewed as a composer in the tradition of Eichendorff. When the young Schumann recommended that those playing or listening to his "Papillons" read the conclusion of Jean Paul's *Flegeljahre,* he was not indicating that a detailed explanation of his music could be found in Paul's writings. Rather, he hoped to provide performers and audiences with a glimpse of the world that had inspired him. He meant to indicate a point of departure rather than an exact model.

Schumann was, however, frequently disappointed: his contemporaries did not understand his music at all, even though Schumann had referred them to the specific chapter of the novel. "I've recommended that they read something of Jean Paul, but still they demand to know exactly where Jacobine hides, where the brother curses and what he is cursing. And when they can't figure it out they talk about secret codes and ambiguous riddles, complaining that a work of art should offer its own explanation. Could it be that it contains too much vague emotion?"

Did Schumann really write music merely to serve the ideas of Jean Paul? He began to ask his listeners, "Don't you think these pieces are clear by themselves?" He begged for confirmation of his belief that he had written nothing but music. But his confirmation was not forthcoming. To his contemporaries, his unusual musical poetry must have seemed an obscure form of shorthand. A few short musical measures often contained the emotion of an entire *Lied* or *Romanze*. There was no "filler:" strictly secondary material or empty virtuosity were avoided. One harmonic subtlety followed another. The rhythm changed from moment to moment. Different styles were mixed, and melodies were mysteriously interwoven, never appearing twice in the same form. With different turns, coloristic changes, and shifts, Schumann provided ever new and exciting nuances to his compositions.

The enormous extent of Schumann's written commentary—which recalls to mind the compulsion today's composers seem to feel to comment on their music—failed to prevent a divergence of opinion between music scholars and practicing musicians. Thus his works, particularly the compositions for piano and for orchestra, are performed today more than ever, and thanks to recordings even his least known works are readily accessible. Schumann's *Lieder,* most of which had sunk into obscurity, are once again regularly performed and recorded. Yet an examination of his music and his place (even in the framework of simple "historical" interest) is seen as fundamentally useless.

But this latter view cannot be sustained, for to this day both Schumann's admirers and critics view his life and works in terms of a creative "break." This distortion has been compounded by the incorrect chronological placement of specific works, which has led to mistaken value judgements. This is true, for instance, for songs which have been assigned misleading opus numbers in well-known editions. The real task before music scholars is to identify the unifying principles in Schumann's work and to seek out his unique contributions to the evolution of musical and cultural thought and practices rather than futilely searching for those works in which he remains true to his Romantic beginnings. They must come to understand and explicate his effort to devise and utilize new stylistic means and larger forms which cannot be equated to the abandonment of his early directions.

No other form is better suited to a full understanding of Schumann's growth and decline than a thorough and penetrating study of his *Lieder.* His songs, though varying in degree of significance, were a continuing and recurring preoccupation throughout his creative life span; further, they reveal his spiritual evolution in his choice of texts. Through Schumann's version of a "musical diary" we can see how his life affected his compositions without actually becoming their subject matter.

Advocates of the theory that Schumann's creative decline began early in his career, basing their thesis on the course of his illness, should consider whether their views of Schumann's fate are not perhaps prejudiced by hindsight. Rather they might ask if it wasn't his spirit which shaped his body. To this end they might search for evidence of deep-seated motivations or alternatively a profound psychic inertia. It is true that Schumann's life was marked by periods of recurring illness which in turn led to creative lapses, followed by periods of hectic activity when his health returned. Self-destructive tendencies, torturous exertion, crumbling resistance and an apparent premonition of having to give up were juxtaposed in Schumann with an extraordinary will to live and create which positively influenced his life, his work, and his goals.

The word "genius" has often been used with reference to Schumann, triggering all those negative associations typical of our present aversion to such labels and the men to whom they are applied. The present era, employing the technological tools of science and social science, is ideologically committed to establishing universal equality. A society devoted to equal rights for all ignores and seeks to deny the role of fate as something that must be conquered. (The fundamental requirement is that the individual is responsible for the outcome of his life.) Yet even today we must understand that in Schumann's case the body was a driving force of inspiration at the same time that it was a burden. That decline, though setting in early, went hand in hand with a growing genius. Surrender was counterpoised with creative impulse. Creation and creator became an internal dialogue, one which was meant to be shared by the ears of all. Uncovering the proper medium to convey this internal dialogue was not only Schumann's problem: the competition between the human voice conveying the word on the one side and abstract instrumental music on the other pervades the entire development of music.

Mozart, Beethoven, and Schubert had already broken away from a strong bias for instrumental music. With the late 18th and early 19th Century revival of German literature, vocal music regained its former artistic prominence. Almost overnight, it seems, the poets Voss, Gleim, and Jacobi appeared, followed by Klopstock and Claudius, along with Herder's scholarly collections of folk songs and Goethe's poetry. This renewal of the written word facilitated the musical expression of emotional states and particularly so when feeling was to be expressed through music. With their newly augmented vigor, texts of genuine literary value inspired music and musicians to incorporate them in song.

Schubert especially benefited from this literary revival, though fewer poems of high literary quality were available to him than to Schumann. Nevertheless, the Austrian was blessed with the treasures of Goethe's poetry as well as that of Claudius, Schiller, Schlegel, and Hoelty. In his use of the poetry of Rückert and Uhland, we have but a glimmer of the extraordinary genius which he possessed. Unfortunately, the first section of Heine's *Book of Songs* appeared only in 1827, a short time before Schubert's death, so that the cycle using these poems remained but a fragment.

No one can dispute the fact that the advances realized by the creator of "Winterreise" were greater and more significant than those made by the *Lieder* composer, Robert Schumann. Schubert's achievement is made even more significant when one considers the extraordinary instability of the language in Schubert's time. Schumann, on the other hand, benefited from newly won literary accomplishments including a newly developed sense of purity of the language and an accepted grammar. The poet Alxinger, shortly before Mozart's death, confessed that he patiently looked up nearly every word in a dictionary before he would dare put it on paper. With this language problem in mind, our respect for the linguistic usage of Mozart and Schubert, neither of whom could be called well-educated by today's standards, can only be heightened. Further, Schubert often composed whatever texts came to hand (for good poetry was still a rare thing), while Schumann was able to pick and choose from a wide variety of first-rate poetry with which he was acquainted through his father's publishing house and book store. "Why select mediocre poems and almost certainly ruin the music?" he wrote. "True poetry encircled with a wreath of music—there is nothing more beautiful. But to waste music on common poetry: why bother?"

Having grown up surrounded with books, Schumann viewed the world through the eyes of a poet and spoke the poet's language. This easy familiarity was reflected both in his acute esthetic sensitivity and his deeply introspective nature. Experience and pleasure were defined and conditioned for Schumann by literary models, and these early artistic impressions profoundly influenced him throughout his life. As a young man, Schumann and his contemporaries passionately espoused the ideals of self-denial, world-weariness, and the transitory quality of life.

Goethe's *Werther* became the symbol for the curious emotional climate of the period: Werther, unable to integrate the realities of life with his emotional life. One is reminded of Schubert's diary entry: "No one understands the pain or the joy of others! We think we grow closer, yet we remain estranged. What torture for those who realize this!" And August von Platen complains, "The most beautiful thing also perishes most quickly. Only pain endures." Ludwig Tieck philosophizes in a similar vein in his "Magelone": "Joy is only deeper pain," "Life is a dark grave." Justinus Kerner, whose poetry Schumann preserved for posterity, writes, "Poetry is unbearable pain, and true song can come only from a heart burning with immense suffering."

Schumann probably perceived his early literary ambitions as a detour from his profound commitment to composition which tinged his early music with dilettantism—but as a mature musician he remained a poet. His music and poetry were of a piece. Even his literary publications clearly confirm this unity of word and music. In an essay on Beethoven, he intentionally uses musical form by creating the literary equivalent of a symphonic first movement with a slow introduction, a transition to Allegro, and contrasting themes which are ultimately integrated.

On the other hand, it is clear that even before he began composing *Lieder* Schumann was sensitive to the constraints which the word imposed on the musical imagination. This is made clear by his frequent reference to his practice of inventing titles for his piano pieces only after he had completed the music. He criticized the titles given to the movements of Beethoven's "Pastoral" Symphony, saying they inhibited imagination. His aversion to the program music of Liszt and Berlioz further illustrates this sense of the strictures imposed upon music by words.

Commenting upon his *Lieder,* Schumann said of the relationship between the word and the musician, "The poetry should be to the singer as a bride in the arms of her groom—free, happy, and complete. Only then will the song realize a divine quality." Further, he insisted the song must express the poem in its entirety, rather than strictly observing the meaning of individual words or phrases. He noted that whenever he concentrated solely on words while composing a ballad or song, an unsatisfactory multiplication of themes resulted. Only with continuing and constant practice over some years was Schumann able to clarify for himself what a song should contain and so gradually overcame his early hesitation in composing for the human voice. He described this content in a discussion of works by Burgmüller in 1839: "Poetic interpretation; animated detail; a felicitous relationship between voice and instrument; the freedom, understanding, and pulsing life which permeates the whole." Here the particulars of the ideal song toward which Schumann was working are clearly defined. Schumann saw the addition of the vocal element as opening up entire new realms of musical imagination. Yet when Franz Liszt, in his essay of 1855, described Schumann as concurring with the idea of program music, he intentionally misconstrued Schumann's views as expressed above. This misconstruction, against which Schumann could no longer defend himself, has persisted in musical circles.

These misapprehensions have persisted to the present, carried forward by commentators accustomed to thinking in terms of musical motifs in the manner of Wagner and his *neudeutsche* friends. Resorting erroneously to familiar and facile canons of interpretation, they attributed symbolic character to particular motifs. Such motifs were surely an element in Schumann's compositional style, but only as they are a part of every composer's body of techniques. Too often such labelling of motifs misses the mark and leads to misunderstanding. If even only one in four attempts to define a motif is inconsistent with the composer's intention, such a canon of interpretation is clearly questionable.

In this light it is worthwhile to consider Liszt's defense of program music. Had he not so overvalued literary references, his views might have converged with those of his friend, Schumann, who assigned an equal weight to word and music. At the beginning of the century, Ludwig Tieck had coined the term "poetic," which he conceived as the essence of "absolute" instrumental music, a view which quickly assumed a central role in Romantic music. Schumann's conception of music developed in quite a different way than Liszt's; he viewed the "poetic" in terms of artistic intensification in contrast to the triviality of mere musical depiction. Schumann's definition of "poetic" does not imply the dependence of music on the text, but rather the equality of the two. But beyond this Schumann viewed the "poetic" as the essence of all art, which is found in its purest form in music. It was this view which transformed Schumann from poet to composer.

Looking back to 1826, the year of his father's death, we can discover the beginnings of young Robert's literary interpretation of his life in his unfinished novel *Selene.* Like its hero Gustav, the author wished to be "silent by nature, full of doubt, ambition and despair, yet whole and vital. He is a painter and a poet, a musical poet (*Tondichter*)."

This is an early description of Schumann's vision of *Lieder.* The text is woven into a complex web of simultaneous meanings, enigmatic and impossible to untangle. Its composition goes beyond the expression of individual words or musical tones, finally realizing an artistic unity, as envisioned by the composer.

This conception of the poem's wholeness should on no account be confused with formless mood painting. Rather, Schumann used the unique perceptive quality of music to infuse each passing moment with a sense of the present. This was bound to lead him to small musical forms—forms that are a continuous whole, often having the quality and characteristics of aphorisms. Following on the heels of Schubert's great works (full of portent), Schumann's goal was a far-reaching (and meaningful) next step. Despite the attempts of a multitude of successors to make Schumann's lyrical ideas their own, none were able to do more than imitate his specific practices. Only Hugo Wolf, of the group inspired by Wagner, and which for over a hundred years has been considered hostile to the Schumann/Brahms circle, was able to master the artistic synthesis developed by Schumann in a uniquely individual way.

We must remember that Schumann had originally turned away from vocal music, since contemporary thought considered "absolute" music the purest embodiment of the Romantic ideal. But Schumann in time rejected the idea of a "particular Romantic school." "Romanticism does not rest in figures or forms; it will naturally occur if the composer is a poet at all," he wrote in 1839. Just as he viewed the prosaic or ordinary as antipodal to pure art, so he thought a slavish devotion to non-musical elements endangered the highest metaphysical values by straying into an empty wasteland of compositional and interpretive virtuosity. He cautioned against depending on programs which inevitably lead to superficial tone painting and resort to common, sentimental, emotional responses.

Schumann's early compositional years were devoted exclusively to the piano, followed by the period in which he devoted himself principally to *Lieder* writing, yet both periods were mutually dependent and closely related. How much so is made clear in a letter from 1840, reiterating his desire to be understood: "I hope I shall accomplish this more easily through my songs." Though unwilling and unable to make artistic compromises, his continuing hope throughout his life was for acceptance by his listeners. Nevertheless, as he moved from composing for the piano to songs he continued to rely upon psychological insight, notably in his use of harmony. The use of "absolute" musical rules diminished. Relative to the practice of his predecessors, the piano becomes more important—indeed the equal of the voice; which is the hallmark of Schumann's songs. This equality distinguishes the song writing of Schumann and Schubert; while the role of the piano was substantial in the latter's songs it is seldom given a position truly equal with the voice. The exceptions include "Gruppe aus dem Tartarus" or "An Schwager Kronos," with their symphonic compactness. Schubert's accompaniment typically only supports the melody, introducing it and surrounding it, but giving it few opportunities for complementing the melody or for independent interpolations. This can only rarely be said of Schumann's songs, in which the voice part by itself often is incomprehensible, and only becomes meaningful when achieving this new relationship with the piano. The shaping of the vocal part is only a part of the creative thought imbedded in Schumann's songs.

In Schumann's work the voice usually shares control of the *melos* with the piano. In some cases, however, the voice alone carries the meaning, at which times the piano must be satisfied with occasional characteristic interjections, as in Heine's *Tragödie II: Es fiel ein Reif in der Frühlingsnacht.* Schumann's intricate piano style serves "to penetrate the life of the poem," especially in an introduction or postlude. The musician becomes the poet's companion, complementing or commenting on that which is unsaid or referred to by allusion, but never becoming mired in programmatic representation.

Thus Schumann's demand that singers learn both the vocal and piano parts equally well has become a matter of accepted practice. Without such attention to the entire piece any understanding of the composer's intentions becomes unthinkable. Certainly, in some folk-song-like *Lieder* such as *An den Sonnenschein,* the melody rests entirely in the voice part, but typically the piano assumes the principal role. Behind Schumann's assertion that the voice cannot express the entirety of a song, we hear the voice of the master of the piano.

Many of Schumann's contemporaries accused him of allowing elaborate piano writing to inhibit the role of the singer. At the end of the last century, most commentators complained of the harmonic variety, which in their opinion stifled the expressive power of the songs. Such objections doubtlessly arose from uncertainty in matters of style criticism. Schumann went considerably beyond Schubert's sharply defined melody lines. If Schumann wishes to produce an unsettled, dreamlike atmosphere, his melodic lines are left incomplete and are not intended to be fully developed. This technique is employed in songs such as *Mein Wagen rollet langsam* or *Resignation.* Especially in late works, such as those mentioned, but also in many parts of *Szenen aus Goethes Faust,* the vocal line has become a musical declamation, while the actual poetic thought is developed in the accompaniment. Schumann's arrogant disavowal of his early melodies and his wistful condemnation of the harmonic style of his youth, saying, "Melody is the war cry of dilettantes," must be understood in this context. Eventually he disclaimed the worth of his early, epoch-making masterworks, calling his C major Fantasy, Opus 17, "vulgar stuff."

All his early creative work through 1839, from Opus 1 through Opus 23, as far as it was completed and published, was dedicated to the piano. Such an intense concentration on a particular genre remained a Schumann characteristic. He exhausted all possibilities within a particular area before moving on. Thus he moved from the piano to *Lieder,* then to chamber music and symphony, and finally to the longer and larger oratorios and operas.

His truly explosive production of *Lieder* which occupied all of the year 1840 proved fruitful for his later work. Out of this effort Schumann learned how to introduce a more elaborate polyphony into his later compositions. He used shifting harmonies to express ideas which were clarified for him by the text, making harmony one of his most precise means of expression. The *Lieder* clearly reveal an enhanced melodic inventiveness when compared to the piano works. Schumann used much melodic raw material from his piano compositions, but a purifying influence of text and voice is apparent. An unreserved obsession with and pursuit of the spontaneous idea was turned aside. Instead a more conscious and controlled use of his wealth of ideas emerged, coupled with a sustained effort to put the tools of composition into the service of the musical phrase and its associated text.

Schumann's study of Bach's works proved fruitful. From it Schumann emerged as virtually a new musician—one who had mastered musical forms. The "new era in music" which he saw dawning in Germany centered mainly on himself. Its watchwords were "strength, nature, truth." In his songs, Schumann included nuances which Schubert had not yet defined—depicting humor, satire, irony, tender femininity, and multi-faceted expression. Though it was not close to his own heart, Schumann expressed the sense of the troubadour's courtly love wonderfully and with unrestrained chivalric exuberance, yet with a powerful command of form. His settings of folk songs from the *Wunderhorn* collection are suitably and appropriately naive, but with a second-hand naïvete,

for on the same day he produced a finely spun fairy tale.

His next outburst of creativity came just three months after his marriage. Though a surprise even to himself, this move into the area of symphonic music was quite consistent with his progress as a composer. Clara Schumann summed up the fruits of their first year of marriage saying, "It is often claimed that marriage kills the spirit. My Robert has produced the clearest evidence to the contrary: three symphonies and over one hundred *Lieder!"*

His frequent turns in quest of new compositional forms were certainly motivated by creative impatience and the search for fresh sources of inspiration. Near the end of a creative phase we can on occasion sense just a hint of fatigue, surely the result of intense exertion. As the exploration of a form neared completion, especially when it involved intense concentration of the magnitude of the "Year of Songs," his interest in the form began to decline as he sought out something new. This sense is confirmed by Schumann's comment in 1837: "Those who remain entrenched in the same forms and musical relationships finally become mannerists or philistines; there is nothing more damaging to the artist than prolonged immersion in familiar forms."

For this reason we must treat careless and oft-repeated references to the so-called "signs of decay" in Schumann's work with considerable skepticism. Signs of decay can only be discussed in the context of his final breakdown. Schumann's musical legacy includes not only the remarkable qualities of his piano style but also his subjective affirmation of faith. He had endowed the miniature form of the *Lied* with a new sensibility. He developed the *Liederspiel* for several voices, and finally the secular oratorio. Unhappily, however, his effort to establish his secular oratorio was denied unprejudiced evaluation and wide circulation due to the fact that he developed it during the last phase of his creative life.

The fluctuations in the quality of Schumann's late works can better be described as the result of musical experimentation than ascribed to problems of health. The issue is further clouded by the many homespun theories about the course of Schumann's illness— theories which ignore the results of medical findings and so do not clarify matters. Clearly Schumann's illness was a formidable handicap with which he had to contend from his early years. Nevertheless, until the catastrophic events associated with his attempted suicide and admission to an institution, he clearly coped successfully with his handicap and worked with clarity and admirable concentration on new problems of style, expression, and form. His artistic gaze remained fixed on developing a new music which he did not live to see—a kind of music which was simple and clear—not intended to overwhelm an audience in the manner of a Richard Wagner. It would be worthwhile to examine the similarity of the perceptions of these two spiritually very different figures.

The completion of Schumann's oratorio *Das Paradies und die Peri* cost him much lifeblood. He considered it something akin to a proof of his musical mastery. "The difference between German masters and Italian and French masters is that we try our hands at all forms and genres. When the virtues of a great composer are extolled, I always ask, 'Where are his symphonies, quartets, oratorios?' " In spite of sickness and fatigue, Schumann's determination yielded an impressive series of comprehensive works during his late phase: the opera *Genoveva,* the *Szenen aus Goethes Faust,* the music to Byron's *Manfred,* a mass, a requiem, and a number of large song cycles. He remained intrigued by foreign thought and set Spanish and Oriental poetry to music with as much understanding and sensitivity as ever.

After 1848, very late in his life and seemingly spurred on by the revolutionary unrest sweeping Europe, Schumann's new departures and explorations became increasingly apparent. Shakespeare replaced the formerly so beloved Jean Paul as the brightest star in Schumann's literary firmament. The dramatist Hebbel became another idol. He planned to compose a *Singspiel* or oratorio based on Goethe's *Hermann und Dorothea* with "music and poetry in a simple, popular German manner." He outlined a plan for a choral oratorio about Luther, presenting Martin Luther "as a man of the people," understood by burgher and farmer alike. Surviving drafts of the text reveal a clearly interdenominational ethos, and a development of the theme which is lifelike and very realistic but quite devoid of Romantic idealization or historicizing.

Schumann had traveled far from the point where, in 1832, he had said to his mother, "I don't want everyone to understand me." His late turn toward religious music only serves to emphasize his amazing intellectual and artistic development. When a former, self-avowed poetic pianist composer undertakes massive works oriented to very definite purposes, we are compelled to acknowledge a decided turning away from Romantic individualism. The first clear evidence of this new direction is found in the *Adventlied* and the motet *Verzweifle nicht,* both written in 1849. It is true, the *Requiem* and *Mass* of about the same time were written in conjunction with his compositional responsibilities at Düsseldorf. But the results do not suggest that he felt forced in writing them. Schumann's religious music marks the end of his writing vocal music compositions, which had begun with the "Year of Songs." The artistic intention of his vocal works was to bridge the gulf between the composition and the audience, between the workshop and the larger world. Only when his mind broke did the springs of creativity and inspiration run dry, causing him to withdraw into himself.

Chapter 2

Several composers, Johann Heinrich Schein, Sebastian Knüpfer, and Heinrich Schütz, closely associated with the development of the *Lied,* lived and worked in Saxony. But certainly the most important was Adam Krieger, one of the first masters of the German *Lied.* A century and a half following Krieger's death, Robert Schumann of Zwickau infused new life into the *Lied* by recasting it in terms of the esthetic and cultural values of the 19th Century.

Like his son, Schumann's father, August, endured many trials, tribulations, and frustrations. August's literary talent went, if not unnoticed, surely unappreciated by his parents. He too was able to realize his personal goals only after years of self-denial and effort so intense that the resulting ill-health brought his life to a premature close. The elder Schumann also had his "Wieck" in the father of his future bride Johanna Schnabel, for whom he was asked to abandon his career as a book dealer and adopt a more lucrative, "materialistic" occupation. Ironically these very literary efforts, such as his compendium *A Handbook for Businessmen,* realized the income needed to become a partner in mercantile ventures in Ronneburg and to marry his faithful fiancée.

He pursued his new business undertaking for four years, only to return to the book trade. Much of what was published by the newly established "Gebrüder Schumann" had a powerful effect on the young Robert. By his 14th year, the future composer had contributed to a body of essays, "A Gallery of the Most Famous Individuals From Every Culture and Every Time." One of the last publishing projects undertaken by August Schumann before his early death was a German edition of the standard works of major English authors. The novels of Walter Scott were translated by Willibald Alexis, while from the works of Lord Byron, by whose poetry Robert was so inspired, August Schumann himself translated "Childe Harold" and "Beppo." Robert devoured not only these translations but the other classics published by his father's house as well.

August Schumann was quiet, reserved, and serious by nature—much like Robert. His mother, who came from a provincial and very close family, tended in her later years toward fanciful eccentricity, occasional fits of rage, and strange behavior induced or compounded by marital difficulties. Robert was born on 8 June 1810, the youngest of five children. His only sister, Emilie, died in her early 20s as a consequence of melancholia. Robert also outlived his brothers Eduard, Karl and Julius.

The baby of the family spent his early childhood surrounded by women. Later, as his talent began to develop, the "beautiful child" became the sheltered darling of the family, whose every wish was granted. Even at an early age he found it difficult to accept opposition. In spite of this, he developed a strong sense of self-discipline which helped him in his life and work and kept him from becoming simply a moody egocentric.

In a supplement to the *Allgemeine Musikalische Zeitung* dated April, 1850, in the 52nd volume of the publication, a biographical account of Schumann noted, "It has been reported, that even as a child Schumann showed considerable aptitude and talent for expressing feelings through music. He is said to have portrayed the personalities of his playmates so precisely and humorously with

Johanna Christiane Schumann,
nee Schnabel, 1810

August Schumann, 1810

passages and figures on the piano, that they broke into loud laughter at the versimilitude of their portraits." These musical sketches became early exercises for the characterizations he would later use in his songs and oratorios, as did the first literary efforts of the youth, who, even while a schoolboy, was convinced that he would one day become famous. Robert wrote comedies which he produced with the help of his father and friends on a makeshift stage and for which he charged admission. These early artistic undertakings raised his father's hopes that the son would follow in his literary footsteps.

In 1820, before Robert entered the third form at grammar school, he and his father attended a concert by the pianist Ignaz Moscheles in Karlsbad. Years later, the composer still recounted the enormous and powerful effect the concert by this accomplished virtuoso had upon his life. The elder Schumann clearly encouraged his son's musical interests, for he acquired a grand piano from the highly respected Streicher firm in Vienna. Musical activity in the Schumann household intensified markedly when Robert came upon the complete orchestra parts for the overture to "Tigranes" by Righini in his father's bookstore. He performed it with a handful of instruments played by family members while he played the added piano part.

His first schoolboy composition was a vocal work—a setting of the 150th Psalm for choir with instrumental accompaniment. His inspiration for this first foray into composition was Friedrich Schneider's oratorio, "The Last Judgment," for which Robert had played the piano accompaniment in a production by his music teacher Kuntsch.

Ignaz Moscheles, 1824

Autograph letter by Robert Schumann
to Henriette Voigt, November 24, 1834

Robert soon found opportunities to exercise his enthusiasm for music outside of his parental home in those of other musically inclined families in Zwickau. One such was the family of the merchant Carus, "where joy, gaiety, and music reigned." He not only performed solo pieces, but also occasionally accompanied choral works on the piano. Schumann's music teacher Kuntsch so frowned upon these self-initiated musical undertakings that he refused to continue young Schumann's lessons. Robert continued his study on his own but Kuntsch subsequently redeemed himself by encouraging Robert to dedicate himself to music—a manifest recognition of his former pupil's talent.

During his school years, Schumann attempted opera on several occasions. But only sketches for overtures resulted. August Schumann, sensitive to his son's musical talents and interests, con-sidered the possibility of a career in music. His mother, however, thoroughly disagreed. She neither possessed any musical interests, nor could she lay aside her prejudices against an artistic career. She remained firm in her opinion that Robert must avoid the regrettable fate of Mozart and turn instead to a respected profession or business.

Finally the elder Schumann took the decisive step. He wrote to Carl Maria von Weber in Dresden asking if he would undertake the education of his son. Weber agreed, but soon thereafter, despite his very poor health, travelled to England from whence he never returned.

So Schumann was once again left to his own devices to develop his compositional skills. Since he had no teacher to criticize his work nor other composers with whom to compare his writings, he inevitably became more than somewhat vain about his achievements. Provincial admiration fostered this conceit and led him to believe that he was on the right path and needed no outside direction. This latter view was especially comforting as his previous experiences with music teachers had led to the sense that he had no need for formal instruction.

As he grew older, Schumann devoted increasing time to reading. *Faust,* which later led him to make grandiose plans for his life, was committed to memory. So involved was he with this fantasy that his friends poked fun at his enthusiastic, endless recitations calling him "Faust" and "Mephisto." Undaunted, Schumann proceeded to translate Theocritus and Anacreon. Stimulated by *The Iliad, The Odyssey* and the dramas of Sophocles, Schumann tried his

hand at writing epics. He was in turn enraptured by Schiller, but finally thoroughly captivated by Jean Paul, upon first reading *Hesperus* in 1827. The story resonated with meaning and significance for Schumann. At last he had found a way of thinking about and viewing life in which he could trust. It was as if he had rediscovered himself and in so doing gained confidence, as if he "had secretly been seeking Jean Paul."

It is no wonder that Jean Paul's *Titan* virtually sent the pliable young enthusiast into a frenzy. So extraordinary was his preoccupation that he broke up with a childhood sweetheart because she did not sufficiently appreciate the poet from Bayreuth. His "Juniusabende und Julitage," also was inspired by Jean Paul. In addition he wrote essays in a philosophical vein ("On the Vicissi-

Zwickau, circa 1840

tudes and Emptiness of Posthumous Fame," "On the Influence of Loneliness"). All were written in his characteristic, barely decipherable handwriting which in later years forced readers to guess at his meaning, especially when written rapidly, as he was wont to do.

Schumann was not alone in his admiration of Jean Paul. The literary panorama of the period was very complicated and changing very rapidly. Despite the large number of stale books by now forgotten hack writers, once the gods of the lending libraries, the good literature of the era was greatly valued. In terms of setting the tone and sensibility of the era, the unbridled enthusiasm for Jean Paul was even more important than the impact of Goethe or Schiller, who achieved his fame only after 1848 in the epoch of awakened liberalism.

It is a great misfortune that modern readers find it difficult to engage with Jean Paul's writings. Present indifference stems from their lack of relevance to our cultural preoccupations, their occasional long-windedness and their often farcical forms which tend to obscure their poetic and philosophical value. The true extent of Jean Paul's role as a barometer for the values and concerns of his time can be found in the moving commemorative address by the usually cool and critical Ludwig Börne. He tells the story of a boat trip on the Rhine on which a fellow passenger was obsessed with off-color jokes. When this irksome passenger fell asleep later, a book fell from his pocket. It was a copy of *Titan*, its pages covered with notes which revealed the unexpected depth of the man's nature.

The Franconian poet who died in 1825 had much in common with Schumann. The works of neither fit simply into the accepted categories of Classical or Romantic. Jean Paul's style is quite unique. Like Schumann, Jean Paul was much involved in subjective concerns which he explored in great variety. A powerful imagination, a love of story-telling and a preoccupation with obscene jokes are characteristics also shared by Schumann—at least in his youth. Schumann too enjoyed grotesque comedy and eccentric characters. Further, he freely employed a wide variety of forms including prologues, interludes and epilogues. He, too, occasionally resorted to a flowery style. Jean Paul's remark that he used sound and not words to best express exuberance reminds us of Schumann's statement when 17 years old. "It's strange," he said; "just at the point where my emotions are strongest, that is where I must stop being a poet."

Young Schumann early lost that sunny and exuberant nature which marked his childhood, becoming reserved and introverted. This restrained outward behavior was retained for the rest of his life, even in the company of friends. Those closest to him found him impassive or preoccupied. Emil Flechsig, a deacon of the Marienkirche in Zwickau, was one of them—a dear friend and associate of Schumann's who later worked with him on the text for the oratorio, *Das Paradies und die Peri.*

Two events of the time had a great impact on Schumann. On October 8, 1826, his father died. With his passing, Robert lost the only friend who could have led him through the shoals of his slowly maturing career.

The other event was his introduction to and later affection for an amateur musician who spent the summer of 1827 in Zwickau awakening his creative impulses with her singing. Agnes Carus, a relative of his friends, the Carus family, was married to a doctor then living in Colditz who later became a professor at the University in Leipzig. She introduced Schumann to several songs by Schubert and encouraged him to compose his first *Lieder.* Inspired by both Schubert's music and Carus' encouragement, he produced a setting—more curious than convincing—of Goethe's "Fischer" which he later published in a supplement to his publication, *Neue Zeitschrift für Musik.*

Schumann's infatuation for Agnes affected him more deeply than previous youthful romances, as she introduced her "Fridolin" to a new world of poetic sounds and musical pictures. Under her spell he wrote additional songs based not only on his own poems but those of Byron and Ernst Schulze as well, to which he assigned the Opus number II. Schumann shortly thereafter stopped using Roman numerals, assigning Arabic numbers to all his self-published works. His plans to publish Opus II were never realized.

Nearly every one of the songs in Opus II begins with a dissonance. Loosely melismatic, they closely follow the sentimental ariettas which were highly favored at the time. "Wenn der

Jean Paul on the way to the Rollwenzel home

Wind sanft entschwand'' was based on a poem by Ernst Schulze (1789–1817), the poet from Celle whose poetry Schubert so highly prized, but another poem ''Zart wie die Rose erwacht'' by the same poet was entered into Schumann's travel diary in the latter part of May, 1829, but not set to music. Another song which opens *Lied für . . . ;* was most certainly a poem from the pen of Schumann (''Leicht wie gaukelnde Sylphiden''). And we can insert in the blank the name Agnes Carus.

The songs in Opus II tell us little about the music of the mature *Lieder* composer; they are but pale imitations of Schubert, who had become Robert's new idol, after whom Schumann also modelled his eight polonaises from the summer of 1828. Only a few weeks later, he entered into his diary, ''Schubert is dead—dismay.'' And a few days later, ''And you, who left us so soon, you heavenly Schubert— if ghosts and doubles had words, they would speak; but if the angels and familiar spirits ever talked, they would speak as you do; you are the flowing, celestial spirit inventing the spring flowers.'' Emil Flechsig later recalled: ''He played Schubert's *Erlkönig* magnificently. . . . He was wildly enthusiastic about Schubert, who was only then becoming well known. He snatched up everything which was available by Schubert. I played bass on the polonaises. . . . When Schubert died the next winter, he was so upset upon receiving this news that he sobbed all night.'' In a letter to Wieck dated November, 1829, Schumann clearly expresses his views on his idol: ''There is no music, other than Schubert's, which is so remarkable psychologically in its sequence and connection of ideas and in its seemingly logical leaps. How few have managed, as he has, to impress a coherent personal view on such a varied mass of musical compositions. So few have so clearly written for the benefit of their own soul. What for others is a diary, in which they record momentary feelings, was for Schubert a sheet of music paper on which he poured out his thoughts and emotions for all to see.''

Schumann found the atmosphere in the Carus household thoroughly congenial. A handshake or other gesture seemed to communicate as much as the spoken word—a manner of behavior consistent with Schumann's views of communicating emotion both personally and in his creative work. He seldom felt the need to openly express the richness of his interior life even in moments of

21

overwhelming emotion. He hoped his music would be understood intrinsically and appreciated directly by his listeners. We must view his embarrassed and stumbling presentation of his poem "Tassos Tod" at his school graduation ceremonies in this context. This difficulty with public speaking became more acute in later years.

Uncertain of his artistic future, Schumann capitulated to the plan devised by his mother and his newly appointed guardian, the merchant Rudel. He was to study law in Leipzig—a pursuit quite foreign to his nature. Well versed in classical languages, he easily passed his secondary school graduation examination in 1828. The decision may have been influenced by his newly developed friendship with Gisbert Rosen, also a law student. Easter, 1828, Rosen transferred from Leipzig to Heidelberg and invited Schumann to accompany him on the trip as far as Munich. The two friends were bound by a mutual admiration for the author of *Titan*. Therefore, they made a stop in Bayreuth to see old Frau Rollwenzel, in whose house Jean Paul had lived for years, and from whom they learned much about their idol. The next day they went via Nürnberg to Augsburg where Schumann presented himself with a letter of introduction to Herr von Kurrer, a chemist whose wife was from Zwickau. Schumann was immediately smitten by the deep blue eyes of the daughter of the house. In order to thwart unwanted advances, her father in turn gave Schumann a letter of introduction to Heinrich Heine in Munich. Making Heine's acquaintance was an opportunity the two young travelers could not resist.

Heine's first widespread acclaim derived from the appearance of *Reisebilder* and *Buch der Lieder,* both of which were enthusiastically received by the younger generation. He lived in a beautiful garden room decorated with the paintings of many of Munich's painters. Schumann recorded his impressions of the encounter in his diary; "Shopping—Matter of taste—Heine—witty conversation—ironic little man—charming fantasy—Walk with him in the Leuchtenberg Gallery—Napoleon's chair—The Graces by Canova insufficiently noble—Magdalena beautiful—Billiards—Dinner together. . . ."

But Schumann did not enjoy Munich. He found the atmosphere in the capital cold and uninviting. Only his introduction to Heine made the stay rewarding. He had expected to meet a sullen, misanthropic genius no longer able to relate to life. Instead he was greeted by an approachable "Anacreon" who immediately befriended him and spent hours with him showing him the town. Heine's scurrilous remarks kept his visitors constantly amused. The relationship made during Schumann's short visit remained but a casual acquaintanceship. Heine's bitter, ironic smile did not go unnoticed by Schumann; he interpreted it as the assertion of pride in his achievement. But simply said, it was the poet's satiric stance rather than his admiration for Napoleon which attracted Schumann.

Chapter 3

After a short stay in Zwickau, Schumann moved into his newly rented lodgings in Leipzig to pursue a career in law. However, this undertaking ended quite differently than had been expected. Schumann quickly became disillusioned with everything about the University. The study of law bored him, so he attended lectures only occasionally and then without enthusiasm. He could not bring himself to come to terms with what he viewed as excruciatingly dry material.

When Schumann entered the University in 1828, Leipzig had about 40,000 inhabitants. The local merchants had created a cultural climate in which both artists and scholars played an important role. The citizens were devoted to the arts, and music in particular. Nearly every household owned at least one musical instrument, and there was much music making in the home. The tradition of male choral societies originated in Leipzig, from which they subsequently spread to other German towns. Contemporary accounts report the anticipation with which the public awaited the weekly presentations by the choir of St. Thomas Church, where Bach had once been active, and where Wagner's teacher, Weinlig, was choirmaster. These accounts add that Leipzig audiences applauded more loudly and enthusiastically than those in Dresden or Berlin. Under the direction of Pohlenz, the Gewandhaus Concerts, having at the time a 50-year history, were in great favor, and even more so after Mendelssohn took over their direction in 1835. The close ties between Leipzig audiences and the performing artists almost assumed the character of a closed, private organization. Leipzig authors and the literati of the "city of book publishers" joined forces to spread their liberal political views beyond the city in the constitutional battles of the times. The news of the successful July revolution in Paris in 1830 brought extended demonstrations, especially by the fraternities of the University. They pledged their allegiance to the liberal nationalism of Fichte and the educational reforms proposed by Ludwig Jahn, the father of physical education in the school system.

The cultural life of Leipzig inspired and stimulated young Schumann, but having no interest in political affairs he disliked the student agitation in support of vague ideals. Though he joined the moderate fraternity, "Markomannia," for a brief period, concerns other than the student activities preoccupied him. However, he did in this short interval learn to ride, fence, and unfortunately, to drink. But the regimented vulgarity associated with the drinking and dueling bouts of his fraternity brothers led to increasing disgust. Though it was not a quiet location, he increasingly retreated to his room, where music became his refuge from everything associated with university life.

Continual assocation with well-educated music lovers encouraged him to pursue his interests in performing on the piano and composing. It was a stroke of good luck that Agnes Carus and her husband moved to Leipzig. Schumann was soon spending a great deal of time in their musically oriented household, receiving much inspiration, as many of the city's leading musicians including *Kapellmeister* Marschner and the composer Wiedebein from Brunswick also were frequent guests. The young man's views of Leipzig began to turn from distaste to appreciation. Ultimately

JUSTINUS KERNER

(1786–1862) Born in Ludwigsburg, the poet and medical writer was educated at the Maulbronn Monastery. Against his wishes, his family intended that he enter business, but in 1804 he entered the university of Tübingen to study medicine and natural science. While there, he cared for the poet Hölderlin during an illness and became a close friend of the poets Uhland and Schwab. Letters to friends written on his journey to Hamburg, Berlin and Vienna, 1809, were the basis for *Reiseschatten von dem Schattenspieler Lux* (1811), his most important literary work. Interwoven through the work are songs and scenes rich with fanciful humor.

He established his practice as resident physician at the baths in Wildbad, where he, together with Uhland, Schwab and Eichendorff, published several literary journals. In 1818 he was appointed chief physician at Weinsberg and pursued research on "Fatty Acids and Their Effect on Animals." He acquired a house at the foot of Weibertreu Castle, the famous "Kernerhaus" which became the focal point of the Swabian school of poets. His investigations into animal magnetism greatly influenced Kerner's thought. In *The History of Two Somnambulists,* he recorded his observations of several cases. In four subsequent publications, *The Seer from Prevort, The Recent History of the Possessed, An Appearance from the Twilight Zone of Nature* and *A Report on an Incident of Possession,* he developed his theory that a spirit-world exists which is projected into the world of matter by a gifted few possessing occult powers. Kerner was also, however, able to poke fun at the occult as in his curious play *Der Bärenhäuter im Salzbade* (1837), which can only be considered a satire of the world of the arcane. In 1853, nearly blind, Kerner closed his office and gave up his practice and patients, among whom was the poet Nikolaus Lenau. The fount of Kerner's poetry, like Uhland's, was folk song, the clarity and earthly reality of which Kerner contrasted with the convoluted and melancholic courtly music so widespread at the time.

he claimed there was no better city in Germany for a young musician.

But was he one? Was his place not in fact in the *Collegium*—was he not to occupy himself with the *corpus juris* rather than attend concerts or play the piano? His letters to Zwickau speak of diligent attendance at lectures. But letters to friends reveal that Schumann almost never attended lectures on law nor opened a law book.

Rather, Schumann read, indeed studied, Wiedebein's book of songs based on poems by Justinus Kerner which Agnes had given him. He purchased Kerner's newly published collection of poems and was at once entranced by the folk-song-like, natural poetry of the Swabian doctor.

Schumann was especially attracted to the song-like character of Kerner's poetry, which is striking, concise, and full of surprising images. It is highly probable that Kerner's *Die somnambulischen Tische* stimulated Schumann's spiritualistic propensities.

Schumann probably used the early collection of Kerner's poems of 1826 when on 29 June, 2 July, and 10 July, 1828 he set three poems by Kerner to music: *Kurzes Erwachen, Gesanges Erwachen,* and *An Anna.* Casting caution to the wind, he sent the compositions to Gottlob Wiedebein for his consideration with a covering letter: "Dear Sir, Please excuse the foolhardy forwardness of an eighteen-year-old youth, who, having been inspired by your most deservedly praised *Lieder,* now dares to enter the sacred world of music with his own inadequate compositions. Treat the youth with forbearance, for he has not been initiated into the mysteries of composition. With passions aroused by poetry, his uncertain hand has assayed a first effort to create a work, which he now lays before you for your gracious yet candid judgment. It was that secret, supernatural force, which is often found in the poetry of Goethe and Jean Paul, that attracted me to Kerner's poems and first gave me the idea of testing my weak powers. For I believe that each word of these poems is infused with the music of the spheres which must be expressed through musical composition."

In his diary for August, 1831, Schumann recalls, "How I trembled as I sent my *Lieder* to Wiedebein." Wiedebein's reply, like Schumann's letter, was influenced by Jean Paul. He found fault with "uncertain handling of the true elements and higher principles of art." Judiciously and presaging modern opinion, he added that the shortcomings of the songs are excusable as sins of youth, since a spirit and a sense of poetry are apparent. He added that wild things must grow wildly, but a wine grape must be carefully pruned and tended. "You should strive for truth in melody, harmony, and expression. But where you do not find these, or where they seem in danger, there you must cut ruthlessly. You have received much, very much, from nature. Use it, and the esteem of the world will be yours."

By Schumann's own account, Wiedebein's assessment was extraordinarily meaningful to him. He took this first professional appraisal of his work and talent very seriously. In his note of thanks he wrote, "In my previous letter I failed to tell you that I am knowledgeable in neither harmony, thorough-bass, nor counterpoint, but am instead a simple student of nature, following a blind and vain instinct, wanting to cast off my shackles. But now I will begin to study composition earnestly!" Schumann related nothing of Wiedebein's encouraging remarks to his mother but his decision to become a musician, which he shared with the Caruses, was firmly taken.

Interestingly, these early *Lieder* by Schumann easily surpass any of Wiedebein's songs, which are pleasant enough but lack both substance and originality. It was therefore fitting that Brahms published, at the end of the last century in a supplemental volume to Schumann's complete works, three of the Kerner *Lieder* which Schumann did not publish in his lifetime. Karl Geiringer wisely published all of the remaining early *Lieder*. (Universal Edition, Vienna, 1933.) Geiringer completed the hastily written manu-

Example 1

Nicht im Tha _ le der süssen Hei _ math beim Ge _ mur _ mel der Sil _ ber _ quel _ le

Example 2

Example 3

Langsam und ausdrucksvoll.

Zieh' nur, du Sonne, zieh' ei _ lend von hier, von hier!

Example 4

Andantino. ♪= 104.
getragen (sostenuto)

scripts, thus revealing to those who will but read them how decisively and consistently Schumann developed his "unprecedented" personal style from his earliest beginning. Wiedebein's kind, well-meant words contain a phrase which became a touchstone for Schumann to which he adhered the rest of his musical life: "Poetic truth." In the handwritten collection of his own poems entitled *Allerley aus der Feder Roberts an der Mulde,* Schumann added the following marginal note next to the poem, "Sehnsucht" (Yearning): "written and composed on Feb. 28th, 27."

Three of the *Lieder* contain themes which reappear soon afterwards in piano works. "An Anna" is recognizable in the slow movement of the *Sonata in F# minor,* Opus 11. This theme in turn seems to have been derived from clarinet works of Carl Maria von Weber (Examples 1 and 2).

We find "Im Herbste" repeated in the slow movement of the *Sonata in G minor* written in 1835 (Examples 3 and 4).

"Hirtenknabe" already adopts the sound of Eusebius. The name of the poet is Ebert, not Ekert as it was incorrectly spelled in 1933 and in later works. The *Intermezzo,* Opus 4, Number 4 (1832) derives its melodic material from this *Lied.*

The most significant friendship which Schumann formed in the Carus' circle was with Friedrich Wieck, the father of nine-year-old Clara. Her performance in a piano trio by Hummel so moved Schumann that he decided to take piano lessons from Wieck. Clara, who loved ghost stories and charades, at which her "Herr Schumann" was most apt and clever, soon dubbed him her father's favorite pupil. But by February, 1829, the lessons came to an end, due in part to Wieck's declining interest in the young man and in part as a consequence of Schumann's plan to pursue the study of law in Heidelberg, apparently not wishing to continue his musical journey with his teacher.

After a short Easter holiday in Zwickau, Schumann undertook the long journey from Leipzig to Heidelberg in the stimulating company of the author Willibald Alexis (actually Wilhelm Häring). Schumann described the journey by stagecoach in letters to his mother, dwelling especially on his views of the Rhine. The

Friedrich Wieck

describe. In the concert halls of Leipzig, I have occasionally been transported with delight but at the same time shuddered in awe of the spirit of music. But in Italy, I learned also to love it. And there on the only such evening in my life it seemed as if God stood before me and for a moment allowed me to see his countenance—and that was in Milan, when I heard Pasta and—Rossini. Do not laugh, Dear Sir, for it is true!" The sound of that heavenly voice remained with him and in later years led to a broader view of song.

His Italian journey was of lasting importance in another way. As a part of his instruction in Italian, before setting out, he made exact translations of the sonnets by Petrarch, which greatly shaped his later sense of poetic rhythm.

Upon his return to Heidelberg, the pendulum swung back in the direction of music. Schumann appeared as a pianist performing the "Alexander Variations" by Moscheles. Soon he was performing at many social gatherings, including the court of the Grand Duke of Mannheim. His law professor, Thibaut, confessing he would much rather have been a musician than an academic, frequently invited Schumann to his home to participate in amateur performances of Handel's works. These musical opportunities, not the study of law, compelled him to remain in Heidelberg. He carefully disguised the real purpose of his stay, especially from his mother. Wieck, however, was advised of Schumann's true intentions when he read, "If you only knew the drives and urges which have compelled me! My symphonies already would have reached Opus 100, if only I had written them down. . . ."

Finally, in July of 1830, Schumann wrote the long letter in which he informed his mother of his decision to turn to music—a decision she could not comprehend. He also requested her to seek Wieck's opinion on the matter. There is a story that the matter was settled in Schumann's mind at a recital by Niccoló Paganini in nearby Frankfurt—Schumann "was aroused and eager to work." Wieck's encouraging response to Schumann's mother was laced with many conditions. Robert would have to study dry theory for two years and learn to play more precisely, distinctly, and evenly. And within six months he must demonstrate his ability to behave in a more learned, robust, and manly fashion. Though Frau Schumann still had misgivings, she left the decision to Robert.

memories of the trip reappear in *Lieder* written much later. ". . . I closed my eyes, in order to be able to enjoy my first glimpse of old, majestic Father Rhine with a full, whole, calm soul. And when I opened them, he lay before me, quiet, still, solemn, and majestic as an old German god, with the entire magnificent, blooming, green Rhine Valley with its mountains and valleys and glorious vineyards. The moon sent out silvery beams, and the hypnotic waves of the Rhine slowly, slowly lulled the wanderer to sleep."

The hoped-for resurgence of interest in the study of law under a celebrated jurist, the venerable professor of law in Heidelberg, Thibaut, actually came to pass.

For the fall holidays, Schumann coaxed funds for a journey to Switzerland and Italy from his mother and his guardian, Rudel. His trip included an unforgettable visit to La Scala in Milan. In a letter to Wieck in November 1829, he wrote, "How often I have thought of you in the Theater de la Scala in Milan, and how often I have been enchanted by Rossini and even more so by Pasta, whom out of reverence and almost out of adoration I will not even attempt to

Chapter 4

Schumann now dedicated himself entirely to the study of music. Without even stopping to see his mother and brothers in Zwickau, he arrived in Leipzig in October, 1830, with an empty purse, but with a stack of musical manuscripts ready for the printer, including the "Abegg Variations," the first version of the "Toccata" and "Papillons." This last piece, a cycle of piano works written under the influence of Jean Paul, clearly demonstrates Schumann's gift for filling miniature forms with life. He had developed the ability to produce such compressed statements through daily improvisation at the piano, the effect of which can be traced in all of his subsequent work. Throughout the 1830s Schumann's world and mind were filled with ideas deriving from wide-ranging and complex relationships with both people and books. It was a rich world pregnant with possibilities from which he emerged with a heightened sense of poetic music, yet music which could stand alone with no need for explanation.

To prove himself as a musician, Schumann undertook lessons in Leipzig immediately. He sublet a room in the house of his teacher, Friedrich Wieck, in which he dedicated himself virtually exclusively to his lessons, practicing the piano as much as seven hours a day. Wieck was a firm taskmaster who spared neither himself nor his pupils. His only thought was the development of a successful musical career, and so it was almost a given that he would become irritated with the imagination and impetuosity of the 20-year-old. Schumann endeavored to adopt a circumspect mental posture—a "Master Raro" (taking the place of Wieck) positioned somewhere between his passionate "Florestan" nature and his dreamy "Eusebius" qualities. But Wieck was concerned only with the "star" quality, with the economic potential he saw in Robert's virtuosity. Clara, Wieck's daughter, had only, in Schumann's view, her great pianistic talent to thank that she, unlike her brother, Alwin, did not suffer the physical abuse of her hot-tempered father. Given this tense environment it is understandable that while displaying no fear of Wieck's temper, Schumann wrote to Johann Nepomuk Hummel in Weimar asking to study under him. The world-renowned pianist and friend of Beethoven refused, however. Hummel's rejection, coupled with Schumann's morbid fear of contracting cholera, then a common disease, cast a long, dark shadow on the life of the diligent student of music theory. He contemplated fleeing to Italy. He suffered anxiety attacks, which were difficult enough to overcome then, but even more difficult to surmount in later years. He took up occult pastimes, such as the "Psychometer" invented by Magister Portius, which only confirmed his lack of self-assurance and desire to escape present tribulations.

Schumann found Wieck's insistence on the strict rules of composition increasingly burdensome. When he later studied with Heinrich Dorn, the opera composer only six years his senior, he openly revolted against "cold, gray theory." Like Schubert, Schumann was able only later in his career to find any pleasure in writing fugues. But Dorn, perceiving Schumann's theoretical inadequacies, terminated his instruction within only eight months, much to his pupil's surprise.

Nowhere in "cold, gray theory" could Schumann's creative

instincts find the means appropriate to expressing his vision. Since childhood a fanatic reader of Shakespeare, he had utopian plans for an opera on the subject of Hamlet. More importantly, in the course of his voracious reading he came across the works of Heine and Grabbe which were to play a central role in his creative life. Incidentally, his notes on Heine should call into question the views of those who blindly doubt his ability to understand the irony employed by this poet. He repeatedly notes the odd turns in Heine's *Lieder,* the "burning sarcasm, that great despair and the devastating caricatures of nobility and rank." In this connection Schumann's remark in his "Motto-book," "I am not capable of bitter sarcasm," is revealing. In "Hottentottiana," a collection of thoughts and poetic fragments jotted down in Leipzig, Heidelberg, and then again in Leipzig, Schumann records his penchant for sarcasm with some regret. "If I could just learn not to let my mind quarrel when my heart is happy and vice versa. I would like to moderate my sarcasm and make my gentleness more sarcastic. I need to find a middle ground. One can accomplish more by means of extreme behavior than through the cumbersome golden mean pursued by ordinary people and the apes." Schumann pursued self-observation candidly and very methodically. He requested on several occasions the return of earlier correspondence which he compared to old notes in order to assess changes in his behavior and views.

In this stormy period of his life, Schumann's regard for E.T.A. Hoffmann and Goethe increased at the expense of his affection for Jean Paul Richter. Because he no longer felt able to deal with musical theory, Schumann took up the thing he found easiest for the time being: writing. His enthusiasm for his contemporary, Frédéric Chopin, whose Opus 2, the Variations on Mozart's "Lá ci darem," had just been published in Warsaw, seems to have been a sort of release for him. His lifelong pursuit of music criticism came into being with his first article reviewing a performance of Chopin's work, published in the *Allgemeine Musikalische Zeitung* in Berlin. He wrote several reviews of performances by a new singer, Livia Gerhard, who later married Frege, the lawyer, and in time was the singer who, Schumann wrote, gave an "unequaled" performance as Peri and would later become a major performer of his *Lieder.* In his first review he noted her "roundness of voice," but found her

;05   806

ALLGEMEINE

MUSIKALISCHE ZEITUNG.

Den 7ten December.   Nᵒ. 49.   1831.

Vorbemerkung.

Wir geben hier einmal über Ein Werk zwey Beurtheilungen; die erste von einem jungen Manne, einem Zöglinge der neusten Zeit, der sich genannt hat; die andere von einem angesehenen und würdigen Repräsentanten der ältern Schule, der sich nicht genannt hat: allein, wir versichern und haben es kaum nöthig, von einem durchaus tüchtigen, vollgeübt und umsichtig kenntnissreichen.

Wir meinen, durch diese Zusammenstellung nicht nur unsere Aufmerksamkeit auf den Verf. des zu besprechenden Werkes auf hier ungewöhnliche Weise an den Tag zu legen, sondern auch zugleich, und ganz besonders, unsern geehrten Lesern zu mancherley eigenen und höchst nützlichen Vergleichungen Veranlassung zu bieten, die mit ihrem grossen Nutzen eine Unterhaltung gewähren, die zu viel Anziehendes hat, als dass sie irgend einem denkenden Musikfreunde anders als höchst willkommen seyn könnte. Mit dem Werke in der Hand wird es wohl am glücklichsten gelingen.

Die Redaction.

I. Von K. Schumann.

Ein Opus II.

— — — Eusebius trat neulich leise zur Thüre herein. Du kennst das ironische Lächeln auf dem blassen Gesichte, mit dem er zu spannen sucht. Ich sass mit Florestan am Klavier. Florestan ist, wie Du weisst, einer von den seltenen Musikmenschen, die alles Zukünftige, Neue, Ausserordentliche schon wie lange vorher geahnt haben; das Seltsame ist ihnen im andern Augenblicke nicht seltsam mehr; das Ungewöhnliche wird im Moment ihr Eigenthum. Eusebius hingegen, so schwärmerisch als gelassen, zieht Blüthe nach Blüthe aus; er fasst schwerer, aber sicherer an, geniesst seltener,

33. Jahrgang.

aber langsamer und länger; dann ist auch sein Studium strenger und sein Vortrag im Klavierspiele besonnener, aber auch zarter und mechanisch vollendeter, als der Florestans. — Mit den Worten: „Hut ab, ihr Herren, ein Genie," legte Eusebius ein Musikstück auf, das wir leicht als einen Satz aus dem Haslinger'schen Odeon erkannten. Den Titel durften wir weiter nicht sehen. Ich blätterte gedankenlos im Buche; diess verhüllte Geniessen der Musik ohne Töne hat etwas Zauberisches. Ueberdiess scheint mir, hat jeder Componist seine eigenthümlichen Notengestaltungen für das Auge: Beethoven sieht anders auf dem Papier, als Mozart, etwa wie Jean Paul'sche Prosa anders, als Göthe'sche. Hier aber war mir's, als blickten mich lauter fremde Augen, Blumenaugen, Basiliskenaugen, Pfauenaugen, Mädchenaugen wundersam an: an manchen Stellen ward es lichter — ich glaubte Mozart's „Là ci darem la mano" durch hundert Accorde geschlungen zu sehen, Leporello schien mich ordentlich wie anzublinzeln und Don Juan flog im weissen Mantel vor mir vorüber. „Nun spiel's," meinte Florestan lachend zu Eusebius, „wir wollen Dir die Ohren und uns die Augen zuhalten." Eusebius gewährte; in eine Fensternische gedrückt hörten wir zu. Eusebius spielte wie begeistert und führte unzählige Gestalten des lebendigsten Lebens vorüber; es ist, als wenn der frische Geist des Augenblicks die Finger über ihre Mechanik hinaushebt. Freylich bestand Florestans ganzer Beyfall, ein seliges Lächeln abgerechnet, in nichts als in den Worten: dass die Variationen etwa von Beethoven oder Franz Schubert seyn konnten, wären sie nämlich Klavier-Virtuosen gewesen — wie er aber nach dem Titelblatte fuhr, weiter nichts las, als:

Là ci darem la mano, varié pour le Pianoforte par Frédéric Chopin, Opus 2,

und wie wir beyde verwundert ausriefen: ein Opus zwey und wie Eusebius hinzufügte: Wien, bey

49

Excerpt from the Allgemeine Musikalische Zeitung, *Number 49, Dated December 7, 1831*

"lacking in depth." The bulk of the review, however, was devoted to Schumann's criticism of her style of execution which, he wrote, lacked animation. Despite this initial response, he later commented on an improved "beautiful and natural execution." Second only to Agnes Carus, Livia Frege was to be Schumann's ideal musical associate and one who held a permanent place in the Schumanns' life. The distinguished singer made her home a center in which the music of her friends Mendelssohn and Schumann found a permanent place.

At this point, Schumann, the "virtuoso apprentice," began to have doubts about a career devoted exclusively to piano performance. Composing and writing on musical matters had seriously reduced the amount of time available for practicing. "Productive and passive accomplishments" were pitted against each other. Only the prospect of interpreting and performing his own works compelled him to remain with Wieck. In order to reduce the impact of the loss of time for piano practice, he constructed a strange device which, mounted near the piano, suspended his middle finger to develop the independence of his ring finger. The device lamed first his middle finger, then his entire hand. No treatment, "allopathic, homeopathic or electrophysiological" proved successful. Amazingly, and perhaps significantly, just before this catastrophe Schumann had written his mother, "I cannot consider pure virtuosity alone. That is a bitter, thankless existence."

Doubtlessly, the decision forced by this affliction to no longer play but only compose and write about music was not completely unwelcome. The pen was now to be both his musical and literary instrument. His writing for the Berlin periodical came to nothing, despite the fact that only two decades earlier E.T.A. Hoffmann had used the same vehicle as the platform to establish the basic foundations of musical Romanticism. A further problem with the journal derived from his unwillingness to refer to himself in his reviews—this despite the fact that he enjoyed talking about himself. He alarmed his editor, Fink, by using instead three fictional representatives: Florestan, Eusebius, and Raro. He borrowed the idea of employing different personages to express one person's opinions from Jean Paul. From this time on, Schumann used one or another of these three imaginary spokesmen in almost all of his publications, including his musical works. Florestan understood "all new and unusual things as well as future events long before they occurred." Eusebius "was a visionary who calmly picked flowers." Master Raro attended to those things "which cannot be learned from books, but must instead be experienced by coming to know masters and masterworks so developing one's own capacities." Together, these three formed the "Davidsbund," or Federation of

David, which for 10 years had a marked impact on the quality and style of the musical reviews. Their writings also provided a continuous and reliable measure of artistic excellence for a decade.

These mystical figures, united in the "Davidsbund" and contending against the Philistines, were the embodiment, so to speak, of Schumann's basic beliefs, quite unlike similar fictitious societies created by earlier writers to circumvent the censorship which prevailed. The "Davidsbund" clearly had less to fear by way of official censorship and repression than their literary predecessors, including Jean Paul; Hoffmann with his "Serapionsbrüder;" or Carl Maria von Weber and his "Harmonischer Verein." The latter two, though, wrote under pseudonyms to conceal their identity, not to voice different facets of a single personality. The objectives of the "Davidsbund" were to expose those artists whose superficial finesse and crowd-pleasing skills made them as popular as genuine virtuosi and to point up the shallowness of contemporary musical criticism. In his chronicle of the period, Adolf Bähr speaks of "those who endeavored to display their compassion and decency by attending the concerts of blind flute players, while others flocked to concerts presented by bravura singers who only performed variations on popular themes (e.g., 'All my pleasures desert me'). In the realm of piano performers, Czerny, Cramer, Dussek, Field, Kalkbrenner, and Henry Herz were the favorites of the day. Another crowd pleaser was the Potpourri, a mixture of operatic excerpts hastily thrown together."

Wieck was among those who gambled on popular taste. He, for example, lost one such gamble on his daughter's behalf in 1831, when, unable to recruit a singer in Frankfurt who would condescend to sing the program of crowd pleasers he had planned for Clara's concert, he had at the last minute to recruit a voice teacher to sing a *Lied* Clara had written based on a text by Tiedge entitled, "Der Traum."

Occasional review columns in a handful of publications which reached only a fraction of those interested in music could do little to improve such a deplorable state of affairs, Schumann felt he must start his own journal in order to seriously come to grips with the shabby state of music. As early as 1833, he laid plans for a journal to give a voice to the "Davidsbund." But it was difficult to find a publisher for such a questionably profitable venture. Breitkopf & Härtel were as unenthusiastic about the journal as was Hoffmeister. Schumann's brothers refused to assist him.

Finally in 1834, C. F. Hartmann expressed an interest in temporarily financing the *Neue Leipziger Zeitschrift für Musik,* to be published by a "Society of Artists and Artlovers." Others gave Schumann's ideas a friendly welcome but no overwhelming support. Consequently, he had single-handedly to win over his audience, until the *Neue Zeitschrift für Musik* had gained a foothold. A planned trial run of two years turned into ten, with Schumann assuming the sole responsibility for seeing the journal through production; initiating new directions; writing the reviews; and dealing with the business correspondence which finally numbered over 3,000 letters.

Along with his idealistic goals and unremitting work to reach them, Schumann also harbored the hope for a settled, secure and more normal life. But the 500 Thalers stipend which Schumann received annually from his father's estate, while enough to support him, would not support a family.

Chapter 5

This is the point at which Clara, a child of the unhappy, first marriage of Friedrich Wieck, must be brought fully into view. Clara was born on 13 September 1819. Her mother, Marianne, the granddaughter of the flutist Tromlitz, divorced Wieck in 1824. She then moved to Berlin, where in 1828 she married Adolf Bargiel, a music teacher. A son from her second marriage became a well-known composer and a friend of Johannes Brahms. In 1828, Friedrich Wieck remarried but his second wife, Clementine Fechtig, had little influence on Clara's upbringing.

The child, who was often left alone, was late in learning to speak and also suffered a slight hearing problem. Beginning at age six, piano lessons came to rule her life. She started in group playing classes based on the pedagogic methods of a man named Logier. Later she started private lessons based on the proven methods of John Fields, which required students to play by ear until their fingers almost moved across the keyboard by themselves, thus leaving the eyes free to follow the music. In 1830, Clara enrolled in a theory course given by Theodor Weinlig. This was her first acquaintance with Bach; and it prompted her to write her first compositions—songs and chorales for four voices. Wieck's plans for his daughter's education were very ambitious, even after she had electrified Parisian audiences as a child prodigy and received the obligatory blessings of Goethe in Weimar. She was to undertake the study of counterpoint; score reading; improvisation; and instrumentation as well as voice and violin lessons.

Clara undertook a seven-month concert tour. Now Schumann heard her play his "Papillons." "She grasped it correctly and pas-sionately and, with a few exceptions, presented it in the same manner." Their musical friendship soon grew into an intimate attachment and a growing sense that they belonged together.

At about the same time, Schumann began to feel that composing only for the piano was limiting his artistic objectives, even though he would continue to compose for the instrument for some years thereafter. After a hurried course in instrumentation, he wrote a symphony which was not published until the 1960s. However, Clara included the first movement in one of her 1832 Zwickau concerts. Schumann was, as a consequence, able to assess his work in the context of a complete program and learned that it had been overwhelmed by Clara's rendition of "Bravura Variations" by Herz. He remained in Zwickau to revise the entire work, annoying Wieck in the process by skipping his lessons. Clara wrote to him for the first time, including critical comments on Richard Wagner whose symphony had "outshone" Robert's own. She thus echoed Wieck's attempt to spur him on, a role she continued to play in later years.

In the spring of 1833, Schumann returned to Leipzig where he took up residence in a garden suburb in order to devote himself completely to his journal. He was amazed that the 14-year-old Clara, with whom he often took walks, had remained unaffected by her success. A love of children and the magic of their innocence was a widespread sentiment of the era. Novalis dedicated his "Hymnen an die Nacht" to the memory of a 15-year-old girl, and the stories, poems, and paintings of those decades are full of children who seem to penetrate and comprehend the deepest mysteries with their simplicity. Schumann's love of Clara helped him reenter the fairyland of childhood for which he was homesick. Did Schumann truly realize the joy of a pilgrimage back to the fountain of youth in the company of this child genius?

The second half of 1833 was filled with work; the dream of his journal had to be realized. To do so, Schumann had to attract the attention and arouse the interest of German-speaking people throughout that divided land in the undertaking. He had to locate and retain correspondents in the musical centers of Europe. But the long hours of editorial work cut short the time he might otherwise have devoted to composing; so following months of intensive work he felt compelled to take up composition again.

Schumann's dearest friend and the one whose views most closely coincided with his own among the members of the "Davidsbund" was the pianist Ludwig Schuncke who was the same age as Robert. The piano-playing son of a French horn player, he had while still a child equaled and then surpassed the concert successes of his father. He came to Leipzig in 1833 after having studied with Reicha, Herz and Kalkbrenner. Because he did not write well, Schuncke's contributions in the area of theory required much editorial effort on Schumann's part. Still, they were kindred spirits and in musical matters spoke the same language. However, his newly won friend developed tuberculosis and after a year Schumann, suffering from deep depression, could no longer bear to live in the same apartment with his dying comrade. He moved in with his mother until Schuncke was buried. Schumann's obituary gives vent to his grief: his friend was one of those unhappy figures who fail to realize their full potential, not due to their failure, but rather to life's adversity. They take their yet ill-formed ideas to the grave with them, but nevertheless contribute to the greatness of others simply by virtue of their qualities. Schumann sent Schuncke's compositions to Felix Mendelssohn-Bartholdy, who was then in Düsseldorf. This gesture opened Schumann's life-long association with the future musical director of the *Gewandhaus* in Leipzig.

Physically and mentally, this was not a good time for Schumann. The family book business suffered financial setbacks. On 2 August 1833, his brother Julius died, probably of tuberculosis, and just two months later, his beloved 23-year-old sister-in-law

Rosalie fell victim to malaria. Schumann had a premonition of her death which led him to believe he was going out of his mind. Melancholy set in, which he described to his future bride, Clara, in 1837, in an attempt to give her "an understanding of my actions and my peculiar personality," as "a heavy, psychological burden," a "deep secret," which she would later come to know intimately.

His mother was forced to wait four weeks for an answer to a loving, sympathetic letter of inquiry seeking news of her son. Robert's explanation: "a series of attacks of serious congestion, indescribable fear, shortness of breath and periodic apathy . . ." Under such conditions it is hardly surprising that the musical harvest of 1833 was sparse. In addition to the "Impromptu," Opus 5; the final version of the "Toccata," Opus 7; and the three sets of variations for piano, later rejected; Schumann had also begun the three piano sonatas, pieces which were intended for Clara, and which in places refer to her musical ideas.

The child had become a shy but beautiful young woman, who charmed everyone with her "mockingly sad" smile (Lyser). The exchange of tender letters between Clara and Robert continued. Robert remained a "pure bachelor"—his previous romantic encounters never went beyond a discreet kiss. Concert tours and Robert's mourning quieted the relationship for a time. In January, 1834, 14-year-old Clara was confirmed.

After the death of his sisterly confidante, Rosalie, his romantic difficulties began. He was unable to place any confidences in his overly sensitive mother. In the meantime Ludwig Schuncke had introduced his shy friend into the home of Carl and Henriette Voigt, a businessman and his wife. In Henriette he found the motherly counsel he sought. Both resident and touring musicians were invited to enjoy the hospitality of the Voigts. Schunck, who held Beethoven in extraordinarily high regard, had introduced only the latter's music to the house. Now Schumann began to introduce the different sounds of newer composers, playing duets with the talented lady of the house. Schumann dedicated his second piano sonata in G-minor, Opus 22, to Henriette, and it was she who introduced Schumann to Ernestine von Fricken.

Ernestine von Fricken from the Bohemian town of Asch had heard Clara when performing in Plauen and could not rest until she became a boarder and student of Wieck. But Clara was not allowed to keep her company. Wieck sent Clara to Carl Gottlieb Reissiger in Dresden to complete her musical theory studies. Above all, however, Wieck wished to assure that Clara and Schumann did not associate overmuch. His plans for his daughter did not include her marriage to a penniless composer, and one who had disappointed his teacher as Schumann had done.

About this time, and before Schumann had begun to compose for the voice, Clara wrote her first *Lied* for solo voice, a "Waltz for Voice and Piano," in A major, based on a text by the deaf painter, Jens Peter Lyser. The unpublished piece can be found in Schumann's "Album" of 1846, and does credit to Clara's talent as a composer.

Clara departed for Dresden reluctantly, for she not only enjoyed her new friend Ernestine but was pleased that she, too, loved Schumann. It was only when she returned to Leipzig for the baptism of her half sister, Cäcilie, and saw Schumann acting as godfather with Ernestine at his side that she became conscious of her own jealous love for Schumann. But she spoke to no one of this.

Ernestine's father, an amateur flutist and the contributor of themes for the "Symphonic Etudes," received reports of the affair between Schumann and his illegitimate daughter. He contacted Wieck to confirm their truth. Did Clara's jealous father wish to be rid of Schumann when he confirmed Captain von Fricken's suspicions?

Wieck portrayed Schumann in this way: "I would have to write a great deal in order to describe more clearly this charming, enthusiastic, talented, very well-educated and likable composer and author." The captain quickly returned his daughter to her home. At about the same time, Clara returned from Dresden. Wieck had the poor taste to write in Clara's diary that Ernestine's gifts had not been realized, because "the sun shone too brightly on her, i.e., Herr Schumann!"

Schumann, hoping to see Ernestine again, returned to Zwickau, through which the von Frickens would pass on their return to Asch. He secretly met with Ernestine and promptly proposed marriage. His mother was aware of his intentions, and he outlined the plot of this "summer novel" in letters to his confi-

Ernestine von Fricken

dante in matters of the heart, Henriette Voigt. The letters reveal considerable doubt about the wisdom of this affair. The voluptuous, alluring girl so attracted Schumann that he overlooked both her poor command of the language and the meaningless prattle in her letters. She also wrote so cunningly of what seemed to be the consent of her father and mother, the Countess of Zedtwitz, that he believed it. In the spring of 1835, if not before, he saw the light and used the farfetched excuse of her illegitimate birth as a reason to break the engagement. Schumann's statement, "Ernestine had to come, so that we could marry," sounds very much like Clara and probably was made in retrospect. Nevertheless, Ernestine would still play an important role in Schumann's life. She sided with the young couple in their quarrel with Wieck by refusing to testify against their union. Schumann later used the letters A-S(=Es)-C-H (which are the German musical equivalents of A, E♭, C, and B) from the name of her home town, Asch, to form one of the principal themes in "Carnaval." We will speak later of his thankful dedication of the three songs in Opus 31.

In the meantime, Clara concertized all winter long, both to her and her father's dissatisfaction. Her mind was on Robert, and Wieck was upset by her indifferent and reluctant performances. He became quite upset with the stereotypical question about Clara's practicing and training regimen so he provided answers to 17 standard questions and wrote them in Clara's diary laced with an irony which he would not have dared use in the green-room.

When Schumann saw Clara again, he discovered a "secret beam of love" in her eyes, but hardly dared to speak with her, which she interpreted as indifference. On August 28, 1835, he finally closed one of his letters to Clara with the line, "You know that you are very dear to me." He sent her his "Grande Sonate pour le Piano-forte" in F# minor, Opus 11, completed that summer with the printed inscription, "Dedicated to Clara from Florestan and Eusebius." She was enraptured by it on the first hearing. By return post she received some articles of Robert's *Zeitschrift,* which was then in its second year. One issue included an assessment of Schubert, whom, contrary to the current opinion, Schumann viewed like Beethoven as "a mortal enemy of the Philistines."

The younger members of the "Davidsbund" celebrated Clara's 16th birthday on September 13th in Leipzig where Schumann met Felix Mendelssohn-Bartholdy for the first time.

Shortly thereafter, Frédéric Chopin passed through Leipzig on his return from a visit to Karlsbad and Clara played several of his pieces for him, and also Schumann's F# minor sonata. This was Chopin's first introduction to the man who had supported him so enthusiastically. However, he ventured no opinion of Schumann's work. The work of his contemporaries was of little interest to him.

One evening that summer, Robert kissed his "Chiara" and decided to break with Ernestine, but he did not have the courage to

Title page of the Piano Sonata, Opus 11, First Edition

voice this decision until the following January. He decided to ask Wieck for Clara's hand, naively assuming that there would be no objection. Wieck did not even allow the subject to come up in conversation, for he had caught wind of this bothersome intruder's most recent advances. In January of 1836 he secretly spirited Clara to Dresden, not even allowing her to answer Schumann who had

35

sent her the Paganini Etudes, and insuring that she was kept busy with concerts and receptions.

Two weeks after their departure, Schumann's mother died, and once again he could not bring himself to attend a funeral, waiting to visit his family only several days later. First he secretly visited Clara, who had been left alone by her father for a day. She wept with him over the death of his mother, who years before had told her, "Some day you will marry my Robert." Wieck, when he learned of their meeting, was furious, demanding all of Robert's letters to her and ordering her to end the relationship. He threatened to shoot Schumann if he ever again approached his daughter.

Schumann found their year-and-a-half of enforced separation his "darkest time." He knew how close Clara was to her father, and was justified in his fear of intrigue, which, ironically, came at the hands, of all people, the composer Carl Banck, a member of the "Davidsbund" who used the pseudonym "Serpentinus." Banck travelled with Clara for the duration of a concert tour as her "voice teacher." When he was forward with her, he in turn forfeited Wieck's "friendship." Banck had tried to turn Clara against Schumann, using Robert's refusal to review her recently composed piano concerto himself, preferring instead to exercise caution and ask another critic to write the review for the *Zeitschrift*. While this episode pained Clara, it did not shake her steadfastness.

In addition to his jealous concerns, Schumann had others as well. One related to Rellstab, the Berlin critic from whose malice an entire generation of musicians was unsafe, and in whose publication *Iris* Schumann was venomously attacked and degraded. Writing for a French journal he criticized Schumann and the *Zeitschrift,* saying "—one could wish he and his staff would flatter each other less." Schumann could demonstrate that in the first seven volumes containing almost 2,000 reviews, only five had been written about works composed by members of the editorial staff. One bit of brightness at this time was Franz Liszt's public declaration of the value of "Robert Schumann and the Leipzig school" in the *Gazette Musicale* in Paris for which Schumann was "overjoyed."

Though he continued unalterably opposed to the desires of the lovers, Wieck recognized Schumann's talent both as a musical critic and composer. Therefore, his decision to "allow" Clara, who had by this time grown quite apathetic, to occasionally perform pieces by Schumann cannot be viewed as a mere attempt to cheer her up. On August 13, 1837, she performed several of Schumann's "Symphonic Etudes" at a morning concert in the *Börsensaal* in Leipzig which the composer secretly attended. Through her friend Becker, Clara begged Schumann to return her letters. Finally, on the 9th of September, as Clara was returning home in the company of her friend, Emilie List, and a servant of the Wieck's, they met again. She found it difficult to hide her shyness and embarrassment. A few days later, on September 13th, Schumann sent a formal letter of proposal to Wieck which included a note for Frau Wieck and the following message for Clara: "You, after this painful separation, may, my dear Clara, wish to support what I have written to your parents. May your love continue to speak where my voice cannot be heard."

Wieck granted the interview, but firmly rejected Schumann's proposal. Schumann was forced to struggle on, seeking that recognition which would change Wieck's opinion, until finally in 1840 he was allowed to make Clara his bride. Periods of happy creativity alternated with periods of anxiety and destructive self-criticism. Schumann had achieved the goals he had set for his three-year-old *Zeitschrift*. Almost without support, he had called into question the musical fashions of the time which had succumbed to the popular taste for music that was easily grasped. Instead he pleaded for high artistic standards.

After repeatedly moving to new quarters, he finally found a place which he found congenial in the "rote Colleg," which he kept until his marriage. "Its windows looked out on the greenest section of the avenue which encircled the old section of Leipzig. Next door was a larger chamber with two windows which also seemed to be a part of his apartment, since there was never any noise from within. It was so quiet and peaceful in the rooms that when the trees in the garden rustled, you could almost imagine that you had been transported to a lonely castle in the forest which glows in the light of the rising and setting sun like something out of one of Eichendorff's wonderful romances." (Jansen)

But without Clara, life in Leipzig was bleak. At the new year she travelled to Vienna, where her talent was widely celebrated. She was given the title of "Kammervirtuosin" (virtuoso at the Imperial court), despite her age, her Protestant background, and her German citizenship. Only Paganini had been accorded such an honor.

This episode further confirmed Schumann's view that his hopes and dreams might be best fulfilled in Vienna, the city of music—that the honor and prestige he sought for his *Zeitschrift* might be fully won there. The Viennese Privy Councillor, Johann Vesque von Püttlingen, an amateur *Lieder* composer, encouraged Schumann to test the waters in Vienna and offered his extensive connections to help smooth the way, for Schumann clearly had no idea how difficult it might be to deal with the censorship and musical cliques which dominated Vienna's musical scene.

The year 1837 was so plagued by anxiety that Schumann found enjoyment only in his work. He was determined to compose for a Beethoven monument in Bonn "Ruins, Triumphal Arches and a Starry Wreath," growing out of his "deep lamentation for Clara." He then changed the name of the work to "Great Sonata," but finally settled on a more fitting title, "Fantasy," Opus 17. The subtitle is a quotation from Schlegel: "Amidst all the sounds ringing throughout this disorderly world, there is a quiet sound meant for the one who secretly listens." Schumann meant the "quiet sound" to be Clara, to whom the "Phantasiestücke," Opus 12, also had been addressed. The latter exemplifies Schumann's love for the lyrical miniature, from his enthusiasm for the evening in "Des Abends," to the question of Fate in "Warum?". He felt the 5th piece of the cycle, "In der Nacht," the most effective. *After* he had written it, he discovered that it could be viewed as a representation of the tale of Hero and Leander.

Schumann's sense of isolation was in some measure relieved by his reunion with Felix Mendelssohn-Bartholdy, in whom Robert found all he felt he lacked: a thorough musical education; familiarity with the ways of the world, and an unusual sense of form. His esteem for Mendelssohn only mounted: "He is the best musician of our time, to whom I look up as if to a high mountain." The creator of the oratorio "Paulus," which stimulated Schumann to once again try his hand at large vocal works, comprehended only in part the artistic stature of his friend, however highly he may have prized him as a person. For a time the two met almost daily for lunch

at the Hotel de Bavière, where they were often joined by Goethe's grandson, Walther, concertmaster Ferdinand David or the composer Sterndale Bennett, to whom the "Etudes symphoniques" were dedicated. Mendelssohn thought Schumann's dedication to the *Zeitschrift* ill-founded and a distraction from more important matters.

Schumann's essays of 1838 attest to his boldness and surety and give lie to the accepted views of an introverted dreamer lacking in resilience and discipline. These traditional portrayals are not only poor representations, but downright misinterpretations as are those of "formless" Schubert or the "demonic" Beethoven. At last the *Zeitschrift* began to receive attention abroad. After the reaction in the Scandinavian countries, Schumann followed with the greatest interest its reception in France, despite his distaste for the "salon atmosphere" which prevailed there, though Clara's successes in Paris certainly helped dispel his unfavorable opinion of the city's musical taste.

Early in 1838, Franz Grillparzer published in the *Wiener Zeitschrift für Kunst und Literatur* a review in poetic form of Clara's performance of Beethoven's "Appassionata" sonata, a work little known at the time.

> A magician tired of life and the world
> Grudgingly locked his magic up
> In a secure adamantine shrine
> And threw the key into the sea and died.
> Mankind bravely tried
> In vain! No key would loose that sturdy door,
> And his magic slumbered like its master.
> A shepherdess playing by the sea
> Watched this hopeless hunt.
> Sensibly, thoughtlessly as young girls are
> She thrust her white hand into a wave
> And grasped, and held, and had it. The key!
> She stood with racing heart.
> The shrine blinked at her, as with eyes.
> The key fit. The lock clicked. The spirits
> Arose and then submitted
> To the graceful, innocent mistress
> Whose white fingers played for and guided them.

Schumann found the poem "the most beautiful ever written about you, and again confirms the poet's godlike stature in revealing with so few words truths valid for all time. In short, the poem pleased me greatly—if your loved one or any lover could both sing and write poetry, this is what he should have created. But putting this poem to music runs counter to the sense of poetry and so diminishes its effect." Clara had probably urged Robert to set Grillparzer's verses to music. Perhaps she hoped to overcome his reluctance to write *Lieder.* But Schumann still felt that composing music and composing poetry demanded two completely different artistic approaches.

Clara's renewed artistic and financial success playing concert programs inspired by Schumann encouraged Wieck to include more of his works in Clara's programs, though he firmly kept the young man at a distance. It was for this reason that Grillparzer first had the opportunity to hear "Carnaval" at a Viennese soirée. Wieck even praised the young composer in public occasionally. To stem Schumann's continuing private hopes he warned, "If I quickly have to marry her [Clara] off to someone else, you alone will be the reason."

Despite Wieck's determined efforts to interdict correspondence, the two lovers left a large collection of letters from these years. They usually wrote every few weeks, he through his friend Reuter, while she, with the help of her maid, transmitted hers at night, living in constant fear of discovery by her father, who slept in the next room with his door open. Clara proposed a regularly scheduled "psychic bridge" between them. Robert's efforts at such telepathic connection strained his nervous state, as he later admitted—"it thoroughly affected me."

Schumann's piano works of those years reflect even more clearly his personal circumstances. He realized that beginning with "Kinderszenen" and "Novelletten" his music had become "calmer, softer, and more melodic." In 1838 he wrote to Clara: "As you have undoubtedly noticed, I am paying special attention to melody; much can be accomplished by diligence and careful observation. But of course, when I speak of the melody, I am not thinking of Italian melody, which is like a bird's song—pleasant, but lacking both substance and thought." The movement of his

musical thought in the direction of the *Lied* is presaged when he writes, "the piano has become too limited." "I often hear in my present compositions a multitude of things I can hardly explain. For example, almost everything I hear when I compose seems to be canonical, yet I can't discover the other voices until after a piece is written. . . ."

It is noteworthy here that Schumann makes two references to vocal music. Even while working on "Kreisleriana," he began to focus on the melodic element. He wrote to Clara, who at this point was quite enthusiastic yet somewhat intimidated in her own compositions, of the "beautiful melodies" which filled his head. Again vocal concepts dominate his account. "Just think, since my last letter I have filled an entire notebook with new *Lieder.* I plan to call it 'Kreisleriana,' for you and my thoughts of you play the main role."

By August of 1838, his sensitivity to the human voice had become significant though not yet decisive. In his diary he speaks of his depression. "Yesterday I thought that I could bear it no longer." Yet that same evening Schumann attended a concert by Pauline Garcia, before which he had felt "as hard as stone," but by which he was "moved to tears"—although Garcia was not blessed with an especially "beautiful" voice and sang in the Italian style, which was quite different from the style Schumann would later adopt. During that same summer Clara had befriended Pauline Garcia, the sister of Malibran and of the later celebrated voice teacher Manuel Garcia. She found the singer charming and devoted to the finest of artistic intentions. Later, probably under Robert's influence, she remarked that Pauline would "never grasp" the sincerity of German music, an opinion entirely shared by Eduard Devrient in later years.

For the period preceding the great *Lieder* compositions, we can assume that Schumann was receptive to the charm of the human voice. However, sincerity of expression was and continued to be much more important in his view than tonal beauty.

Following a lengthy discussion with her father in Vienna, Clara suggested in a letter that Schumann should consider moving the *Zeitschrift* to Vienna. Wieck had given his consent (as Clara much too optimistically termed it) to their marriage, on the condition that Schumann move to another city. In truth, Wieck, as was his wont, had written in Clara's diary that Clara would need at least "2,000 Thaler a year" on which to live, a sum far beyond Schumann's means.

Vienna, the city of music, had always been Schumann's ultimate goal. So when father and daughter had returned to Leipzig, he discontinued his secret visits with Clara to prepare for his journey and the training of his colleague, Oswald Lorenz, in the editorial duties which the latter was to assume. Occasionally, though, he permitted himself to stand for an evening under Clara's window listening to her practice his "Novelletten," the first of which she found especially "thrilling." On the 27th of September, they bid adieu at the home of a friend. Schumann travelled via Dresden and Prague to the Imperial City only to learn in a letter from Clara awaiting his arrival that Wieck had only feigned consent, counting upon Schumann's unwillingness to relocate. In this Wieck had been grievously mistaken.

Schumann urged Clara to resolutely assert her independence from her father's renewed intransigence and deposited 1,000 Gulden with a friend in Leipzig for Clara's use, which would permit her to travel to Paris without her father's support. She did not actually take this step until early in 1839.

Schumann soon discovered, "I am not comfortable with these kinds of people; if the decision were mine alone, I would return to Leipzig tomorrow. The *Zeitschrift* would clearly fail, if it were to be published here." A public enamoured with the music of Josef Lanner and the Strauss brothers and which flocked to Rossini's operas hardly seemed prepared to accept the intense emotional content of Schubert's genius, something that Schumann had assumed almost without question.

In addition to attending to the affairs of his *Zeitschrift*, Schumann found time and energy in Vienna to compose several important works for the piano: "Scherzo, Gigue und Romanze," Opus 32; "Arabeske," Opus 18; "Blumenstück," Opus 19; "Humoreske," Opus 20; "Nachtstücke," Opus 23; and "Ein Faschingsschwank aus Wien" (A Viennese Carnival Tale), Opus 26. In the last, Schumann scored a point against and outwitted the Imperial censors bent on frustrating his effort to print his journal in Vienna. Innocently hidden among the dance motifs, we hear the *Marseillaise,* the performance of which was then forbidden in Vienna. The "Nachtstücke" (Night Pieces) very closely approach the formal design of a *Lied.* "There is a passage in that piece to which I must always return. It seems as if someone is sighing 'Oh God!' from the bottom of his heart. As I was composing, funeral processions, caskets and unhappy, desperate people passed through my mind's eye, and when searching for a title, my thoughts repeatedly returned to 'Leichenphantasie'" (a title borrowed from Schubert).

Schumann's stay in Vienna was marked though by happy episodes—his friendship with Mozart's son and a visit to the graves of Beethoven and Schubert, which Clara had previously described to him in letters. On the way home from the Währing cemetery, it occurred to him that Schubert's brother, Ferdinand, was still alive. He looked him up, and while going through a 10-year accumulation of Schubert's papers, was thrilled to discover the great C major symphony. He immediately sent it to Mendelssohn, who gave the work its premiere at the *Gewandhaus* on March 21, 1839. Schumann also convinced Breitkopf & Härtel to print the work.

The illness and death of his oldest brother Eduard, who had continued to operate their father's bookshop, led Schumann to prematurely end his stay in Vienna. His journey home was difficult, overshadowed by yet another death in the family. For a time, Schumann seriously considered the possibility of taking over the business, having inherited his father's business sense. Schumann's occasional references to his indifference to money have been incorrectly interpreted or overstressed. Rather, he detested the unremitting drive for financial success in men like Wieck.

After his return, Schumann determined to confront Wieck with the warm reception which several Vienna publishers had accorded his compositions, not only to overcome the latter's objections but also to stiffen Clara's diminishing resolve to break away from her father. Interruptions in their correspondence reduced Schumann to a deep melancholy: "It seems as if I have been wrapped and packed away in black clothes; an indescribable state."

In January of 1839, Clara travelled to Paris accompanied only by a maid. Her first concert trip without her father not only proved the 19-year-old's independence, but also her skill in organizing a concert series. At that time, there were no concert agents as we know them today, so Clara, like other artists, had to arrange for the hall, tickets, etc.; act as publicity manager, and then perform the concert. Additionally, following her performance, she was obliged to host a reception at her hotel. On one evening she was among the illustrious guests at Meyerbeer's table.

Heine made the strongest impression on Clara; the banality of those who laughed most heartily at their own jokes repelled her. She found him melancholy and unhappy, for his progressive illness led him to fear that he would lose his sight. Clara found nothing of the cheerful nature Robert had described to her. He spoke bitterly of Germany but promised to visit her in Leipzig, as did Auber, Onslow, and Halévy. Those visits were never made.

Wieck wrote Clara a letter filled with emotion and worries, which she said "almost broke my heart." Her resolve vanished. She wrote Schumann of her love and faithfulness, but added that she could not proceed further until the questions of their future and means of livelihood had been resolved. She added that her father would accompany her on a tour of Belgium, Holland, and England that summer, since a female artist was more favorably received when accompanied by a man. Her alarming letter crossed Schumann's optimistic letter to her, the woman who was to be his wife "at the earliest possible moment." Despair was inevitable, as was Schumann's angry reply. Wieck sent a list of insulting "conditions" aimed at excluding Schumann from her life, which he demanded she sign. He had gone too far: Clara refused. Nearly simultaneously she signed Schumann's petition seeking legal permission for them to marry and turned it over to an attorney.

In July, 1839, the couple turned to Clara's mother to request her permission for their marriage following Frau Bargiel's request that Schumann travel to Berlin so that they might discuss the matter. The result of their very frank conversation was a letter from her mother advising Clara to return home to her father, whose concerns she had ignored. Clara cancelled her London debut and began the journey home. Along the way, at Altenburg, Schumann and Clara met for the first time in nine months. They spent only three days together in Schneeberg at the house of Schumann's sister-in-law before Clara continued on to her aunt's house in Leipzig, where she met her mother, who requested that Clara remain with her.

Schumann returned to Leipzig to complete several articles including a major essay on Franz Liszt for the *Zeitschrift*. The musicians and composers whose performances or work Schumann reviewed were usually pleased with his assessments. Stephen Heller wrote from Paris: "Above all I thank you for your critique of the sonata. . . . No one writes as precisely, delicately and sensitively as you. I showed your review to Heine who said it was 'extremely well written'."

In addition to the extensive writing for the *Zeitschrift*, Schumann also began "about 50 new compositions." The productive "year of songs" was about to begin. In a letter to the composer Hirschbach, in the summer of 1839, Schumann still confessed that he had always placed music for the human voice "below instrumental music and never considered it a great art." But he added, "Please tell no one." It is understandable that Schumann did not wish this opinion to be widely known. In his *Zeitschrift,* he put it more mildly: ". . . . thus we cannot grant the composers of vocal music a place in the sun, any more than painters grant it to landscape artists, if that is all they paint." It is no wonder that as a critic, Schumann always passed reviews or articles dealing with vocal music on to his "Liederminister," Lorenz. Schumann clearly felt that such music did not belong in his department.

Chapter 6

It is even more astounding then, how strongly Schumann's interest in the *Lied* was renewed shortly thereafter, despite his interest in this medium at the beginning of his musical career. This renewal may well have resulted from the appearance of the oratorio "St. Paul" by his friend Mendelssohn. Simultaneously Schumann also returned to writing articles on the *Lied* in his journal. He wished, as a writer and composer, to assist his readers in these articles in understanding the esthetics of his creative intentions, and he particularly struggled to develop a critical position reconciling the expression of the composer's personal views with the artistic demands of the *Lied.*

Schumann found it very "informative and rewarding" to compare two songs based on the same text and he strongly adhered to psychological truth as a measure of success. He was bothered by Carl Loewe's compositions, in which it seemed "each individual word of the poem was subjected to 'tone painting'." He found Heinrich Marschner's music more convincing, for the composition depended upon more formal connections between text and music: "Everything lives and whispers. Each syllable, each note is enhanced." Before he could bring himself to write *Lieder,* Schumann had to reconcile himself to the sad fact that the profusion of *Lieder* being written "could have buried all of Germany annually."

After spending the Christmas holidays with Clara and the Bargiel family, Schumann nervously awaited the court's judgment, which was to be handed down on 4 January 1840. Before the judgment would be handed down, the court had given Wieck 45 days to present evidence to support his charge that Schumann was addicted to drink. All of the other objections brought by Wieck had already been rejected by the judge based on a "letter of reference" in which Schumann summoned all the evidence he could muster. In it he presented evidence not only of a yearly income of 1,500 Thaler and of his landlady's trust by giving him a key to her house (an element in Wieck's allegations), but also testimonials from Liszt and Moscheles vouching for the quality of his artistic and musical talent.

He determined to go beyond these testimonials by obtaining his doctorate to add further confirmation of his capacities. One of the *Zeitschrift* writers, Pastor Dr. Keferstein, who wrote under the pen name K. Stein, presented the dean of the faculty of philosophy at Jena with a selection of Schumann's compositions and articles, as well as the plans for a thesis on Shakespeare's relationship to music to be written by Schumann. In less than four weeks, and without presenting a thesis, Schumann was awarded the degree of Doctor of Philosophy.

When Wieck read the press notice of Schumann's degree, he renewed his agitation more vigorously, but he now directed his venom against Clara as well, who had just undertaken another concert tour. He had a notice printed which repeated his objections, those which had only recently been rejected by the court, and sent it to influential persons in the cities Clara was to visit as well as to friends and acquaintances. From Hamburg she wrote, "I am so terribly nervous, especially since no one here understands anything about music—just imagine, they prefer Dreyschock to

Thalberg. . . ." The following engagement in Bremen was also difficult for Clara. Schumann blamed himself for not accompanying her in order to support and defend her. "There are reasons for as well as against accompanying you. I would have liked to prove my talents as a concert artist on tour with you. But of course, it is also nice to stay here, in this warm room, diligently working for humanity. . . *Adieu* now, my dear, thought and composing have exhausted me, so that I almost perish. Oh, Clara, what bliss it is to write for the voice. I was without it for so long. . . ."

Clara could not restrain a passing sense of jealousy. "How nice that you've been composing so intensively! Your preoccupation with *Lieder* sounds suspicious. Is there perhaps a young nightingale, who has so inflamed your passion?" But, among the singers Schumann knew, there were none who might fit Clara's description.

Wieck plotted against his daughter's recitals as vigorously in Berlin as in the cities visited earlier in her tour. He tried to prevail upon Alderman Behrens to refuse Clara's request to use his grand piano for her Berlin concert, suggesting that being used to a hard English action, she tended to batter all other instruments. Just before her Berlin concert she fainted, but encouraged by her mother, she played after all. As a result, however, she developed a painful neuralgia in her face. Something of what Schumann had been enduring at the hands of her father began to dawn on Clara. We begin to detect more forbearance and understanding in her letters.

While Wieck's obdurate cruelty had wounded Schumann, it had not destroyed him. On the contrary, he was overflowing with musical thought, completing numerous sketches at a frenzied pace—he could barely contain the creative inspiration which drove him. On 16 February he wrote Clara, "I just wanted to tell you that I have finished six notebooks full of *Lieder,* ballads and quartets. You will like some of them. . . ."

Schumann's first biographer, Wilhelm Joseph von Wasielewski, has claimed, probably correctly, since he was able to rely directly on the composer's statements, that Schumann returned to the *Lied* out of a personal need to achieve a higher level of clarity in expression. He believes it quite understandable that Schumann turned to the use of words at this time in his career "in order to express his sensibilities and emotions more clearly than he had before." Walter Dahms wrote, although not entirely convincingly, that Schumann's outpouring of song derived from his sense that Clara did not entirely understand him. But we can rule out any notion that Schumann was aware of such thoughts at the time. Rather, this explosive productivity seems to be a part of a personal cycle which Schumann recognized, having developed a keen sense of self-observation in such matters. In a letter to Clara on 7 February, he wrote, "I am overflowing with music, just as I usually am in February." Of the many pieces Schumann left unfinished in 1839, most are *Lieder.*

In a paper entitled "Robert Schumann's *Lieder:* First Versions and Revisions," Victor Ernst Wolff recounts his review of the music notebooks which Schumann rapidly assembled during February, May, and September of 1840. They include more than 100 *Lieder,* a number of them first drafts. Comparing these preliminary sketches with their printed versions, he discovered numerous changes, both large and small, including improvements in the relation of text to musical expression and the more precise formulation of musical intention. Frequently, an initial, unusual thought was replaced by one more "understandable." Some of their circle of friends attributed this extensive reshaping to Clara's influence. Wolff ascribes the changes to Schumann's wish "to take classical tastes into account." The magnitude or extent of these changes, however, is not of such import as to compel us to join Hans Joachim Moser in dismissing many of these *Lieder* as worthless. The detailed examination of these changes need not detain us further at this point, though we must point out before moving on that the abundance of sketches in these notebooks has made it much easier to date those *Lieder* which bear no specific date. In this, we follow, with few exceptions, the convincing arguments of Eric Sams.

Schumann's artistic direction now took a radical turn. This new direction was foretokened by the *Lied* "Der Nussbaum," which he sent to Clara with a note saying, "Sing this quietly and simply, just as you are." At about the same time, Schumann announced his ballad "Belsatzar," a group of songs for four voices, and seven collections of *Lieder.* "I can hardly explain how simple everything has become for me and how happy I am about it. For the most part, I composed them while standing or walking, not at the piano. This is a very different type of music, which is not initially realized through the fingers."

He seized upon the poetic word with a passion, producing no less than 138, that is more than half of his solo songs, during this single year. The choice of poems attests to the fundamental element Schumann sought for his texts; they must reflect the poetic spirit. As with his self-styled piano technique and its unique form of expression, he developed a style of *Lied* which continued and expanded upon Schubert's style. In this context, it is especially important to point out that improvisation at the piano, which had heretofore always preceded the written version of a piece, was now replaced by Schumann's thought and imagination, an undertaking of the mind quite independent of the piano. This approach was subsequently articulated as a principle of composition in Schumann's *Musikalische Haus-und Lebensregeln.*

Clearly, the piano had proved a valuable tool for Schumann for a time. Schumann's technical refinement placed him ahead of his contemporaries, even the much-admired Chopin. But he had exhausted the possibilities of the instrument as a compositional device and so had to turn to inner resources to portray the emotional intentions he wished to express. The transition to the *Lied* occurred quite smoothly, for the forms of the *Lied* which had been clearly evident in piano works such as "Nachtstücke" and "Romanzen" were now simply drawn upon.

Schubert had provided a model for simplicity of expression, tenderness of tone, and a natural grace which provided a special atmosphere for these miniatures. "A poem should be like a breath," said Goethe, who often referred to a poem as "Lied." This became a basic formula for Schumann's work. He often surpassed Schubert in creating colorful moods, though he was not always able to equal Schubert's use of powerful dithyrambic pathos. This may be why Schumann produced very few successful ballads; though he was never able to suppress the lyric poet within him, particularly in his operas. Longing for spring, autumnal melancholy, feelings of love, joy, anxiety, twilight, the woods, and homesickness—all these challenged Schumann's compositional genius. Every flash of imagination or insight served to ignite his creative instincts.

By learning to trust the inspiration of the moment, Schumann, like Schubert, began to achieve some of the immediacy of folk song. He selected texts which were unaffected and singable, preferring simple quatrains. Within the natural structure of the verse, he often emphasized the voice, while the accompaniment was written to indicate that he was attempting to create something more than a popular melody. Unlike the songs of earlier composers, Schumann's melodies do not dominate the other elements.

Shakespeare ushered in the "Year of Songs." Schumann's posthumously numbered Opus 127, Number 5, "Schlusslied des Narren" from *Twelfth Night,* based on the German translation by Schlegel and Tieck, points to an unfinished anthology planned to reflect the opinions of several poets on the relationship between word and music. Schumann jotted down these sketches during the period when he was enthralled by Jean Paul and called his collection "Dichtergarten" (The Poet's Garden). It opened with a text by Shakespeare, whom Schumann revered as a "universal genius of the same stature as Mozart and Beethoven." Shakespeare's relationship to music was, as noted earlier, the topic Schumann had chosen for his doctoral dissertation, but the ideas were but poorly roughed out since he received his degree without submitting it.

Schumann shortened the lyric epilogue of the comedy (from which Otto Nicolai had adopted Falstaff's speech in *The Merry Wives of Windsor*) by deleting the second and fourth verses. He had just become acquainted with the incidental music to *A Midsummer Night's Dream* by his friend Mendelssohn. Thus, it is not surprising that the goblin from Mendelssohn's *Overture* reappears here (Example 5).

This was the only composition for which Schumann turned to Shakespeare for text material, but it is important to note that the poet of his youth accompanied him into the world of the *Lied.*

Schumann's relationship to Heine, whom we meet in the second piece included in "Belsatzar," Opus 57, is quite unusual. This song has frequently been ridiculed and criticized, particularly by those who, despite careful study, fail to find Heine's bitterness, sarcasm, and scintillating irony reflected in Schumann's music. However, numerous instances support a contrary view. Schumann

Example 5

Robert Schumann: "Belsatzar," *autograph score (choral version)*

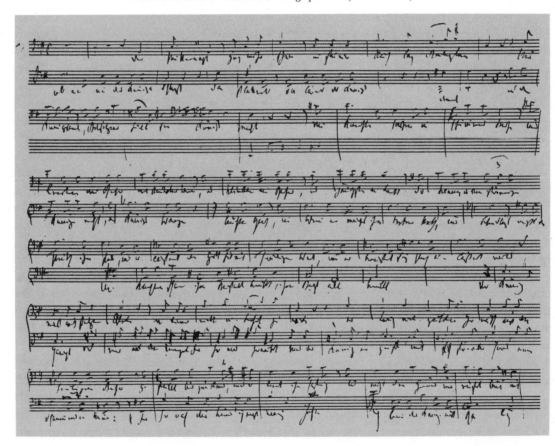

set aside only those texts which depended upon that eroticism which Heine found so irresistible. But the old Florestan-Eusebius creative conflict which marked Schumann's inner being is most evident in Schumann's artistic relationship with Heine. Rarely do we encounter an artistic expression so similar to Heine's, with its tortured, almost pathological qualities and its intensity.

The Heine texts which Schumann selected seemed those which most fittingly represented the inner contradictions of his own nature. From intentional exaggeration to sentimentality, Schumann was able to reanimate Heine's poetry through the genius of his music. Sometimes he used the poetry only as a vehicle; at other times his music gave substance to shallow verses. Nuance, a broken spirit, joy turning to melancholy, sadness turning into exuberance and sarcasm, tone painting of twilight, the images of death staring over the shoulders of young girls—Schumann drew upon all of these states of mind and images found in Heine's poetry and from them developed his unique style of the *Lied*. Though it was not always implied by Heine's verses, Schumann tended to set them in four- or eight-measure phrases, endeavoring to make them more "folk-like." Later, Schumann was to find the simplicity he sought in the poetry of Eichendorff as it was written.

In the genre of the ballad—"Belsatzar" was his first and most successful—Schumann, whether he wished to or not, was forced to compete with Carl Loewe, the composer from Stettin whom he greatly admired. "If we had to choose any living composer who from the beginning of his career to the present [1835] captured the German spirit and soul, expressing them now tenderly and then with wild abandon, speaking sometimes in the language of young love and at others in an outburst of the greatest fury, then we must select Loewe." Schumann was not referring to the few Loewe "hits" which are still performed, but to his enormous influence through his choice of texts and his support of relatively unknown poets such as Mörike and Rückert. Schumann wrote of Loewe, who was at the time travelling throughout the country singing and playing his own works, as the "rare union of composer, singer, and virtuoso."

Schumann marked his newly found relationship to songs with a touching gesture: in February of 1840 he planned to print Heine's poem separately, preceding the music, as was indeed done when the work was published in 1846. The music for "Belsatzar" has often been criticized. Too many motifs, it is claimed, interfere with the free flow of the ballad; the use of the "primitive device" of increasing tension; the lack of dramatic sensibility (attributed to the hushed delivery of the terrifying last verse); an awkwardly structured singing line—these are but a few of the allegations from which the work still suffers today. Its critics do not seem to understand the fact that they are dealing with a bold device—conceived, amazingly enough, by a "beginner"—which portrays the heavy brooding quality of the poem's opening by arousing the listener's senses through the nervous restlessness in the piano part, then carrying the listener to the catastrophic climax through the use of an ever quieter and simpler musical line, finally closing in a hushed, stifled mood. Schumann, to be sure, confronted in his ballads the same problems with which Schubert wrestled in "Taucher" or "Einsamkeit:" the overwhelming number of characters and complicated plot result in a growing number of musical motifs, in a musical overload. Schumann only solved this problem in *Die beiden Grenadiere* when he limited himself to a single theme.

The story of "Belsatzar," the king who blasphemes the Lord and whose servants kill him, possesses the character of a dramatic scene, the setting and story line of which Schumann's music subtly suggests. It also maintains the dense, foreboding mood to the very end, despite the continuous diminuendo leading from the noisy feast scene to the stillness of death. Every element of the composition, from the pridefully emphasized "ich" ("I"), sung on high G (Example 6), to the sinister and eerie writing on the wall is carefully woven and integrated into the work, making it an organically artistic whole.

Example 6

Without doubt, Schumann's affinity for the emotional world of Byron's life and writings incited his admiration of Heine.

Schumann did not always share his contemporaries' proclivity to take Heine seriously. Conversely, he often devoted great effort to some relatively insignificant texts, giving them an importance of which Heine would have made light had he been familiar with Schumann's *Lieder.* Their meeting in Schumann's youth had not led to any kind of recognition. Only as a writer did Schumann receive Heine's approval.

In *Liederkreis,* Opus 24, based on poems by Heine, and dedicated to Pauline Garcia, we follow Schumann into a musical domain which was in no way strange to him—the song cycle. Schumann adopted the form of the song cycle from Beethoven ("An die ferne Geliebte") and Schubert's masterpieces. He only added his own grandiose, bold touch.

He rarely published songs singly; more commonly he collected them and set them into a larger context, though these assemblages were seldom presented in the form of a continuous story. A group of songs set to the texts of a single poet or merely a similarity in the mood of the poems were often enough to justify bringing them together. Schumann arranged the nine poems from Heine's "Junges Leiden" in a sequence that suggests a single plot line. "Recently, I have been working on a great cycle of songs by Heine and now it is completely finished. . . ." (Again we see "completely finished," just as we did after his first vocal composition!) After thus informing Clara he continued, "While I was composing, my thoughts were only of you. Without such a bride, a person could not write such music."

The cycle begins with a dream-like *Allegretto* in D major entitled "Morgens steh ich auf und frage," a poem also set to music by Robert Franz and Franz Liszt. The poet's question as to whether his love will come today is accompanied by a regular, pulsating rhythm which is repeatedly broken into by freer rhythm. Such improvisatory agogic notation had never been previously used. "I wander as if in a dream the day long"—these words determine the mood of the music: there is little hope that the dream will be fulfilled. The piece ends in a form which would soon become typical Schumann, with a triple grace-note on the beat—not on the upbeat! (Example 7.)

HEINRICH
HEINE

1797 (?)–1856. Heine was the son of Jewish parents; his father, Samson, was a textile merchant. He was born in Düsseldorf, the exact year of his birth being uncertain. Before Harry (his given first name) undertook his studies, his father went bankrupt. His mother, Betty, née von Geldern—the daughter of a physician and herself an enlightened follower of Voltaire—had a greater influence on him. His brother Gustav founded a newspaper in Vienna and was awarded a baronetcy. His brother Max was a physician to the Czar. Heinrich became Germany's most famous poet after Goethe, despite the fact that the head of the family, his Uncle Salomon of Hamburg, still wrote his letters in Yiddish.

Düsseldorf had been under French control since 1806, under the command of Murat. Heine viewed Napoleon as the embodiment of freedom, a belief which lay at the base of his decision to leave the land of his mother tongue—as well as favorable professional prospects in Munich—for "voluntary exile" in Paris. The decision was facilitated because his hopes of a professorship in Munich were dashed by Ludwig I. The falling away of friends and supporters resulting from his quarrel with Count Platen and a falling out with his rich uncle in

Example 7

Hamburg contributed to his decision to emigrate. The matter was finally settled when he read with enthusiasm newspaper accounts of the July Revolution. But political pressure and persecution followed him, including the censoring of his writings by the Frankfurt Bundestag, the same restrictions falling heavily upon other members of the literary party, "Junges Deutschland" (Young Germany).

From his 3 3rd year, Heine remained in France living in Paris, Montmorency, Dieppe and Boulogne-sur-Mer, eventually marrying a French woman, Mathilde. He spent the last eight of his remaining 2 6 years on his sick bed. He died in his "mattress grave" on 1 7 February 1 8 5 6. Though he had declined physically, his spirit, his imagination, his awareness of world events, his productive powers, and his charm never faltered nor failed.

His poetry displays natural folk song quality inspired by the "Wunderhorn" poetry, and is evidence of his rebellion against the overly refined and intricate poetry of the time. The figures which fill his epic and dramatic poems all reflect qualities and characteristics he found within himself. He later judged his early tragedy, "Almansor," as not sufficiently "drastic." "William Ratcliff" derived its theme of the lost bride and unhappy love from the "Buch der Lieder," and transforms it into a gruesome ballad. His only short story, "The Rabbi of Bacharach," is not just a fable of pogroms, but also a portrait gallery of Jewish eccentrics. Heine's "Französische Zustände" (The Situation in France) and his Parisian letters under the title "Lutezia," mark the beginning of a new genre, literary journalism. As a critical historian, he chronicled the intellectual movements of his time in *The School of Romanticism* and *On the History of Religion and Philosophy in Germany*. He expressed his despair most clearly in his poetry—as much by resorting to frivolity, arrogance, and sarcasm as with a sweet, dark, or heartfelt tone—a poet who unflinchingly acknowledged the hopelessness of the human situation.

Title page from the first edition of Liederkreis, *Opus 2 4*

Critics have suggested that the music of the second song in Opus 24, "Es treibt mich hin," is at variance with the meaning of the poem—that the massive chords denote resignation rather than impatience. They further contend that Schumann's belief that Clara would remain in Berlin for some time and not just for "hours" affected the form of the piece. This view may be the consequence of overly heavy interpretations of the piece by some artists. The fast tempo demands extreme concentration on the part of both the pianist and the singer, especially for precise ensemble during the rubatos. Careful attention must also be given to the clarity of the consonants. The impassioned restlessness which characterize the *Lied* is symbolized by its key, B minor, which foretells the unhappy outcome, the imminent disappointment of the waiting lover. Schumann does not ignore Heine's subtle mockery, which resonates throughout the lover's lament when he celebrates the "most beautiful of beautiful virgins" with a distorting five-note turn, or when he describes the dragging "lazy hours" with a humorous canon (Example 8).

The inner peace of the third song, "Ich wandelte unter den Bäumen," contrasts strongly with the mood of its predecessor—it is marked *Adagio* and is in B major. Schumann did not use the poem's original title, "Das Wörtlein Liebe." Perhaps he did not know it. The rich polyphony of the prelude remains sketchy and it is never fully worked out. The connecting point in the dialogue between the lovesick lover and the birds is very significant: "Dann tut es noch einmal so weh. Es kam ein Jungfräulein gegangen." (Then it will hurt even more. A young maiden came singing.) No answer to the question is sought, for the lover wishes to rid his thoughts of her who taught the birds the loving words. But, against his hope, the answer comes after a downward skip of a ninth and a rather daring, deceptive cadence (Example 9).

Though it is not expressly indicated, a change in the singer's timbre is required at this point. Here, as in innumerable other cases, the usual tone production without special attention to tone color will not do. The boldness of this transition, though written long ago, continues to be exciting. Schumann used doubled thirds in a high

Example 8

Example 9

register, to portray the birds, as he often did when birds appeared in later poems. The song ends on a six-four chord, like an unanswered question.

"Lieb' Liebchen, Leg's Händchen," is the second song in the cycle. While the previous song expressed anticipation, this one is dominated by the melancholy of death. Death was a thought never far from Schumann's mind, but 1840 was a year full of hope. So this song, in which Schumann expresses Heine's ironic views, is quite a remarkable accomplishment. The conclusion of the song is unprecedented: the piano accompaniment comes to an end, and the voice is left alone to confront the hopelessness of death (Example 10). Syncopation, rests, and breaks, occasionally in the middle of a phrase, form the character of this miniature which Reissmann, in his Schumann biography of 1870, indignantly denounced as an unnatural and outrageous assault on the sacred, serious theme of the poem, due to his misunderstanding of Schumann's intentions.

Example 10

schla - fen kann.

Schumann placed the musical high point of the cycle, "Schöne Wiege meiner Leiden," at its midpoint. For the first time, as he would frequently do in the future, he altered the poem, expanding it by repeating sections of the text to suit his musical requirements. Notwithstanding, Schumann's treatment is justified: the mood of Heine's hectic departure from Hamburg is reflected in the music. The singer first assaying the piece may question the possibility of realizing the "beauty" of the melody at the indicated tempo ("lively"). But it will soon become clear that the composer's musical intention can only be achieved at this rapid tempo. It is a song whose theme is at once hectic yet luxuriant in self-pity and sorrow. The piece, shaped by contrasts, is in the form of a dramatic scene. The third, fifth, and sixth verses distance themselves from the floating syncopation of the principal melodic line with their panting accompaniment.

After the phrase "Lebe Wohl!," the repetition of which supports the theme, has been heard for the last time, the composer introduces a piano epilogue. Just as in *Dichterliebe,* this epilogue seems to interrupt the cycle. It is as if a departing traveler turns back once again, seeing in a single panorama the sum of the injustices he has suffered.

The sarcastic side of Schumann's complex character makes itself known in the sixth piece of the cycle, "Warte, Warte, Wilder Schiffmann." Regularly rolling rhythm pervades the bitter "departure from Europe." The composer sustains the poignancy of the original poem throughout. Schumann has added "gleich" ("at once"); and the groaning "oh," neither of which appear in Heine's text, to avoid a deeply tragic tone yet achieve a feeling of unmitigated angry bitterness. Pain and rage are embodied through the use of sharp contrasts in the harmony of the accompaniment and tritone jumps in the vocal line. In cutting off the voice on the seventh of the dominant chord, Schumann introduces despair. At the conclusion of the piece, after so many bitter protests, the protagonist's power to continue is broken; he collapses in exhaustion.

The intermezzo of the seventh song, "Berg' und Burgen schau'n herunter," opens with the simplicity of a gentle folk song. The inner conflict is only suggested by the strophic arrangement. Heine's analogy between the river and the lover is only hinted at in the sound of the wave at the end of each verse. At the time of composition, Schumann could hardly have imagined being deceived by his fiancée. The last line of the third stanza, in the first edition of the poem which Schumann used, begins with the word "bringt" (brings). Schumann corrected this to read "birgt" (harbors).

Moving from the gentle conclusion of the seventh piece to the resignation of the eighth, "Anfangs wollt' ich fast verzagen," Schumann avoided the heavy use of accents to which other composers, including Liszt, have resorted in setting this poem. This short song possesses numerous musical connections, including

Bach's chorale setting of "Wer nur den lieben Gott lässt walten," and Chopin's Prélude Number 20, from Opus 28. Of the composers known to have set this quatrain to music, including Schumann, all overlooked Heine's humor, which led him to write these lines about a pair of patent leather shoes ("und ich hab' es doch getragen"). ["I have borne it" or "suffered it"—another meaning of *getragen* is "worn it" (Ed.).]

Of course, Schumann was critized for his setting; it was seen as a prime example of his "misunderstanding" Heine. In two musical phrases, fascinating in their conciseness, Schumann repeats the final words, "Just don't ask me how!" as a questioning half-cadence on the dominant. The way in which Heine eludes explaining "how" prepares the way for the conciliatory conclusion to the cycle (Example 11).

Example 11

a - ber fragt mich nur nicht wie? nicht wie?

Thus it is difficult to understand why the concluding song in the cycle, "Mit Myrten und Rosen," (with Myrtle and Roses) was deleted in the Peters Edition and published instead in the first volume of Schumann's "famous" pieces. There is a clear similarity and continuity in the sound quality between these two songs. The placement in the wrong volume as well as the fact that the title is taken out of context usually results in a sentimental interpretation.

The mood of the middle of the song is "as wild as a stream of lava spewing forth from the depths of Mount Etna." Only at its conclusion, obscured by an impressionistic harmonic haze that foreshadows Ravel, does Eusebius voice his "melancholy and gentle love." The song's piano part is reminiscent of the *Novelette,* Opus 21, and like it succeeds in combining romantic sensitivity with clarity, passion, and artistic discipline. Schumann has entirely mastered the form which he has created here.

In February, 1840, immediately after the completion of the cycle, when Schumann offered his latest work to the publishing house of Breitkopf & Härtel, he was, of course, exaggerating when he described its creation as an "extended" period "of enjoyment and happiness." "Since I am known only for my piano works, I think this may arouse some interest. I would appreciate it if it could be published soon, under the conditions previously agreed upon. I hope you will not mind providing me with a few more free copies, about ten or twelve. You may wish to publish the collection in two volumes, but I would really prefer to keep it intact, since it forms a single unit."

On the 23rd of May, Schumann gave Friedrich List a copy of his *Liederkreis* to take to Heine in Paris. The enclosed letter reminded Heine of their meeting in Munich. Apparently, the package never reached Heine's hands. Perhaps List was never able to contact Heine so sent only the letter to him. On the 6th of July, Schumann asked Stephen Heller to remember him to Heine. Heller answered on the 30th of July: "I have not yet seen your *Lieder,* nor have I seen Heine, who moves in closed circles, and who in general seems to be an unpleasant, mysterious person, whose works are much more likeable than he is." Later, in "Lutezia," Heine complained that he had "never received one complimentary copy of any of the many hundreds of compositions using his poems which have appeared in Germany." This remark is reminiscent of Goethe's mysterious silence after Schubert sent him a copy of his most important *Lieder.*

Chapter 7

Schumann's relationship with Friedrich Rückert (1788–1866), from whose work he adapted the poems for his collection entitled *Myrten,* was much different from that with Heine. Rückert's verse was more easily and successfully set to music; occasional triviality could be rendered innocuous by a carefully contrived melody. If the composer followed the text too faithfully, the poetic weakness or lapses were more easily detected, which is often typical, as in the cases when geniuses such as Schubert, Mahler, or Strauss attempt a literal interpretation of a weak poem. Like Paten, Rückert transformed the poetic medium, moving it in new and previously unexplored directions, as well as imprinting a new sense of rhythm and color.

Schubert and Hetsch were the first composers to set Rückert's poetry to music, but they now were joined by Schumann. He was entranced by Rückert's mastery of the rhythmic and technical aspects of poetry, which, however, was not so academic as to lose the strength and simplicity of folk song. However, Schumann had no sympathy with that aspect of Rückert which, with similar skill, celebrated death and insanity in works like "Kindertotenlieder" ("Songs on the Death of Children").

Schumann called the introductory song of *Myrten,* Opus 25, "Widmung." He employed a different musical approach to the portrayal of the emotions of love here than he had with Heine's poetry. He turns to a passionate form as he sings a profoundly felt hymn to his loved one in the middle of the piece with the line, "You are the silence" (one of Rückert's favorite metaphors). The characteristic sweeping keyboard passages and the enharmonic progression (A^b major to E^b major) to the central section—these are devices

we shall encounter again in many Schumann songs. In the final measures, Schumann creates a meditative instrumental effect which surpasses that of the text itself. In these measures, a new motif is introduced, independent of the voice. It becomes apparent in this first song that Schumann agrees with the poet's heartfelt remark, "Unless I have sung it, I have not experienced it."

In the *Myrten* collection of songs, we find great diversity of subject material and styles loosely connected to each other, just as in "Carnaval," "Faschingsschwank" or "Nachtstücke." Feldmann theorizes that not the Heine cycle, which seems to have been inspired by thoughts of a lover, but *Myrten* was meant as a wedding present for Clara. Schumann's artistic objective was not a uniting theme but a reflection on a variety of matters touching on religion as well as love. Thus it is that Schumann requested a "green or blue" cover on the published work, "because the songs are for the most part cheerful," whereas he suggested a "silver" or "ash-gray" cover for the later Eichendorff songs.

Five songs from Goethe's "Divan" are included in the *Myrten* volume. "Freisinn'" from "Buch des Sängers," is characterized by high spirits, much movement, energy, and a dotted rhythm which successfully avoids becoming march-like. The instructive yet contemplative middle verse, "Er hat euch die Gestirne gesetzt," is especially effective. In this verse, only the straight chords remain untouched by the rhythm. It is interesting to note that Schumann almost never changed any words in Goethe's poems, a liberty he took with the work of other poets.

Text changes occur in *Der Nussbaum* (The Nut Tree) by Julius

FRIEDRICH
RÜCKERT

A scholar and poet, born in Schweinfurt, Rückert was the son of an official of the treasury who was transferred to the village of Oberlauringen in Lower Franconia in 1792 to take up duties in the justice office of the baronial lord-high-steward. In 1829, Rückert recorded his impressions of his early youth in a poetic and humorous cycle entitled *Memories of the Son of a Small Town Official.* After finishing his schooling in Schweinfurt in 1805, he undertook the study of law at the University in Würzburg, where he remained until 1809, after having turned almost exclusively to the study of philology and esthetics. He delved so deeply into philology that he later said of himself, "Every language written by men is alive in me."

For a short time after 1811, he lectured in Jena and briefly taught in a secondary school in Hanau. Rückert gave up public employment and settled in Würzburg, devoting himself to his own studies. For the next few years he lived from time to time in Würzburg, in Hildburghausen and with his parents in Oberlauringen. He expressed his sympathies with the movement for political freedom by writing "Geharnischte Sonette" and "Spott—und Ehrenlieder" which he first published in a volume of *German Poems* under the pseudonym Freimund Reimar. In 1816, Minister von Wangenheim convinced him to go to Stuttgart to become the poetry editor for Cotta's *Morgenblatt.* He saw a great deal of Ludwig Uhland in Stuttgart, despite the fact that they held differing views on the question of the constitution for Württemberg. In the fall of 1817, Rückert travelled to Italy where he was actively involved with the German artistic community in Rome until his return to Vienna in 1818. There he undertook the study of Persian, a step which was to be important for his later writing. After several years, in which he lived in several towns in Franconia, he married Luise Wiethaus-Fischer. After his marriage he established his "poet's retreat" in Neuses near Coburg where, for the most part, he lived during his later years. In 1826, he was called to the University at Erlangen as professor of Oriental languages and literature. By then both his academic work and poetry focused almost exclusively on the Orient.

The mass of translations and adaptations Rückert produced from Near Eastern, Indian and East Asian poetry was overwhelming. After the ascension of Friedrich Wilhelm IV to the throne of Prussia, Rückert was summoned to Berlin. He did not feel at all comfortable there, and in 1846 he returned permanently to Neuses. As a poet he remained extraordinarily productive. His name quickly became widely recognized in Germany, thanks not only to his songs contained in *Liebesfrühling* (Spring of Love), which countless composers after Schumann set to music, but also to his meditative and educational poem, *Weisheit des Brahmanen* (The Wisdom of the Brahman). He also wrote several historical dramas which were of a lesser consequence.

His importance lay in his rare ability to place didactic and introspective themes in a lyrical setting. Much of his poetry is unique, both in its great wealth of thought and knowledge and the power of its expression. However, much of Rückert's voluminous writing is of little value. His skillful handling of language often resulted in an affectation which stood in the way of true poetic achievement. Rückert's masterful skill lay in his ability to infuse even trivial matters with poetic life. He expresses a cultural epoch which could and wished to be enthusiastic yet tough-minded, scientific yet sentimental. He does this through his manner, occasionally doctrinaire, and through a sometimes cold, formal style of the old poetic school.

Goethe's collection *West-östlicher Divan* had interested the public in the poetry of the Orient and prepared the way for the enthusiastic response to *Östliche Rosen* in the early 1820s. But for some time, Rückert's dual role as poet and scholar foreclosed his popular success. His poetry appeared only in journals and yearbooks, but not in collections over his own name. Furthermore, his scholarly papers and translations reached only a limited audience. When his *Collected Poems* was finally published as a single volume, this state of affairs was completely altered.

Mosen. Departures from a text which in Schubert's case might have been a typical transcriptional error or perhaps a slip of the memory was always a conscious, intentional act for Schumann. Thus, in the case of *Der Nussbaum* he separates some of the verses to express the fullness of its dreamy quality in the music, unimpeded by Mosen's words. Thus, when Schumann substitutes "Blätter" (leaves) for "Äste" (branches), he does better justice to the portrait of a twig on a nut tree. However, this alteration led to an undesirable word repetition, which Clara retained in editing his collected works.

The spontaneity of Schumann's music makes *Myrten* unique. In *Der Nussbaum* especially, a poetic mood is created by the interplay between piano and voice. The word, bound by its physical nature to the voice, is enveloped in the otherworldly musical atmosphere created by the piano. Often the song retreats behind the piano, surrendering the initiative to that "quiet melody" which can no longer support the word. The coquettish quality to which interpreters of this song occasionally resort is entirely out of place.

Mosen had greatly impressed Schumann at a particularly convivial party. Schumann later wrote, asking, "What was it that I discovered in your eyes? Was it something like a ruby which not only absorbs but also radiates? Or was it something else—but I think I had seen that look before, and after you disappeared so suddenly, I often dreamt of it."

Schumann used as the text for the fourth piece of Opus 25 "Jemand," one of Gerhard's translations of poems by the Scottish poet, Robert Burns. In setting this song, Schumann resorted to the style of folk music, as he would again later, especially in the Spanish songs.

While Haydn and Beethoven had composed original songs set

JULIUS
MOSEN

(1803–1867) Mosen attended secondary school in Plauen and in 1822 moved on to Jena to study law, during which time he travelled to Italy. Upon graduation, he took a position with an attorney near his home town and in 1831 he was appointed to the bench in Kohren. In 1834 he established a law practice in Dresden where he soon gained literary distinction. He was requested to be the producer at the Oldenburg *Hoftheater* in 1844, but the onset of an incurable illness affected his work and resulted in total paralysis which forced his retirement in 1850.

Despite his physical infirmities, he remained intellectually and artistically active. He achieved artistic recognition with the publication of his epic poems "Das Lied vom Ritter Wahn" (1831), a free rendering of an old Italian saga, and "Ahasver" (1838). These volumes provide clearer evidence of his gift for philosophical reflection than for poetry. Schumann acquired a copy of his "Gedichte" (Leipzig, 1836) and was impressed by Mosen's fresh, folk-tale-like stories. A number of Mosen's ballad-like poems, "Die letzten Zehn vom vierten Regiment," "Andreas Hofer" and "Der Trompeter an der Katzbach," became a part of the popular vernacular. Mosen also wrote novellas and plays. He became absorbed in writing for the theater, but his plays were so dominated by abstract rhetoric that their mostly historic content was often obscured. Mosen's play "Cola Rienzi" was among those considered by Wagner when he was drafting his opera.

to texts by Burns, some of which are still sung in Scotland, Schumann created his own restless, passionate music for the poet's verses. He was attracted to Burns's poetry by its purity and its unpretentious, natural quality. Sams is of the opinion that the English text could simply be substituted, since, he claims, Schumann altered the German translation rather carelessly. This criticism seems inappropriate, since Schumann was simply attempting to create a work possessing the feel of Scottish folk music.

The texts for the next two songs were derived from Goethe's "Schenkenbuch," a part of his *West-östlicher Divan.* "Sitz ich allein" (I Sit Alone), Opus 25,5, and "Setze mir nicht," Opus 25,6, are a pair of short, related poems of a humorous turn. Their humorous interplay is so concentrated that the songs demand careful attention. The low voice part (indicated by the bass clef of the original) must be given special attention, so that it is clearly understood. Though other composers might be tempted to write quiet music in a leisurely tempo for "Sitz ich allein," Schumann filled this song with merriment and sprinkled it with rubatos and complex accompaniment, such as the coquettish slur on the last syllable of "eigenen Gedanken" (Example 12).

The short epilogue of "Setze mir nicht ein" in the form of a landler is a model of Schumann's pianistic delicacy.

"Die Lotosblume" (Opus 25,7), with a text by Heine, is among Schumann's most famous compositions. The sultriness of the poem led Schumann to previously unheard musical effects and harmonic tensions, reflecting the poem's twin poles of tenderness and passion. This song employs one of the composer's characteristic devices, which has led some to question his understanding of the requirements of vocal music, namely the placement of rests in places which break up the contextual meaning of the poem. Schumann slavishly honored the length of the lines in Heine's poem, charging the singer to support the line to the end, sustaining it dynamically and avoiding a pause. The criticism that these rests mar the work is unfounded when it is understood that we are not dealing with caesuras in the traditional sense (Example 13).

The two line endings finish on the third. At a time when only the tonic was heard as providing the effect of a conclusion, the thirds sound inconclusive; they then move on to the fifth of the next phrase, though its entry is delayed by either a half or a whole measure rest. The transitional nature of these rests is indicated by the accompaniment, which hints at, yet delays the chord. The rests, therefore, are intended to generate suspense. They portray the tightly closed flower's fear of the sun, while also portending imminent opening and radiance. Neither Robert Franz's setting of this poem nor that of Schumann for three-part chorus (transcribed for two soloists by Carl Reinecke) equal the magic of this song.

In the eighth piece we again encounter Goethe, who under the title *Talismane* collected and integrated five short, independent groups of aphorisms. Schumann used only the first three. He repeats the opening verse, following it with the third poem, then adds a repetition of the first verse, and finally repeats the "Amen" from the second.

Schumann avoided any sense of folk music in delineating the qualities of "uncertainty and confusion" as Goethe termed them, vividly and intricately (Example 14).

The eighth notes creep along legato and *piano* without any sense of motion, gradually entwining themselves in mired repetition. These lines impart only temporary divergence from the sure, firm character of the rest of the song. Schumann carefully resists creating any radical departure from the inner meaning of the balance of the work, so this passage does not stray markedly from the song's tonality. Schumann's treatment of Goethe's poem recalls a letter to Therese Schumann in 1836, in which Robert described his intimate acquaintance with inner turmoil: "Sometimes I am truly terrified of being on top of things, of moving on, of struggling, of remaining independent, despite my innermost convictions. I become quite confused—." But the song returns to the solemnity and majesty of the poem and its expression of faith and trust. The C major trumpetlike flourish for the voice returns, just before the concluding "Amen" over the low bass line.

It was Marianna von Willemer in her poem, "Lied der Suleika," and not Goethe, as Schumann must have believed, who answered Goethe-Hatem's "Abglanz" in the *West-östlicher Divan.* "Wie mit innigstem Behagen" (With the Greatest of Ease) is a five-part song developed out of two double verses with the repetition of

ROBERT
BURNS

(1759–1796) Burns suffered a childhood filled with hard labor and poverty. As a child, his mother taught him the folk melodies which were later echoed in his poetry. By age 16 he had read Pope and Shakespeare as well as Locke and Bayle. He found these authors even more stimulating than the private lessons he had come to enjoy. Smitten with love for a country maid, he tried his hand at his first poem which would bring him fame, "Handsome Nell." At 19, Burns was to have become a surveyor in Kirk-Oswald, but his love affairs and roistering set his father against him, forcing the young country poet to leave home and open a flax shop in Irvine.

When his father died in 1784, Burns returned to support his family, and together with his brother, Gilbert, acquired a lease on a small farm. But despite their hard work, harvests were meager. He portrays in "The Cottar's Saturday Night" the behavior to which this desperate situation had led him and satirizes the views of the orthodox clergy ministering to a country congregation. On the banks of the Ayr he became acquainted with Highland Mary, a milkmaid from nearby Montgomery Castle to whom he dedicated some of his finest poems. Even before Mary's premature death he began an affair with the beautiful Jean Armour. She was anxious for marriage, but her strongly Calvinistic father, a master mason, opposed their plans. The despondent poet had just about decided to become the overseer of a plantation in Jamaica when he learned that a collection of his poems, which he had published by subscription, had received an enthusiastic acceptance in Edinburgh.

Burns returned to Edinburgh and published a second printing there but after a year returned to his rural solitude. In spite of impassioned love letters to a lady in Edinburgh he clung to Jean, who in the meantime had borne him twins. Jean's father shortly thereafter consented to her marriage to the celebrated poet. In the following years, Burns first endeavored unsuccessfully to rescue a neglected estate near Dumfries, then became a customs inspector, a post he resigned when the work no longer suited him. During those years he wrote many poems and political essays for various daily newspapers. His open support of the French Revolution cost him the favor of many friends. His situation was aggravated by his scarcely disguised affection for the deposed Stuart dynasty. Alcoholism and the stress of his situation undermined his health. Gout necessitated a journey to the seashore, where he died at only 37 years of age. His wife bore another son while his funeral was in progress.

Burns wrote of young love, of devotion to his home, the joy of friends and of political and social injustices. His poetic immediacy greatly influenced Scott and Moore as well as Byron and Shelley.

Example 12

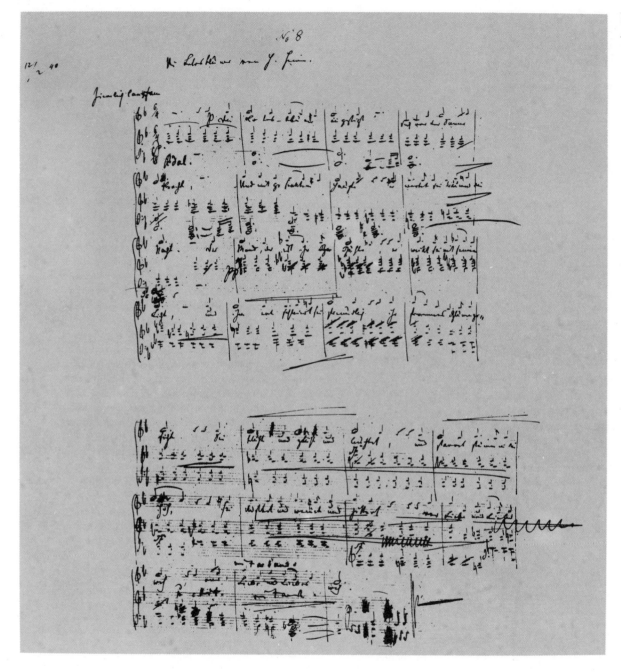

Robert Schumann:
Autograph of
"Die Lotosblume"

Example 13

Ziemlich langsam

Die Lo_tos_blu_me äng_stigt
sich vor der Son_ne Pracht, und mit ge_senk_tem
Haup_te er__war_tet sie träu_mend die Nacht.

half of the first verse. Polyphonic voices creep seductively; chromaticism woos with longing and growing intensity. Schumann repeats sections of the text for the sake of the melody, just as he does with Burns' "Hochländer witwe" (The Highlander's Widow) (with the word "blieb's").

With the two *Lieder der Braut* (The Bride's Songs) Schumann expressses well what must have been felt by Clara. Together with *Widmung* (Devotion) and *Zum Schluss* (In Conclusion), they form the most passionate outpourings in the collection Schumann presented to his adored Clara. As he was increasingly wont to do, Schumann altered the text by repeating the final verse.

In Burns' "Hochländers Abschied" (The Highlander's Departure) Schumann drops the final verse and instead repeats the first verse. With a different melody the poem became a true folk song in Burns' homeland. Schumann captures the restlessness and passion of the text in his music. In Burns' "Hochländisches Wiegenlied" (A Highland Lullaby) Schumann introduces a new form of musical expression, by in effect veiling single notes and harmonies behind atmospheric chords and pedal points. As with many other songs, aggressive use of the pedals is prescribed to accentuate these pedal points. It is interesting that in this song the original English text can also be sung to Schumann's music.

Schumann chose as the text for the fifteenth piece in this cycle a poem from Byron's "Aus den Hebräischen Gesängen" (From the Hebraic Psalms), translated by Theodor Körner. Those who do not associate Byron's poetry with Jewish sources should be reminded that Byron travelled to the Orient with his friend Hobhouse in 1809.

Byron's admiration for Thomas Moore's *Irish Melodies* is recalled in his *Hebrew Melodies* of 1815. Clarity of expression and melodic beauty give "Aus den Hebräischen Gesängen" a significant place in Schumann's work. He attempted to recreate a romantic, dreamlike sense of "foreign lands and peoples," and succeeded in creating a vision of Oriental melancholy. Although the music is conceived on a large, sweeping scale, it retains a sense of both inscrutability and sorrow. The arpeggios which accompany the lamentation do not simply sweep to and fro, as in the popular "background music" of the period, but are used harmonically so that each note contributes to the expressiveness of the piece. Such complicated figures closely approximate those used by Chopin. The magic circles in which the accompaniment swirls, seemingly

Example 14

Mich ver_wir_ren will das Ir_ren; doch du weißt mich zu__ent_wir_ren. Wenn ich

GEORGE NOEL GORDON
LORD BYRON

(1788–1824) Byron was related to Scottish royalty through his mother. His father, a captain in the Royal Guard, known as the "mad blade," wasted his wife's fortune before deserting her. Whereupon Byron's mother, a woman of a stern but passionate nature, returned to Aberdeen to raise her son. The narrow constraints of school coupled with unrestrained sojourns in the mountains of Scotland formed young Byron's willful and insolent character as well as his lifelong sensitivity to natural beauty. At the age of 10, Byron inherited his title from his uncle and was also placed under the guardianship of his great-uncle.

Following an unsuccessful effort to correct his club foot, he was enrolled at Harrow and later entered Trinity College, Cambridge. There, under the spell of old ballads, he wrote his first poems. Upon leaving Cambridge he led a carefree existence at his ancestral estate and in Edinburgh, where he relived Walter Scott's epics at night-long parties.

After coming of age, he undertook the maintenance of his estates and took his seat in the House of Lords, only to leave London in 1809 with his friend, Hobhouse, on a journey to Greece and Asia Minor. Upon his return in 1812, the first canto of *Childe Harold* appeared, describing the journey in a style which combined the sentimentality of Werther and the polish of Scott's epics. After Napoleon's abdication Byron recorded his disappointment in "Ode to Napoleon Bonaparte."

His unhappy marriage to Anna Isabella Milbanke was terminated in 1816 after the birth of his daughter, Ada. With public opinion heavily against him, Byron (who liked to adopt a posture of "reverse hypocrisy," feigning baser motives and behavior than he actually possessed) left England for a second time in 1816.

He travelled through Belgium, up the Rhine and into Switzerland where he took up residence on Lake Geneva, spending much time in the company of the Shelleys, as reflected in the second canto of *Harold.* An excursion with Hobhouse to the Bernese Oberland provided, along with Goethe's *Faust,* the inspiration for Byron's first dramatic work, *Manfred* (1817). The profound and mature work, *The Prisoner of Chillon,* was also written while at Lake Geneva.

During the fall of 1816, he travelled to Italy, remaining in Venice through 1819. There he completed *Harold, The Lament of Tasso, Beppo* and *Mazeppa.* The idea for *Don Juan* and the first cantos of that work also have their origins in this period.

While in Venice he fell in love with the 16-year-old Countess Teresa Guiccioli, née Gamba, whom he followed to Ravenna, and who was his adored consort for years. In 1819, the Countess's family drew Byron into the patriotic movement of the Carbonari, dedicated to lifting the Imperial yoke and regaining the independence of Italy. Teresa's husband had, in the meantime, presented evidence of her adulterous affair with Byron to the Pope, who allowed a divorce on the condition that she live in the house of her father, Count Gamba. The Count gave her the option of returning to her ancestral home or entering a convent. But the revolution ended disastrously and the Gambas were exiled. They moved to Pisa, then occupied by the French, and Byron followed. He completed *The Two Foscari, Sardanapalus* and *Marino Falieri* while in Pisa, but was forced to depart for Genoa in 1822 due to trouble with the police. Before leaving, however, he fulfilled a promise to his friend Shelley by having the latter cremated after he had drowned while on an excursion.

Tiring of his unsettled existence, Byron determined to dedicate himself to the struggle for Greek independence from the Turkish Empire. He embarked from Livorno with weapons, money, and medical supplies to support his new cause. Following his warm reception and meeting with the new Greek government, he outfitted two ships in an attempt to save Missolonghi, and took sail for the threatened city. He hoped by providing an alternate model to moderate the cruel and vicious warfare between Turkish and Greek armies, but a mutiny and quarrels so thoroughly dashed these hopes and the poet's sensibilities that he suffered repeated attacks of fever, which culminated in an acute and ultimately fatal respiratory infection, leading to his death on 19 April 1824.

Example 15

without beginning or end, assures its independence, yet allows the piano to join the voice as if in a duet—each with its own role while pursuing an independent course. By suppressing the traditional use of the caesura as it had been used in strophic song, an unending melody is achieved, which provides new freedom of expression giving direction to the *Lied* from the beginning with merely a sigh (Example 15).

Schumann surely shared Byron's romantic discontent, for the latter's work influenced him more profoundly than that of any other foreign writer. Despite this shared identity, Schumann frequently revised translations of Byron's poems to suit his musical and personal needs—changing "The heart" to "My heart," for example.

Although *Rätsel* has been attributed to Byron, it more likely came from the pen of Catherine Fanshaw, and was translated into German by Kannegiesser, an author published by the elder Schumann. Schumann fashioned his setting of the poem into a humorous musical riddle, which depended for its solution on the listener's musical ear. The solution lies in the final note, an "H," the German equivalent of "B." Listeners lacking absolute pitch, and so not catching this musical cue, must understand all of the quickly sung words which is nearly impossible. Of course, this clue is anticipated in the piano part where it is sounded in four octaves. The playful repetition of "Was ist's?" ("What is it?") is Schumann's addition (Example 16).

Venetianische Lieder (Songs of Venice) *I* and *II* are witness to the charm of Schumann's sense of humor; songs using poems written by the Irishman Thomas Moore.

Example 16

Schumann was so taken by Moore's comparatively slight verse that with very simple means he produced a stunning multi-faceted composition. Using triple counterpoint, his gliding rhythms interweave the movement of the rudder, the swaying of the gondola, and the voice of the gondolier. Again, the composer chose to alter Moore's text by repeating some of the lines to fit his musical needs.

The song to which we now turn grew out of, as Schumann recounted in several letters to Clara, a memorable and exciting encounter with Franz Liszt in early March, 1840, in Leipzig. His letters describe both their meeting and his impressions of the world-famous virtuoso. Following a brief period of initial uncertainty and reticence, Schumann found the encounter both enjoyable and stimulating. Before their encounter, they had publicly supported each other and the friendship which developed from this meeting was to last until Schumann's death, despite the artistic differences of their careers.

On the 13th of March, Schumann shared important news with Clara: "You will be astonished with what I am producing. I'll have quite a few works for you when I come to Berlin. . . . Also more *Lieder. Des Hauptmanns Weib* (The Captain's Wife) seems very fresh and romantic to me. . . ." The first draft of the song based on Gerhard's translation of Byron's poem may have been composed during Schumann's residence in Vienna, since it was written on music paper acquired from the Diabelli Company. A minor variation in the melody line occurs at the phrase, "wohnt mit ihm vereint in des Friedens Schatten." The opening of the version for male

chorus of the "Lotosblume," which later became the third selection of the choruses contained in Opus 33, is found on the back of that same sheet of paper.

Schumann adopted the very unusual A-B-B-A form from the form of Heine's poem, which he used for "Was will die einsame Träne." A very moving, elegaic tenderness pervades the song, and the somewhat unfortunate metaphors of the verses are presented so matter-of-factly and seductively that the listener easily overlooks them. The piano part supports the voice through the simple use of chords. The melody line follows the model of folk song, save for Schumann's typical pauses and indications of changes in harmony, such as the dissonance on "Qualen" (Example 17). The feeling is consciously restrained in order to maintain the cheerful character of the *Myrten* cycle.

Example 17

Following *Niemand* (No One), the energetic Florestan-like counterpart to *Jemand* (Anyone) with its Scottish coloring, comes "Du bist wie eine Blume" (You Are As a Flower), one of Schumann's best-known songs. It was probably written during the transitional period of 1839, since on 21 August 1854 Brahms wrote to Clara, "Your husband showed Fräulein Remont all of the songs in the Scherer songbook which he had composed earlier. Of them, he told her 'Du bist wie eine Blume' was the first. That is true." Heine's masterful manipulation and control of vowels and consonants must have been especially appealing to Schumann. For example, we may observe Heine's skillful use of similar sounds (Du bist wie eine Blume: *bist wie—so hold—mir ins—mir ist*), as well as Heine's systematic use of soft initial sounds which he incorporated

THOMAS
MOORE

(1779–1852) Moore was the son of a wine merchant. At the age of 15 he entered the University of Dublin to study law. He had been deeply influenced by the execution in 1803 of his childhood friend, Emmet, for the latter's enthusiastic support of the Irish uprising of 1798.

About the time of his friend's death, he began to exercise his musical talent by introducing, in Dublin's musical circles, songs written to accompany his poems. After graduating in 1799, he went to London seeking a publisher for his translation of *Anacreon*. In the end he was forced to published it himself. Fortunately, it was very successful, thus freeing the author from financial pressure. His first poems, similar in style and feeling to *Anacreon,* greatly influenced Byron. So successful was his poetry that he was asked to be the Poet Laureate, an appointment which he rejected. Supporters in the Whig Party then secured a posting in Bermuda, where Moore

resided for only three months as the Whigs were returned to power. Moore was about to take an official post in Ireland, but just at that point the police had to intervene to prevent a duel between Moore and the editor of the *Edinburgh Review* over an insulting review of Moore's recently published *Odes and Epistles.* A similar confrontation with Byron, who had satirically alluded to the incident, was also peacefully settled, and happily resulted in a close friendship between the two.

Schumann drew upon Moore's principal work, *Irish Melodies,* which had been partially translated by Freiligrath. *Irish Melodies* were conceived as the texts for a group of national Irish songs arranged by John Stevenson. Like the songs, the poems are a mixture of "grief and recklessness." Allusions to the unlucky fate of Ireland and to Moore's friend Emmet surface frequently. In addition to his greatest work, *Lalla Rookh,* which provided additional material for Schumann, Moore also wrote humorous epistles in which he poked fun at the Conservative Party, the Prince Regent and the Holy Alliance.

Following his marriage in 1811 to the wealthy heiress, Miss Dyke, he devoted himself to literature, London social life, and his estate in Wilshire until he was forced to flee to Paris as a result of financial difficulties. Upon his financial recovery he wrote a novel entitled *The Epicurean,* as well as several historical studies which reached their zenith in his history of Ireland. Following the publication of his friend Byron's memoirs in 1833, he capitulated to the censors and destroyed Byron's papers entrusted to him.

into the meaning of the poem (the H in *Hauch,* the soft B in the "Bitt"-consonant), which Schumann greatly admired. Schumann abjured a sentimental musical setting of this text, unlike other composers. Rather, he adopted first a devout and then a melancholy feeling. The highest and lowest pitches in the voice part occur together on "so hold" and on "aufs Haupt" and sensitively trace the motions of a loving caress. The two sections and epilogue of Schumann's *Lied* mirror the two verses of the poem. Two errors are frequently made in the interpretation: some performers sing "erhalte" with a suspension, a practice found in Baroque music,

failing to notice that the same motif in the accompaniment is not written in such a way. There is no sighing or entreating. Instead, the sentiment is cautiously stated, lacking any sense of confident expectation. Secondly, in many editions the text reads "so schön und rein und hold," perhaps because Schumann inadvertently used this word order in the undated manuscript.

In the delicate ghazal, "Aus den östlichen Rosen" by Rückert, we arrive at Schumann's first encounter with the Orient, which at that time embodied all things distantly romantic and unknown. In Herder's wake, the esthetic of August Wilhelm Schlegel had established the East, as distinct from classical Greece, as the root of Romanticism. Schumann's musical settings of Rückert's "Aus den östlichen Rosen" and Goethe's *Divan* poems point to the extraordinary orchestral color he later employed in *Das Paradies und die Peri.* On the margin of the manuscript dated April 1 8 4 0, we find the inscription, "Expecting Clara," which makes the anticipation animating the *Lied* understandable. (Schumann changed "An ein Auge frühlingslicht" to "An ein Aug voll Frühlingslicht.")

In contrast to the stormy opening pieces in this group of *Lieder,* which can be attributed to the nature of the poets whose poems Schumann used, stands the concluding song, Rückert's "Zum Schluss." It is thoughtful, contemplative, yet not without inner tension and simplicity of expression, and perhaps best illustrates the objectives of clarity and simplicity which Schumann later set as the "new way."

This insistence upon simplicity clearly separates it from Liszt's compositional style at that time. Yet to Schumann's astonishment and pleasure, Liszt had incorporated his own transcriptions of songs by Schubert, among others, into his Leipzig concerts. As early as 1 8 2 8, Clara included several of them in her repertoire. In his review, Schumann noted both the virtuosity and the clarity of the performance. "We cannot imagine hearing anything more beautiful than these songs by Schubert imbued with feminine artistry. The human voice could not have rendered them more beautifully." Liszt later also arranged some of Schumann's songs, as did Clara following the death of her husband.

But we also learn of a different assessment of Liszt: "He plays so unusually, so bravely, so frantically, and yet so tenderly and delicately. I have never heard anything like it. But, Clara, his world is no longer my world. For all of his display and splendor, I would never surrender the sense of the art as you practice it and as I often have while composing at the piano. His is a bit tawdry."

Schumann put all of his songs started up to this point in final form within two months. They were published amazingly quickly thereafter. The speed with which the Heine Cycle was published may be attributed to the desire to acquaint the public with the "new" Schumann and his songs. It is also likely that Schumann did not wish to dedicate a group of songs to his bride written in a genre for which the world of music did not yet know him. The speed with which the Heine *Lieder* went to press is even more remarkable when we consider that many other products of the "Year of Songs" were published years later, many with late opus numbers.

His enthusiasm for his newly discovered *Lied* encouraged Schumann to try his hand at choral arrangements, a genre which continually posed problems for him. *Sechs Lieder für vierstimmigen Männerchor* (Six Songs for Four-Part Men's Chorus) was published as Opus 3 3. Schumann surely hoped to explore the timbre and other possibilites of this genre which was so popular in Germany. But unfortunately, he barely went beyond vertical harmony. Schumann's choral version of Goethe's *Rastlose Liebe* is easily surpassed by Schubert's solo version. In *Der Zecher als Doktrinär,* he did realize to some degree the humor implicit in the text. But his choral arrangement of *Lotosblume,* which is only slightly inferior to his arrangement of the same piece for solo voice, avoids the trite.

A choral arrangement of a romantic *Lied* can at best be viewed as a contradiction in terms. The 1 9th Century did not smile on polyphonic a cappella songs for multiple voices, although in the works of Zelter and Mendelssohn the musical world approached a rediscovery of the Baroque—a development upon which Brahms was able later to build in his choral works. But the period did not possess the natural communal spirit which was evident during the "Golden Age" of polyphonic music.

Dr. Keferstein, the clergyman who had assisted Schumann in obtaining his doctorate and who was also a member of the editorial board of the *Neue Zeitschrift für Musik,* complained to Schumann of the latter's reduced dedication to the journal. Schumann replied on 1 8 February 1 8 4 0, "Though I cherish my work on the journal, it must take a secondary place. Is not every man solemnly bound to develop his greatest talents? If I remember correctly, you yourself gave me this advice years ago, and I have taken it to heart. I write this, my honored friend, because I detect some slight criticism of my attention to editorial matters in the last few lines of your letter. I don't deserve it. It is true that I have not fully discharged my responsibility to the journal, but that is simply because I am so heavily involved with other work, which is the more important. It is the higher destiny which I must fulfill in this life. I have been com-

EMANUEL GEIBEL
(1815–1844)

This poet from Lübeck made the gypsy theme fashionable. Geibel was the son of a minister and studied in Bonn and Berlin, first theology, but later Greek and Latin philology. He resided in Athens in 1838, working as a private tutor in the household of the Russian ambassador. Together with his friend, Ernst Curtius, he translated a number of Greek poems, which were published under the title *Classical Studies* (Bonn, 1840).

Geibel returned to Germany in 1840 and published his first volume of poetry. It was from this collection that Schumann selected the texts for his Opus 30 and numerous other later songs. Geibel had intended to become a professor of Romance languages, but his poetic gifts led him to abandon an academic career. With the publication of "Zeitstimmen" (Voices of the Times) he entered the ranks of the political poets of the decade of the 1840s, despite his opposition to radical politics enunciated in the poem, "An Georg Herwegh" (To Georg Herwegh). During the winter of 1842/43 he wrote his first play, *König Heinrich* (King Henry), a work, which like other theatrical pieces of the period, was more proper than effective.

In 1843, Friedrich Wilhelm IV awarded Geibel an annuity, which provided financial independence. His poetry gained widespread attention at about the same time. "Zwölf Sonette für Schleswig-Holstein" (Twelve Sonnets on Schleswig-Holstein) and his short epic "König Sigurds Brautfahrt (King Sigmund's Bridal Journey)

bespeak his stature and independence. After spending the summer of 1843 with Freiligrath in St. Goar on the Rhine, he went to Berlin in 1844, where in 1846 he wrote the libretto for Mendelssohn's opera *Loreley*. This work was never completed due to Mendelssohn's death. Soon afterwards, the *Juniuslieder* (Songs of June) were published, which surpassed their predecessors in perfection of form and content.

In 1851, King Maximilian of Bavaria summoned Geibel to Munich to take up a post as professor of esthetics at the university there. He was made an officer in the newly founded Order of Maximilian and raised to the nobility. He became a friend of the king, who was devoted to literature, and also became the acknowledged leader of the group of poets then living in Munich. He seemed unusually blessed with good fortune, until in 1855 he lost his young wife, Ada. The climate in Munich proved detrimental to his health, so that even before the death of his friend the Bavarian king, Geibel began to spend part of each year in the more congenial climate of Lübeck. In 1869 he finally resigned his positions to remain there. His Bavarian pension was cancelled, but Wilhelm I of Prussia awarded him an annuity equivalent to that received in Bavaria.

Geibel's most important poetic accomplishments were realized during his years in Munich. His work was diverse and rich. It included lyric and epic poetry and drama. With Schack, Heyes and Leuthold he made translations and paraphrases, mostly from the Spanish. Schumann employed texts from *Volkslieder und Romanzen der Spanier* (Folk songs and Romances of Spain) (Berlin, 1843). Though Geibel is now all but forgotten, his poems were among those most frequently set to music by his contemporaries, and he was widely acclaimed and appreciated by the public. His place in his times was described by Fontane in a letter written in 1851: "The nobility vie for his friendship and seek the favor of his company. He hears arrangements of his poems played on out-of-tune barrel organs. 'Geibel's Poetry' is advertised in all the store windows in gold letters. Twenty-five printings in 10 years. Money in the bank, beautiful women at his side, and clever friends at his table. Everything, everything— and yet such a cold frog. No luck at all!"

posing: these days I am writing only vocal works, small and large, including quartets for male voices which I would like to dedicate to my honored friend, if when he reads these words he will refrain from diverting me from composing. May I? I can hardly tell you how much more I enjoy writing for the voice than for instruments alone. I feel inspired and invigorated in my work. My eyes have been opened to new things, and I am even thinking of doing an opera, which of course would only be possible if I completely stopped working on the journal. . . ."

It may be safely assumed that a large part of Schumann's output during this period was meant to be performed in private, domestic circles. This is especially true of the duets with piano accompaniment, Opus 34 and 35. They are idyllic in a pensive way and occasionally develop into dialogues between male and female voices. The degree to which they were intended for amateur performers is best revealed in the tendency of the piano part to take over the melody and so lead the singers. But it is entirely incorrect to insist that these works are mere social or popular songs, typical of the Biedermeier era. The inappropriateness of such a categorization is best demonstrated by such pieces as the two serenades based on poems by Burns, *Liebhabers Ständchen* (Lovers' Serenade), Opus 34, No. 2, and *Unterm Fenster* (Under the Window), Opus 34, No. 3, which require genuine virtuosity to master their passion. Schumann traces the movement of the dialogue so precisely that it is necessary to follow markings such as the allegretto in *Unterm Fenster* exactly and to carefully sing the rallentandos and accelerandos, which are indicated but which produce only an allusion of rubato. With this in mind, Schumann's omission of the indication "a tempo" should not be confusing.

In Opus 29, based on poems by Emanuel Geibel, any indication of solo or choral performance is missing. They are simply intended for multiple voices. *Ländliches Lied* (Rustic Song), Opus 29, No. 1, towers gracefully above this group. Here Schumann displays the lightness of Mendelssohn, although he improves upon it with rich harmonies and ingenious intertwining of the voices. *Zigeunerleben* (Gypsy Life), Opus 29, No. 3, was composed for small chorus with the optional accompaniment of triangle and tambourine. This song marks Schumann's first use of Geibel's gypsy poems—poems which he would use frequently later. *Zigeunerleben* describes a wildly romantic scene around a gypsy campfire in the woods. The magic flavor of ancient songs and stories, a wild, ecstatic dance by torchlight, and at the conclusion, the unanswered question of the next destination, are all described by a four-voice choir reflecting the artist's images, so that save for the temper of abandon which permeates it, it does not differ from the other pieces in the collection. Though their parts are not written out, a tambourine and triangle help to convey the atmosphere. Neither the language, the music, nor the poetry of the gypsies is used. This would change drastically only with the arrival of Brahms.

Schumann's well-known Opus 15, *Kinderszenen* (Scenes from Childhood) for piano, include a title which reflects one of the principal elements of Romantic longing: "From Foreign Lands and People," the life style and songs of (then) distant countries and remote times including early Europe. The enthusiasm for the mythical bard, Ossian; for the various versions of the *Nibelungen* Legend; and for old folk legends as collected by the brothers Grimm and others all attest to the preoccupations of the Romantic mind. The Romantic artistic imagination was particularly fired by the popular image of the gypsies leading free and wayward lives, of which ordinary citizens living within the narrow, well-ordered conventions of the Biedermeier era could only dream. The simple, vital gypsy music, known to most only second-hand, added to their appeal.

Schumann combined texts by Geibel and Hebbel in a single collection, despite their very different poetic sensibilities. He used a Hebbel text for the first song in Opus 27, "Sag An, o lieber Vogel mein," (Tell Me, Lovely Bird) which he probably obtained from a journal or a private copy, since Hebbel's (1813–1863) first volume of *Gedichte* (Poems) was not published until after 1842. It should be noted that the poems Schumann selected from Hebbel's large output show little of the passion, of the crass and bizarre which marked much of the poet's work.

Upon reading Hebbel's first tragedies, *Judith* and *Genoveva*, Schumann was immediately taken by their unusual power. He was particularly drawn to the forcefulness of characterization as well as their passion and immediacy. He quickly recognized Hebbel as a

FRIEDRICH
HEBBEL

The first 33 of Hebbel's 50 years were pure hell. He was born in Wesselburen near Dithmarschen, the son of a mason, and grew up in poverty, physically and spiritually hungry. He continued in these circumstances until 1846, when he married Christine Enghaus, a Viennese actress. She not only had money and influence but was also a member of the Burgtheater.

His earlier years had thoroughly humbled the man.

He had been dependent on patrons, scholarships and the meager income of his first wife, Elise Lensing, a seamstress who loved him selflessly and bore him two children, but whose love he could not find it in himself to reciprocate.

Hebbel dropped out of law school in 1835, thus losing his scholarship. Without any resources he travelled that winter from Munich to Hamburg on foot. At the age of 30 he received a two-year travel grant from the King of Denmark, spending 1843/44 in Paris and 1844/45 in Naples and Rome. On his return journey through Vienna he met Christine Enghaus.

With her support he found his life's purpose and reason. He gained entry to the court in Vienna and was in a position to make yearly trips to Munich, Weimar, Hamburg, Paris or London. Christine invariably played the lead role in his plays. He was awarded the prestigious Schiller Prize for his play *Nibelungen*. Before his death, he had been awarded an honorary doctorate and made a Privy Councillor.

In his poems as in his plays, Hebbel identified the vision which drove him: "The feeling of complete contradiction in all things." Hebbel's strength lay in his ability to depict tragedy without guilt.

first-rate talent. Though he was somewhat taken aback by Hebbel's nihilistic reflections, some of the poems revealed a nature capable of tenderness and affection.

All of the texts by various authors which are united in Opus 27 under the title, *Fünf Lieder und Gesänge,* deal with love, either tenderly or playfully. Schumann has echoed the miniature-like character of the texts by using a small format. He satisfied both himself and the taste of the age with his flowery style. The one extant copy of *Dem roten Röslein gleicht mein Lieb* (My Love is Like a Little Red Rose) is dated 15 May 1840. The song may have been written earlier, but was not completed in time for inclusion in *Myrten*. The rather old-fashioned text by Robert Burns (translated by Gerhard) contains numerous flower metaphors which the modern mind finds embarrassing. Schumann treats it in a graceful, folk-like style, with some chromatic niceties. Had Schumann's work consisted entirely of *Lieder* such as these, he would now probably be viewed as a

typical Biedermeier song writer.

His choice of *Was soll ich sagen* (What Shall I Say) probably reflects Schumann's thoughts at the time he married, for he had met Clara 12 years earlier when she was but 9 years old. Interestingly, Adelbert von Chamisso wrote the poem when he was 38 and about to marry an 18-year-old girl, whom he had also known since her childhood.

Great economy of means characterizes both Chamisso's anguished, questioning text and Schumann's music in *Was soll ich sagen,* (What Can I Say). Opening on a descending bass line beneath soft, supporting arpeggios, and a hesitant melody with a pair of seemingly strangled sighs in the accompaniment, it allows the words and music to speak eloquently. Schumann added "Ist ein Gebot" (It is a command) in measures 11 and 12.

Though *Volksliedchen* (Little Song), Opus 51, No. 2, on a text by Rückert is slight and quite undemanding, it is typical of the minia-

ADELBERT
VON CHAMISSO

Actually Louis Charles Adelaide de Chamisso, he was
born in Boncourt Palace in Champagne, France, on
January 30, 1781. In 1790 he and his parents fled the
revolution, settling in Prussia after a period of much dis-
tress. He became a page to Queen Luise in 1796, and in
1798 was commissioned to an infantry regiment under
Friedrich Wilhelm III. When his parents later returned to
France, he remained in Berlin.

His love of poetry brought him into contact with
Varnhagen von Ense, Theremin, Hitzig and de la Motte-
Fouqué. Even after they had all gone their separate ways,
they maintained contact through the publication of a
volume of poetry to which they all contributed. All the
while Chamisso devoted himself to the studies which he
had been unable to pursue in his youth, particularly
Greek and natural history.

When Hameln surrendered to the French, Chamisso
refused, despite urging, to participate in the betrayal by
the Prussian commander. Indignantly, he resigned his

commission and returned to Napoleonville in his
homeland, hoping to obtain a teaching position.
Although it did not materialize, he was introduced into
the circle of Madame de Staël in Coppet where his interest in botany was kindled.

He returned to Berlin in 1812 to pursue formal
academic training. He was haunted by conflicting loyal-
ties through the course of the Wars of Liberation:
unwilling to either join his friends in fighting the forces
of his homeland or join the French to fight his friends.
He therefore happily accepted in 1815 a commission as
naturalist to accompany Captain von Kotzebue, the son
of the author, on an around-the-world scientific expedition. But, this venture too was fraught with difficulties.
Other members of the party, and particularly the ship's
captain, interfered with or thwarted his research and
collecting undertakings in every imaginable way. In addition, Kotzebue so misused Chamisso's journals and
notebooks in his account of the expedition, and without
Chamisso's permission, that Adelbert viewed it as
thoroughly dishonorable. His own account, *Journey
Around the World,* did not appear in its entirety until
1836.

In October of 1818 he returned to Berlin where he
was made curator of the Botanic Gardens. He then
married and was soon promoted to the position of
Director of the Royal Herbarium. He was made a
member of the Academy of Sciences in 1835. He published his first poems between 1804 and 1806 in a joint
venture with Varnhagen entitled *Musenalmanach.* His
famous tale *Peter Schlemihl* tells the story of a man who
loses his shadow; and it reflects his own restlessnesss and
purposelessness. Chamisso died in Berlin on August 21,
1838.

tures in which Schumann displays his complete mastery of the small
form. The postlude characterizes the insecurity and impatience of
the girl—a touch which is unsurpassed in subtlety. Very little
original music was composed for this song; strains of *Widmung,
Schöne Wiege meiner Leiden* and *Im Rhein, im heiligen Strome* appear
throughout. It is clear that Schumann placed great value on such a

little folk song, for he intended to include it in a "Mozart Memorial
Album." This album was to have been published in 1839 in conjunction with the unveiling of the Mozart Monument in Salzburg, but
did not actually appear until 1843. Given Schumann's intentions, we
can certainly assume the song to express the reverence in which he
held Mozart. Judging by the choice of texts and the musical style the

piece was probably composed in the spring of 1840. George H. Spencer found an additional verse of text in an anthology compiled by a certain Johann which was not included in the complete Rückert edition. This lost verse could breathe interesting new life into the song.

Wenn ich im Wald mit Freuden geh'
In meinem grünen Hut,
Wärmt mich ein froher Gedanke
In voller Liebesglut.
Der Himmel ist so blau,
Die Liebste ist doch mein,
Ich weiss es ganz genau,
So wird es ewig sein.

When I walk happily in the forest, wearing my green hat,
One glad thought warms my loving heart.
Blue is the sky—my loved one is mine—
And I know: thus it will always be.

Schumann's use in Opus 53, No. 2, of Wilhelmine Lorenz's poem *Loreley,* dated April, 1840, can be attributed to the fact that her husband, Oswald, was a friend of the composer and worked with him on the *Neue Zeitschrift für Musik.* Schumann even had dedicated his song cycle *Frauenliebe und -leben* (A Woman's Life and Love) to him. In setting *Loreley,* Schumann pays homage to Schubert's *Die Stadt* (The Town) in the way he depicts the waves. He takes the closing words, "gedenke mein," literally by using portions of his own, earlier songs. As was often the case, the key of E major appears here in connection with the image of feminine seduction. This same key was to appear again in *Waldesgespräch* (Voices of the Forest); it had already been used for the same musical coloring in "Schöne Wiege meiner Leiden." (Wagner's Venusberg motif in "Tann-häuser" is also in this key.)

"Ich wandre nicht" (I Wander Not), Opus 51, No. 3, based on a poem by the correspondent for the *Neue Zeitschrift für Musik* in Hamburg, Carl Christern, is especially interesting in light of Clara and Robert's intention of seeking some surcease from Wieck's con-tinuing meddling by travelling to England for a time. In February, 1839, Schumann, writing from Vienna, asked Clara, "Are you brave enough to go to England with me?" The plan was dropped in the summer of 1840, but Christern may have alluded to it in his poem, and Schumann may have written this song to thank him. Before he included it in Opus 55 he had published the song separately on two different occasions, once in 1843 and again in 1844. He must have thought a great deal of it, perhaps because it embodied his notions of the virtue of simple music.

Schumann encouraged Clara to come to know the joy of com-posing songs, since she was not only his source of inspiration, but also because he admired her talent for composition. In March of 1840 he suggested she set a poem to music. But she believed she could not compose, and added that she was disappointed by her inability. "I am not a talented composer. Don't think it's laziness. To compose a *Lied,* that I cannot do *at all.* To really understand a poem—that requires genius. . . ." As Robert's wife, she proved herself incorrect in light of her splendid contributions to Rückert's *Liebesfrühling* (Spring of Love). Her musical talent was also evident not only in her piano concertos, but also in her chamber music and piano works. Though her compositions follow the same lines as Schumann's and are conceived within narrower artistic boun-daries, they are of permanent and enduring stature.

Meanwhile in April, 1840, Schumann returned to Heine's texts. The exact date of composition of *Arme Peter* (Poor Peter), Opus 53, No. 3, is uncertain, but the placement of this trilogy at the beginning of the *Buch der Lieder* (Book of Songs) indicates that it was written during the "Year of Songs." Both the poet and the com-poser sensitively treat the pseudo-folk theme, the rare outcome of a successful collaboration. The inflexible rhythm of German folk song has been employed by countless poets for lullabies or dirges and dances of death. Heine turned to this meter to produce his characteristic and farcical joining of tenderness and cruelty. Schumann follows the lead of the poet only in the opening. In the first section, based on a leisurely bagpipe tune, we meet the silent hero, Peter, immersed in sorrow. Octave leaps played by the right hand set a plaintive tone while creating splendid polyphony (Example 18).

Example 18

The central figure of these three mini-scenes speaks for the first time in the second song. The accented D minor chord bespeaks his tortured soul, which in fleeing from itself discovers only the evidence of its own weakness. Schumann quite curiously has the voice descend deeply, as Peter climbs "to the mountain top," as he seeks to find himself in solitude (Example 19). Then his final disappointment is realized, and he can only weep as the piano, in a falling sequence, drops Peter's motif.

Example 19

In the third poem, Peter's great misery is presented. The villagers point accusing fingers at him and insist that he must change his ways. No one understands his tragic dilemma, so they ridicule "him." Juxtaposed to the belief of the crowd is the sympathetic poet, quietly setting things straight through his own understanding of "him" (Example 20). The moving comparison of the two perceptions of Peter is accented in the music by the register and modulation in this section. Peter is accompanied to the grave by a dirgelike passage, and his burial is denoted by the postlude. With two sixth chords in G minor and D minor followed by a reconciliatory D major chord, the composer concludes the "tragedy."

The fact that Schumann made many textual changes in *Der arme Peter* while deleting only one "and" in Heine's *Abends am Strand* (Evening Along the Seashore) demonstrates how strongly this latter poem intrigued him. Without resorting to tone painting, the calm of the evening, a dreamy atmosphere, and adventure stories are captured by the inner "ear and eye." Again we encounter the harbor in the "beautiful city" of Hamburg, visited earlier in *Schöne Wiege meiner Leiden* (Beautiful Cradle of My Sorrow). The continuous gliding motion of eighth notes over the calm bass line (suggesting violas) could not picture water or fog more clearly. Then the story comes to life with the portrayal of foreign visitors; here Schumann refrains from using folkloristic touches. Schumann's first biographer, Wasielewski, found the comic touch of the Laplanders' exaggerated cries, gradually dying away in the ocean air, objectionable and said it called the stature of the song into question (Example 21).

Immediately preceding the conclusion, an Indian scene in E major is unexpectedly injected. At the end, the original mood returns, uniting the varied elements of the music, which despite their diversity never exceed the musical limits of the *Lied*. The eighth-note motion mentioned in the opening and repeated at various tempos throughout the song returns at the end in its original shape, thus integrating the song rhythmically.

Example 20

Example 21

Die beiden Grenadiere (The Two Grenadiers), Opus 49, No. 1, or as Heine titled it, "Die Grenadiere," recalls an episode in Düsseldorf when the poet was 19. He was among those who saw the return of the first French prisoners of war from Russia, as we read in his *Buch Le Grand.* In Schumann's hands, the short but vivid impression of Heine's poem becomes timeless.

It is obvious that Schumann liked the "Marseillaise"—a melody popular during the French Revolution. Elsewhere, he used it less obviously, more or less carefully disguised. In his piano work, "Ein Faschingsschwank aus Wien" (Carnival in Vienna), for example, he disguised the "Marseillaise" by changing the meter to 3/4 time, in order to deceive the censors who had forbidden its use. He used the "Marseillaise" again in the overture to his incomplete *Singspiel* (light opera) *Hermann und Dorothea,* Opus 136 (1851). While he most certainly patterned *Die beiden Grenadiere* after Loewe, Schumann's sparing use of thematic material and the impressive power of musical expression clearly set the work apart.

Within the "through-composed" form of the piece, there are hints at strophic, repeated patterns, marchlike, with lyrical developments. The high point of the piece occurs with the triumphal entry of the "Marseillaise" at the end. Schumann, through the ingenious use of the piano postlude in the last phrase, traces his Grenadier from his initial patriotic fervor to his death. No victorious *fortissimo,* no organ postlude closes the ballad, but rather the image of the French military collapse is clearly portrayed in the epilogue, using a musical style different from that employed in the rest of the piece.

Wagner, whose power in depicting such scenes is unquestionably highly effective, set the same ballad and also used the "Marsellaise" as its finale, but not so successfully as did Schumann. His version was written during the winter of 1839/40, shortly before Schumann completed his setting. When Wagner heard of Schumann's composition he wrote an anxious letter from Paris. "I hear that you have set Heine's *Grenadiers* to music and that it ends with the "Marseillaise." Last winter I set the same poem to music and also used the "Marseillaise" as the conclusion. That is of some significance! I used a French translation which I commissioned here and which Heine approved. It was sung repeatedly and earned me the order of the Legion of Honor and a yearly pension of 20,000 Francs which I draw directly from the private treasury of Louis Philippe." Schumann's version did not receive the same accolades and rewards.

The simple, undemanding setting of Heine's *Die feindlichen Brüder* (The Duelling Brothers), Opus 49, No. 2, completed in April, 1840, is consistent with the poet's penchant for sarcasm. Listeners who recall similar folk legends treated by Heine, such as the *Loreley* or Flying Dutchman's subjects, and expect more from Schumann's music than the simple interpretation provided, will find themselves deceived. The phrase which begins "Gräfin Laura" should inform our ears that this is a satire on the nostalgia for the medieval, typical of the period. It is musical recitation in Gothic type, the same style from which much of Hugo Wolf's sarcasm derived.

Chapter 8

Schumann joined Clara in Berlin in April, 1840 for a month, and among other things met with Mendelssohn. On April 4th, Clara noted in her diary that Schumann had showed her "many of his *Lieder,* which exceeded my expectations." Mendelssohn, too, was generous with praise when Schumann played several pieces from his *Liederkreis* (Song Cycle) for him on April 19th. Shortly after his return, Schumann put to paper the songs based on Eichendorff's texts. Clara's biographer, Litzmann, views the song *Mondnacht* (Moonlit Night) as a reflection of those "happy, carefree, spring days."

It is difficult to establish the exact dates of these *Lieder.* On May 15th, Schumann wrote to Clara, "There are twelve Eichendorff songs, but I have already set them aside and begun something new." His account implies that he had finished them, though the "Noten-bücher," which contain the manuscripts, date some of them after May 15th. Perhaps he had finished a draft, but added the dates later. In the "Notenbuch" the songs follow *Dichterliebe* (Poet's Love) immediately; they thus were composed between May 24th and June 1st. Thus both cycles were being worked on simultaneously in the same period. While *Liederkreis* was shaped as a group as it was being composed, *Dichterliebe* was conceived as a cycle from the beginning.

In Eichendorff, to whom Schumann now turned, he recognized not so much the poet of romantic nature scenes—the wandering minstrel so common at the time—but rather a poet who was the "soul of the world," one who sought to encapsulate the meaning of life in his poetry. Schumann rarely commented on Eichendorff; he wrote much more extensively about Jean Paul, Shakespeare and Goethe. But Schumann included him in the "new school of German poetry," which, for the first time, made possible "a more artistic and profound form of song." For "only the new spirit of poetry can be reflected in music." All told, Schumann set 21 poems by Eichendorff to music, assuring him an important place in Schumann's total vocal output.

That which is perceived and dealt with as eternal truth is expressed in the poetry and music of these songs. In the music as in the words, we find symbolic representation of the human condition. The limits of time and fashion are here surpassed, for the songs bring the past into meaningful relationships with the present, because they are infused by timeless truths. Eichendorff's natural and direct style appealed to similar propensities in Schumann's artistic nature, though Schumann did not hesitate to maintain his creative independence by freely altering Eichendorff's texts. Images of one's homeland; the legend-filled past; the magic of twilight and night; the mystical sense of faith in life and God—all are enhanced by the new light in which Schumann casts them. Thus *Liederkreis,* Opus 39, is unusually animated because of the novel and unprecedented ideas dealt with in this cycle. Every song in it is marked with a profusion of new musical invention. Never before in the history of the *Lied* has the poet influenced the composer more than in this collection of songs. "This cycle is my most romantic," said Schumann, though such a statement does not do his artistic achievement full justice. To Clara he added, "There is much of you in it," but this says little about the perfection which can be found in

JOSEPH,
BARON VON EICHENDORFF

Eichendorff was born on 10 March 1788 in Lubowitz palace near Ratibor in Upper Silesia, which at that time was part of Austria. His family, ennobled long before, had lived in Silesia only since the end of the Thirty Years War, whence they had moved from Brandenburg and Bavaria. The family income derived largely from land holdings. As the child of "farmers," he enjoyed a childhood in the country. The child, who also spoke fluent Polish, was raised on Polish and German folk songs and fairy tales. One of his tutors, Kaplan Ciupke, instilled in the ten-year-old a profound religious belief which is particularly manifest in his novel, *Ahnung und Gegenwart,* but which greatly influenced all of his poetic output.

In 1801 the brothers, Joseph and Wilhelm, entered a Catholic secondary school in Breslau, connected with a theological seminary and staffed by priests. In 1805 they embarked on their advanced studies at the University in Halle, later transferring to Heidelberg. During their holidays they hiked in the Harz Mountains—outings of the kind the author of *Aus dem Leben eines Taugenichts* (From the Life of a Ne'er-do-Well) could in later years no longer take, as his studies, writing, and, after his marriage, the demand of obtaining a livelihood consumed all his time and energy. Though called "countrified" by Brentano, the brothers turned out to be a lively pair in Heidelberg, though they regularly attended morning mass. Joseph's diary mentions the "divine" lectures by Görres and meetings with him. The combination of the man's spirit and personality enthralled Eichendorff. As a student, Eichendorff, having mastered the art of linguistic analysis and interpretation, began to explore the means to integrate his poetic and religious insights.

the natural art and artistic naturalness of this cycle. Not only are time and space dissolved, but so too are the limits on the esthetic sense of human fate, which is accomplished by successfully and assuredly combining the conflicting elements of life. Schumann would never again achieve such a level of seeming effortlessness in his work. As a mark of his abilities both as a poet and a composer, it has been pointed out that he arranged the specific order of the texts within the cycle without depending upon a connecting, narrative framework.

Scholars have analyzed the order of the 12 pieces in terms of their tonal relationships. Hans Joachim Moser points to the preference for sharp keys for the representation of things glittery, ethereal, angelic. K. H. Wörner examines the architectonics created by the rhythmic choices made, noting the alteration between duple and triple meter. However, such crutches aid the listener but little in the attempt to discover the inner meaning of this work of art.

Schumann included two poems from Eichendorff's *Ahnung und Gegenwart* in each of the two halves of the cycle. In each case, a song of Erwin is followed by a song of "warning." The character of the two halves is such that the less melancholy songs are located in the first half, while the "darker" *Lieder* are placed in the second. This arrangement of the songs demonstrates Schumann's use of the principle of alteration; a tendency also apparent in his choice of keys.

All of the poems include the image of a wanderer, which Schumann imperceptibly develops within the structure of the cycle. The dynamic marks must be considered a characteristic of the cycle rather than an indication of development. All but two of the songs are marked *piano;* an expansion to *forte* is found only near the end of each half, in Nos. 6 and 12. The indication *forte* is used elsewhere

As was customary among those of his class, he set off on a period of travel and study after he had finished at the University. He went first to Paris and then on to Vienna by way of Nürnberg, after which he returned to Lubowitz for two years, where with his brother, he prepared for his future as a farmer. During this period Eichendorff also entered into what was to prove a happy union with Aloysia von Larisch, the daughter of a neighboring family. In the fall of 1810 it became clear that the Eichendorff estate would not support Wilhelm, Joseph and his wife. Joseph went to Vienna to finish his law degree, but unable to find a position upon graduation, he enlisted in the Lützow Fusiliers in 1813. After unremarkable service at a fortress he obtained in 1816 a position as a clerk in the logistics section of the Ministry of Defense. Later he became a government attorney in Breslau. When he was made a Privy Councillor in Danzig in 1821, he and his wife already had four children. In 1831 he was appointed a Privy Councillor in the department of Catholic church and school affairs at the Cultural Ministry in Berlin. He was plagued by ill health and professional frustration during all the 9 years in East Prussia and 13 years in Berlin. He particularly disliked Berlin, and in a quarrel with his superior in 1844 asked to be discharged.

With his health improved, Eichendorff moved frequently. He spent 1846 in Vienna as an intellectual historian. There he came into the company of Grillparzer, Stifter, and his old friend of earlier days in Vienna, Raimund. In the course of his life, Eichendorff associated with many of the leading intellectual and cultural figures of his day. He especially valued his friendship with Friedrich and Dorothea Schlegel, who, like Adam Müller, offered him not only intellectual stimulus but also critiques of his work. Eichendorff also came to know Arnim, Tieck, Kleist, Hoffmann, Fontane, Gneisenau, Gentz and Metternich. He wrote little poetry in his later years, occupying himself principally with journalistic and scholarly work in the field of literary history as well as a translation of the works of Calderon. He did produce three epic poems as well as a cultural-historic picture book. In 1855 he moved to Neisse to live with his daughter's family, where shortly thereafter his wife died. Eichendorff began to write his memoirs, but he took ill and died 27 November 1857 at 70 years of age.

only for direct conversation between the two speakers in No. 3, and to contrast the spatial relationships of closeness and distance in No. 11. Feldmann's comment that Schumann's music is at its best when sung quietly—or as previously stated, "sung as if from heaven"—is particularly apropos in performing this cycle.

The only extant copy of *In der Fremde* (In a Strange Land) is in Clara's handwriting. For some years, the composition was attributed to her, but this attribution proved to be incorrect. Premonitions of death and loneliness, both familiar companions to Schumann, dominate this song, but it is devoid of the air of inner strife which was so fashionable during the period. The expression of yearning is conveyed by a simple melody. The contrast between the rising and falling sixteenth notes on the piano and the voice part that moves within the range of a seventh is a particularly effective means to portray the world-weariness of the "innocent." The modulation employed recalls the telling of a story; the traditional opening, "Es war einmal" (Once Upon a Time), is especially well characterized by the harplike accompaniment, which continues throughout the song. This technique seems natural, for the song was sung to a guitar accompaniment in Eichendorff's story *Viel Lärmen um nichts* (Much Ado About Nothing). Schumann often increased the intensity of a piece by lengthening melodic phrases, in this case from four measures to six. In the tenth measure he adds a counter-melody to the song in the piano, which Sams, who was given to identifying motifs, called the "Silence Motif." More appropriately, it may be viewed as an intensification of the exclamation, "Wie bald" (How soon), since the note B in the vocal line is picked up and the two words are repeated on the interval of a fifth (Example 22).

At the end of the song an archaic effect twice appears through the use of a plagal cadence. Such allusions to the ecclesiastical

Example 22

modes are also used in Nos. 8 and 11, which focus on mortality and death. This usage is a conscious attempt to establish religious allusions. The text of the poem is altered, mostly through the repetition of words, to meet Schumann's melodic needs. As a result Eichendorff's "kennt mich auch hier" becomes Schumann's "kennt mich mehr hier."

The ecstasy of the love song *Intermezzo,* floating, entranced, above the syncopated accompaniment, seems intended to erase the sense of prevailing sorrow. The first verse focuses on the image of the loved one, the second on the lover's desire to be with her. Though the poem ends with this thought, Schumann returns to the image of the first verse, a practice for which he was often reproached by critics, especially in his later works. In *Intermezzo,* however, this return does not conflict with the poet's sense, but rather proves a precise understanding of Eichendorff's poetic intentions: the poet also returns to the image of the lover at the end of the poem when he writes "und zu *dir* eilig zieht." Clearly it was this reference to the first verse which led Schumann to repeat it with slight variations. Schumann distinguishes the two verses by having the voice and the piano proceed together in the second verse. An

intensely introspective poem has been transformed into one which is "on the tip of one's tongue." This sense of immediacy is further enhanced by the syncopation in the piano line.

No. 3, *Waldesgespräch* (The Voice of the Forest), from (together Eichendorff's *Ahnung und Gegenwart* is almost a documentary of the other-worldly, for which Schumann provides a musical explanation. In the song, the voices of magic speak to a human being who has entered the world of the unknowable. This is not a simple ghost story with witches and senseless incantations. All of the elements of normal discourse are employed to produce the illusion of demonic spirits, just as they had been used in dialogue form in Eichendorff's novel. Schumann defines Loreley's "balladlike" version of her story with an archetypical harp accompaniment against which the knight's vigorous horn motives stand in contrast. The construction of the melody is noticeably naive, as is the harmony, which relies on a simple alternation between tonic, subdominant, and dominant. The only exception to this simple construction is found in the transition to a diminished seventh chord when Loreley sings of her grief-filled "heart."

In *Die Stille,* also taken from *Ahnung und Gegenwart,* the secrets of the text are expressed through a parlando which advances only with small intervals. A delicacy of feeling seems to lead the listener from the wayward uncertainty of *Waldgespräch* to the intense soliloquy of the girl, Erwine, who like Goethe's Mignon, is dressed in men's clothing to accompany her secret lover Friedrich. Erwine sings this song after a scene in which she finally overcomes her shyness and confesses her feelings to Friedrich, feelings of which he is not aware. The secret, of course, involves not only her lover, but also her ability to solve the riddles of his childhood. Schumann recreates the sly, happy mood of the poem with a scherzo in six-eight time. By deleting the third verse and repeating the first, a sensitive alternation of the text which we already have witnessed, Schumann creates a sense of incompleteness and uncertainty. The forces of circumstance pressing for remaining silent are intuitively balanced by the personal desire to be open. This effect provides similar outer sections around a contrasting middle section.

We will linger over the fifth song of the series a bit longer, although, or perhaps because, it is one of Schumann's best-known songs, which every aficionado of the art song claims to understand. *Mondnacht* (Moonlit Night), with its sense of calm and reserve, is one of the high points of the *Lieder* repertory. Eichendorff's words "still" (quiet), "sternklar" (starlit), and "träumen" (dreaming) create the basic mood of the piece. To this Schumann adds the direction, "tenderly, secretly," which does not indicate much about the tempo, but does tell us a great deal about how it should be performed. The melodic material appears to be relatively simple. Five of the poem's six verse-pairs are set to the same eight-measure phrase. The prelude which returns between the verses serves both to separate the verses yet consolidates the song. Adorno noted the form of this piece "is similar to medieval barform." In keeping with this parallel, the first two verses make up the *Stollen,* and the last the *Abgesang,* which is not inconsistent with the content of the poem. Wiora correctly understood the repetition of the eight-measure opening melody as Schumann's effort to realize a "fundamental sound" which "encompassed all the sounds of the world." The break in the phrase, "und meine Seele spannte—weit ihre Flügel aus . . ." which, we already noted in *Lotosblume,* is not intended as a caesura, but rather as the kind of extension or expansion of the thought one often comes across in Romantic poetry. Such a break is not cadential as in the tradition of 18th Century music and poetry, but rather a stop for a breath, as if to expand the space of the song endlessly. The suspended fifths at the end of the phrase, which play such a characteristic role in *Mondnacht,* have their roots in the same artistic objective (Example 23).

At this point, the melody and harmony deviate from the path they have been following, but this departure does not diminish the internal cohesion of the song. The rhythm in the accompaniment remains unchanged, and the piano prelude is now woven into the accompaniment. A single melodic motif is used until the end. The continuous accompaniment, the quiet rustling of wings of the piano between vocal phrases, the furtive, independent life of the middle voice, the quiet innocence of the conclusion which becomes increasingly lineal, all speak to Schumann's talent for uniting his innermost thoughts and feelings with his heart and sense of nature.

Example 23

Und mei _ ne See _ le spann _ te *ritard.* weit ih _ re Flü _ gel aus,

This song had a far-reaching influence on Schumann's successors, including Johannes Brahms (*Feldeinsamkeit*). A look at the second line of the poem reveals that Schumann set the line "von ihm *nur* träumen müsst'," probably due to an error in transcription by Clara. It should read "nun." Schumann once wrote Clara that E-h-e (the German word for "marriage" and the letters which denote the German equivalents of the musical notes E, B, E) is a very musical word. He uses it frequently in this piece in the left hand, probably meaning to indicate the reluctance of completely surrendering oneself to a mystical union with nature, such as Eichendorff recounts in the poem (Example 24).

Example 24

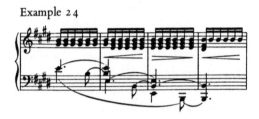

Neither the dynamic marking's "secret" whispers nor the dreamlike floating should slow the tempo. Only at the end, when the soul is freed of all earthly trappings and imagines itself ready to fly "home," should the song slow somewhat. The frequently used mordent from the twelfth measure should be executed as shown in the *Neue Zeitschrift für Musik* (Example 25). Raimund von Zermühlen, the famous baritone who sang this song with Clara at the piano, reports that Schumann thought of it as a barely perceptible "shudder." Von Zermühlen passed this interpretation on to those who followed him. *Mondnacht* is the quiet midpoint of the cycle. The serene key of E major leaves little room for harmonic nuances—shimmering, whispering—until the last line of the text flows into a mystical dissonance which is not resolved until after the last note of the song, which should therefore not be sustained too long.

Example 25

Clara and Robert spent May of 1840 together in Berlin. It was probably the happiest time of their lives together, and was the setting for the creation of this masterpiece. They played for each other the pieces which aroused their interest. Clara took out some of Robert's older pieces as well as a handful by other composers, while he turned to some of his most recent works. Both confirmed their love of the other and the other's art.

When returning home after one of their visits with Mendelssohn, who had been living with his parents for some time, they presented Clara's mother with a copy of *Mondnacht* for her birthday. The verses were taken from a small book of poems which Clara had planned to set to music. It is possible that Mendelssohn was the first to sing this music, for in a letter to Dr. Eduard Krüger Schumann wrote, "I wish you could meet Mendelssohn personally and hear him. Among artists, I know none who can compare to him. He knows I like him, and he likes me and some of my music too. We spent several unforgettable hours together at the piano in Berlin. Lately, I have written a great deal of vocal music. He sang a number of my songs, accompanied at the piano by my bride (she plays well, as you may know). I felt quite blessed. I know him quite well, since before his marriage we were together almost every day."

It is no accident that some of the qualities of Mendelssohn's musical style can be detected in the Eichendorff *Lieder*, though they represent the strongest and most original of Schumann's works to that time. The songs sung by Fortunatus (guitar in hand while wandering from room to room) in Eichendorff's *Dichter und ihre Gesellen* (Poets and Their Companions) have been moved by Schumann to an outdoor setting at night. The copy of the manuscript for *Schöne Fremde* (Fair Distant Land) is marked "speech-like whispering." This characterizes the appropriate manner of singing this hymn dedicated to the "visionary night." The intensity of the work derives its strength from a powerful spirituality, which would be destroyed by playing the postlude *fortissimo,* merely for the sake of an "effective" ending. The rising feeling of happiness is suppressed, even before it is completely realized. Throughout long passages at the beginning of the piece, the key is uncertain; not until the end is it clearly established. Schumann commonly employed the same stylistic technique in his piano works. We also see here how

Clara Wieck, ca. 1840

Robert Schumann, ca. 1840

aphorisms find their way into the songs, which may then suddenly lead to action. Schumann often used this musical and artistic device in his song cycles. An introduction then becomes superfluous; it might be dropped completely or at the most shortened to just a few notes. In the case of this song, as if compensating for the shortened introduction, the postlude is made all the longer, echoing the vocal line, even though it has long since faded away. Brahms, in the postludes to both verses of his song, *Meine Liebe ist Grün* (My Love is Green), shows his indebtedness to Schumann's *Schöne Fremde*—the text of which was written by Schumann's son Felix.

Auf einer Burg (The Old Castle, Opus 39, No. 7) conjures up a fairy tale world in which Schumann sketches the sultry midday heat and the petrification of the century-old knight, using ethereal strands of static parallel melodies in the piano and voice parts. The "Draussen" (outside) in the third stanza is quickly lost in the mist and forgotten, and in the course of the song the feeling of death and ruin gives way to the melancholy of loneliness. Within the self-imposed limits of an "old style," Schumann attempts to capture the atmosphere of the poem with a great economy of means. Drone-like passages which seem to wind around themselves, suspensions which tend to obscure phrasing and tempo, "improper" accentuation, harmonies which are without direction—all of these musical devices create the impression of lifelessness and timelessness which the poem suggests. Schumann's aphoristic precision could not be

Example 26

more evident than at that point at the end where the rigidity is relaxed, and the persistent line of descending fifths and ascending sixths is abandoned (Example 26) with the sobbing of the bride heard in the final measures. Schumann's music presents the sobbing as a fact, but also as an unanswered question.

When listening to this gem, we are reminded of its relationship to another late Romantic composer who also set poems by Eichendorff to music, Hans Pfitzner. In his *Aesthetics,* commenting on *Auf einer Burg,* Pfitzner first noted that "correct" declamation was not a criterion in understanding or judging this song. "That this song was not created for musicians who are interested in what is currently fashionable is clear when Schumann emphasizes the first syllable '*Musi*kanten' rather than '*Musikanten*'. For me, so few notes have never created so intense and meaningful an atmosphere. I know for certain that it is around 2:00 in the afternoon. Nature's deep quiet. The forest devoid of people. Hot, shimmering air—everything floats as if in a daydream—even the heavens are asleep—voices rising from the Rhine far below a distraction—a sad chord on the word 'munter' (lively)—why does all this affect us so strongly? It is as if something is touching an exposed nerve, but just as this would cause intense pain in the physical realm, it causes a feeling of intense delight in the spiritual realm."

A jagged, muffled figure pervades the second song entitled *In der Fremde* (In a Strange Land); it also represents images of a rushing brook and mysterious forest lights. The sixteenth notes continue throughout the song, but the accompanying melody is interrupted in the second measure, in somewhat too hackneyed a way, by a measure of alternating sixteenth notes and rests, as if the interrupted tonal line can only be improved upon in the mind's ear. Feelings of constraint, of searching, and of hopelessness mark both this two-measure melodic motif and its harmonic accompaniment (Example 27). The piece does not conjure up a variety of specific images, but instead depicts a state of mind. Schumann's unique ability to focus upon and delineate the most significant elements of a text is best illustrated by comparing his version of this poem with that of the Austrian composer, Joseph Marx.

Example 27

The Adagio, *Wehmut,* is restricted to legato lines in the harmony. The modulation to the sub-dominant on the word "Sehnsucht" momentarily opens up the song's cocoon, but the light that enters is dreary and subdued. With D major thus spotlighted, the morbid coloration of the principal key, E major, becomes even clearer. In Eichendorff's story, *Ahnung und Gegenwart,* Friedrich hears a lone voice singing "Wehmut" without any instrumental accompaniment—a notion which seems foreign to Schumann. Yet he has set the poet's words to a sweeping adagio melody which the piano follows in unison for almost the entire work, making it the prominent element in the song. The intensity of feeling finds free expression in the cantilena, the sense of grief finds relief in tears. Then the built-up tension is relieved by calm. The broad register of sixths and octaves in the accompaniment creates the wistful character of the *Lied.* At one point in the 9th measure, the voice becomes independent, moving on its own. In the epilogue, this same plaintive element, now marked by chromaticism, appears again, the very element that was to remain "secret," and which was kept down in the vocal part.

The tenth song, *Zwielicht* (Twilight), probably one of the most fascinating of Schumann's compositions, once more touches on the fantastic elements of human existence. It too is taken from *Ahnung und Gegenwart* and is sung as if resounding through the woods from a distance, warning of man's faithlessness. The opening measures in the piano are written in that confusing, intertwining, restless style which we have already encountered in *Talismane* (Example 28). These four measures introduce the melodic and harmonic material contained in the entire song. Schumann based his handling of this

Example 28

material on Bach's two-part polyphony, foregoing the fullness of sound which chords would provide. In the last verse, Schumann intensifies the restlessness and uncertainty in the voice line, while the bass line, which has been driven by a syncopated rhythm, falls away from its supportive harmonic role. An air of suspense and uncertainty prevails, and we seem to find ourselves on the edge of the abyss of mental confusion. All the while the listener is held fascinated by the artist's handling of these intimate and terrifying themes.

Schumann's portrayal of the threat to mankind is remarkably "modern," and exposes his central inmost concerns. His profound understanding and premonitions of the ambiguity of the human condition was then emerging—at the time when relationships threatened to become increasingly complicated, convoluted and mendacious. For the first time in the recitative concluding the piece, language becomes an independent, external, musical element "Hüte dich, sei wach und munter" (Be on your guard, be awake and alert!)—a recitative, barely audible. Both music and words whisper and stammer almost like a scarcely-heard or understood inner voice (Example 29).

Example 29

Im Walde (In the Forest), Opus 39, No. 12, also suggests the accord between aloneness and communion with nature and the harmony of light and darkness. Schumann repeatedly interrupts the suggestive 6/8 tempo with ritardandos, which are positioned like question marks between the "external" impressions—a challenge for the interpreter. The "dropped off, casual" ending, typical for Schumann, once more returns to a speech-like style, expressing anguish and anxiety. All along, the song describes the dying away of the noises of the forest, so that it is appropriate that the song concludes without a postlude. It should be noted that nine years later Schumann used the same text for an a cappella chorus, Opus 75, No. 2.

The cold silence of the previous song is shattered by *Frühlingsnacht* (Spring Night), Opus 39, No. 12, voicing a lover's bliss and the glory of nature in joyful song. The last line is ecstatic—"Sie ist deine, sie ist dein!" (She is yours, she is yours!)—and could only be sung by someone who sees the imminent realization of his dreams. The two verses are so densely filled with a great diversity of thoughts and emotions that one wonders why editors at the turn of the century felt compelled to append additional verses in order to extend the ecstasy beyond what is convincing. The heart of the melody is an embellished seventh chord which soars above the thirds and seconds as if to escape the constraint of the composition's framework. The young Brahms used the same pulsating beat in *Nachtigallen schwingen* (The Wings of the Nightingale), Opus 6, but was unable to equal Schumann's unsurpassed exuberance.

The printing of the last pages of *Frühlingsnacht* was so inept that in 1850 Schumann complained to his publisher, Whistling: "The

Felix Mendelssohn-Bartholdy, 1846

last pages are a holy mess. Just imagine: Lind was singing it at a concert in Hamburg using a new copy, but when she turned to the last page, she found an entirely different song. She continued singing without hesitating. After it was over, she calmly told me what had happened. She knew it by heart; she had to, because of your defective copy."

Eichendorff's *Der frohe Wandersmann* (The Happy Wanderer) was not included in Opus 39, or to be more precise, he removed it from the second edition of *Liederkreis* and replaced it with the first version of *In der Fremde*. With an anonymous melody, the poem came close to being a folk song. Schumann's version never achieved the popularity which he had hoped for. His fascination with the poem's subject is understandable in view of the interest in travel which marked the period. After Wackenroder and Tieck, readers now travelled through Germany with Uhland, Chamisso, and Eichendorff, viewing a land still abundant with reminders of the Middle Ages. Sometimes high-spirited, sometimes melancholy, these accounts of journeys through space and time bear witness not only to the longing for communion with nature but to the pleasure found in the chance adventures which could be found waiting at the next bend in the road as well. Such journeys also familiarized the poets with the world of the common rural folk. For Brentano and Arnim, such travels became the source of the songs and ballads—naive, ironic, or cruel—which they collected in *Des Knaben Wunder-horn* (The Youth's Magic Horn). Not everything in this famous collection can be attributed to folklore, for the compilers added their own poetic and balladic material to the anthology. Whatever its origins, this collection greatly influenced both the content and form of the literary works of Eichendorff and Uhland.

Schumann's setting of *Der Frohe Wandersmann,* Opus 77, No. 1, in a lively march tempo, is somewhat forced and elaborate. The epilogue conveys the feeling that the composer gladly separates himself from Eichendorff's cheerfulness to express his own thoughts about courage, joys and dreams.

Schumann's musical output increased markedly during this period. In the evenings he wrote only short, exhausted letters, as all of his energy was spent on composing. "Above all [I] want to write *Lieder*—in the morning, beginning at six o'clock, so please think of me then. By the time you come I shall be exhausted by it. . . ." At another point he wrote, "My earnings from my compositions are not insignificant, and will continue to improve. Do you know that I've earned almost 400 Thalers during these six months? Yes, it's true. I sell no five-sheet notebook of *Lieder* for less than six Louisdor. That adds up, because when I am in good form I can write two sheets of songs in a day, sometimes even more, if you, for example, asked me to . . . By the way, I hear that the Heine cycle is much talked about, which makes me quite happy."

Chapter 9

Schumann had hardly completed the first drafts of the Eichendorff *Lieder* when he undertook a new cycle based on poems by Heine, which has become known under the title *Dichterliebe* (Poet's Love). He dedicated this cycle to the singer Wilhelmine Schröder-Devrient. It recounts something of the story of those months during which Robert and Clara drifted apart and were then reconciled. The title itself hints at the cycle's personal content. In Rückert's volume, *Liebesfrühling* (The Spring of Love), from which Schumann also derived the text for two songs contained in *Myrten,* we find the lines "Dichterliebe hat eignes Unglück stets betroffen. Hohe Götter, lasset mich das Beste hoffen!" (The love of the poet has always met with ill fortune. Great gods on high, let me hope for the best!)

Observing this uncertainty, we may ask ourselves if, despite their obvious affection, Schumann truly loved Clara, or if his life with her was only an eagerly-pursued game of hide-and-seek. Upon reflection, it seems plausible: at a time when he truly hoped for a happy outcome, the texts he chose reveal his characteristic anxiety—a deep uncertainty as to whether he could be happy with the woman he loved. At a time when we would least expect it, he was obsessed with the thought of unrequited love, with fear of the "other" coming between the bride and groom. He falls victim to Heine's despair, almost to the point of satire, but only when it has a tragic bent as it does in this cycle. This "Story in Songs" freely assembled by the composer from Heine's *Buch der Lieder,* is guided by Schubert's example in *Schöne Müllerin.* Here the poet willingly exposes his innermost feelings, but also displays a kind of naiveté

which is also expressed in the epilogue, quiet and resigned in mood.

The piano introductions to Schumann's songs, though often no more than a series of chords, set the emotional state for the upcoming text. In the short introduction to *Im wunderschönen Monat Mai* (In the Beautiful Month of May), the tonality fluctuates between F# minor (without actually using the chord) and A major, and even when the voice enters, all harmonic turns are unexpected (Example 3 o). The independent, dreamy, Chopinesque style of the piano arabesque might suggest that the vocal line had been added later. The "open" ending brings to mind the term "aleatoric," as used by Pierre Boulez for some 2 oth Century music. Be that as it may, the unresolved dominant-seventh chord at the end indicates that Schumann was moving in that direction, avoiding any clear conclusion of the piece.

In *Aus meinen Tränen* (From My Tears) the music surrounds the text like a deep, ironic veil, yet it reveals all the more clearly the poet's frame of mind, which Schumann shared. The morbid sentimentality of this, the first of many "flower" songs, contrasts profoundly with *Die Rose, die Lilie* (The Rose, the Lily), whose text seems inconsistent in the context of this song cycle: this short, breathless admission of bliss seems out of place in the atmosphere of bitterness and sadness pervading the cycle. It may have been chosen to provide a contrasting tempo to the songs which precede and follow it. Richard Tauber's virtuosic tour de force of whispering the entire piece in one breath, as he does on an old recording, is hardly to be recommended, though it has often been imitated. Such display

Example 30

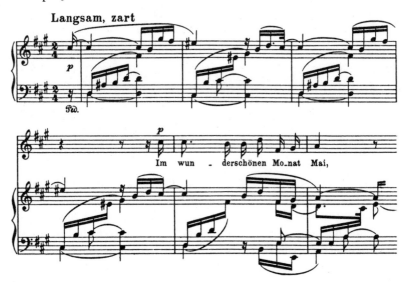

Langsam, zart

Im wun - derschönen Mo_nat Mai,

of bravura is likely to result in a hurried, careless rendition; the one simple motif disappears almost before it is ever heard.

For *Wenn ich in deine Augen seh* (Whenever I Look in Your Eyes) Schumann employed a persistent, recitative-like dwelling on a single tone. The melodic line is compressed, interrupted by occasional, sudden flourishes. Here, as in other songs of the cycle, the optional notes that go *with* the piano line are preferable, the piano part being melodically dominant.

Ich will meine Seele tauchen (I'll Hide in the Heart of the Lily) also possesses a fleeting character. The text speaks of music; an unsung song provides the nucleus of this poem. Bits and pieces of memories appear in the patterned accompaniment, but the melody is alluded to only in single daubs of color, never being fully developed. The middle voices seem to be almost incidental. In the *pianissimo* passages, which are a reflection of the poet's reveries (the notation *con pedale* refers to the left pedal!), the vocal line has little melodic significance or text declamation. When all the text has been sung, the song is not completed, for the piano forsakes its repeated patterns and carries the real vocal line. For a moment, we have a brief insight into how the melody might have sounded. This piano

passage is followed by the true epilogue, again bringing undulating harmonies: brittle chords introduced by grace notes; the tinkle of the lily goblet, now turned to glass. The oscillating, arpeggiated harmonies have collapsed.

The vision of the Cathedral of Cologne inspired not only the *Rhenish Symphony*, but prompted Schumann to add *Im Rhein, im heiligen Strome* (On the Rhine, on the Sacred Stream) to the long list of works whose structures were inspired by Bach. These loosely-based Bach studies seemed new and unusual to his contemporaries. The motif is treated polyphonically, but the rhythm is inflexible. They suggest Gothic works in the spirit of Caspar David Friedrich; Gothic ruins as seen through early 19th Century eyes. Schumann writes an organlike bass line, with embroidery in the manner of a Bach chorale prelude. They evoke the sun's shimmering reflection in the nave and the cherubs in Lochner's painting "Madonna im Rosenhag", as well as the emotional reaction of the viewers of the scene. Robert Franz's setting of the same text expressed grace and charm, here the scope of interpretation has been expanded, so that the poem is surpassed. Once again we see Schumann's ingenious use of repetition as the singer repeats "die Lippen", stammering in

Example 31

Frau; die Au _ gen, die Lip _ pen, die Lip _ pen, die Wäng _ lein,

astonishment, and then continuing with the melisma of the main theme after a quick breath (Example 31).

Accented repeated notes in the Schubert manner permeate the song *Ich grolle nicht* (I Blame Thee Not). But they develop into amazing progressions of unresolved seventh-chords, a musical technique which Arnold Schönberg particularly notes in his *Harmonielehre* published in 1911. The piece is in C major, a key which has incorrectly been labeled optimistic. This therefore might come as a surprise, but the choice of key turns out to be appropriate for portraying the overcoming of resentment, the transforming of resignation into unhappy love, and for evoking the singer's half-ironic resolve never again to succumb to weakness. For the high point of the vocal line, Schumann offers a high A, which the author often has used in performance. It is preferable that the singer then go on to the following D. Some tenors have transported the song to E♭ major in order to use their high C and so avoid the dangerously low notes at the end, but this is not advisable. The line "Ich grolle nicht" appears twice in Heine's poem, but Schumann repeats it six times for added effect.

Und wüssten's die Blumen (If Only the Flowers Knew) begins weightlessly as if it had no roots. The quiet voice line above the uninterrupted whisper of the accompaniment suggests formlessness. The flitting opening leads at the end to the lover's desperate disappointment, flowing into an epilogue whose dramatic effect is reminiscent of the forceful opening of *Kreisleriana*. The gentle complaint has become an accusation.

In the next song, *Das ist ein Flöten und Geigen* (I Hear the Flutes

and Fiddles), the mood changes to bitter detachment. The piano seizes the initiative, assigning to the voice a melodic recitative. In the postlude the irony collapses; a striking effect which led Gustav Mahler to use an almost identical figure in the conclusion of his satire, *Des Antonius von Padua Fischpredigt* (St. Anthony's Sermon to the Fishes). However, the irony does not crumble as it does in Schumann's piece (Examples 32 and 33). The waltz in the piano part does not represent the resounding music at the wedding party, but rather its effect on the soul of the tortured listener. To accommodate the piano line, Schumann has made numerous changes in the

Example 32

Example 33

g'fal - len!
les - sened!

text (*Drein* in measures 10 and 22, the addition of *wohl* in measure 21, *ein Pauken und Schalmei'n* in measures 46 through 49, *lieblichen* in measure 63 and the repetition of a number of words). The pianist must not hurry through the strong dance rhythms and thereby rush the tempo. The internal contrast between the devastating sadness and the wedding dances must remain clear.

"Hör ich das Liedchen klingen" (When I Hear the Song) begins with a lonely, free-sounding, syncopated melody comprised of seven notes. It is heard in the four-measure introduction and continues in augmentation in the epilogue, where the accumulated pain is released as tears. The piano (not yet the voice, not even with the final words "übergrossen Weh!" [enormous grief]) describes the tearful outburst, then introduces the idea that these emotions can be overcome, though this outcome is not realized until the end of the cycle. Schumann set his version of this poem between those of Meyerbeer (1832) and Robert Franz (1843). These three versions and that composed in the 1880s by Edvard Grieg have much in common, but Schumann used the piano most sparingly and most effectively. At the end, the abrupt introduction of chromaticism in the piano part, strongly emotional, contrasts quite effectively with the simplicity of the voice line.

Though skeptics fail to see it, "Ein Jüngling liebt' ein Mädchen," (The Youth Who Loves a Maiden) demonstrates Schumann's ability to do justice to Heine's sarcastic tone. The bitterness of the disappointed lover is cast as a popular ballad with an intentionally simple theme and a hackneyed closing using repeated chords. Only in the last line, "Dem bricht das Herz entzwei" (His heart breaks in two), with a dramatic ritenuto, does a serious, anguished musical utterance emerge. Prior to this statement, contempt for the "old story" is unmistakable, expressed through constant repetition of the boring subdominant-dominant-tonic cadence. The piano seems to make fun of the hint of sentimentality in the voice line; it contrasts such feeling in its rhythmic cross-accents. Heine's use of the word "heuratet" (marries) was insufficiently crude for Schumann's intentions so he replaced it with "nimmt" (takes).

"Am leuchtenden Sommermorgen" (On a Brilliant Summer Morning) moves us largely by the striking modulation from B♭

major to G major at the point where the flowers ask the poet "Sei unsrer Schwester nicht böse" (Do not be angry with our sister). At this point the elegy, carrying no hint of bitterness, seems to pause and the flowers recall the melody of the last piano epilogue, hinting again at the possibility of overcoming grief.

In "Ich hab' im Traum geweinet" (I Wept in my Dream) Schumann ignores the satiric undertone which Heine almost certainly intended and concentrates on the lover's obsession with having been abandoned. In the third verse, a subtle accent in the poem is suddenly given great importance. The whispered recitative is set aside when the sense of the song is revealed in the final "Tränenflut" (flood of tears). In this song the vocal line is marked by meaningful pauses, while the piano part is characterized by its reserve. Its dotted-rhythm motif stands in clear contrast with the vocal line. (The identical treatment is repeated in Schumann's setting of Lenau's "Der Schwere Abend" [The Heavy Evening]). (See Examples 34 and 35).

Example 34

Example 35

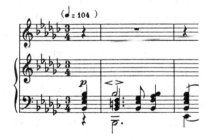

85

"Allnächtlich im Traume" (Every Night In My Dreams) depicts the awakening lover's repeated efforts to recall his recurring dream. The hesitant, groping pauses should be clearly observed by the singer. Not just for musical reasons, but to emphasize the lover's effort to recall his dream, Schumann repeats the word "freundlich" in the second line and later repeats "schüttelst" and "den Strauss". He can barely remember his thoughts just before awakening, but the "word" upon which all depends eludes him.

From the dream world, the cycle moves into the imaginary realm of the fairy tale with "Aus alten Märchen" (From Old Legends). The expansion of the main motif to twice its former dimensions toward the end of the piece produces the moving effect which Schumann intended by the indication *Mit inningster Empfindung* ("with greatest sensitivity"). The short epilogue "tempo primo", seems to look once again for the motif—but in vain: the dream has dissolved "like evanescent sea foam". This tender, poetic piece, with its richness of images, demands all of the singer's abilities to express its many hues. With steady pace, the song moves forward with increasing tension to the rising phrases "ancient melodies", to the sweeping seventh-chords of the "reflection" and to the two sighs "Ach!" (Schumann's own repetition), and finally to the yearning legato lines of the last verse. The reader should pay no heed to discrepancies in the present-day text, since Schumann used the first edition of Heine's work for his text.

The poet is thrust back into reality with a percussive broken chord in B minor. "Die alten, bösen Lieder" (The Old, Evil Songs) are carried to the grave in a grotesque and extravagant show piece. Angular figures in the piano part and a powerful deployment of the voice in the low register (problematic for the singer) accurately portray the poet's sarcasm. Schumann's B minor theme to a rigid rhythm gives a hard-toned quality, which remains unchanged up to the phrase "Wisst ihr warum". Then at the adagio line "Ich senkt auch meine Liebe und meinen Schmerz hinein" it seems to weep. Once again the voice line ends on the subdominant E minor, until the piano begins the quiet yet ecstatic epilogue in B major. Resorting to the usage typical of his epilogues, Schumann expands upon the meaning of this song by recalling his declaration of love for Clara made in "Am leuchtenden Sommermorgen." This instru-

mental conclusion summarizes and at the same time defines the essence of the cycle.

Again, Schumann omitted two songs originally intended for the cycle. The content of "Dein Angesicht" (When I See Your Face), Opus 127, No. 2 did not seem to fit into the context of this grouping. This impressive study was not published until 1854 (together with Heine's "Es leuchtet meine Liebe" [My Love]). This slowly-paced piece is in 2/4 time and thus poses some tempo problems for performers. Each sixteenth-note must be given full weight and expression; which should determine the proper tempo.

"Lehn deine Wang" (Rest Your Cheek on Mine), Opus 142, No. 2 was also originally intended to be included in the cycle. However, it would have introduced a sentimental quality despite Schumann's instruction to perform it "passionately", and it therefore was omitted. Nevertheless, this composition strikes one as much more original than the frequently-sung setting by Adolf Jensen, Opus 1, No. 1. It is important to note the omission of the epilogue in this piece, as it illustrates Schumann's reluctance to introduce a new thought in the final notes of the piano if the poem has already provided a clear conclusion. Schumann never saw the publication of this song; it was published with "Mein Wagen rollet langsam" (My Coach Rolls Slowly) two years after his death.

"Es leuchtet meine Liebe" is an exciting and ingenious reflection on Schumann's experience of deprivations, with Wieck as the central villain—the "Riese der Wüste" (giant of the wilderness) of the poem. Clara is the virgin, and Schumann the bleeding knight to whom measures 25 through 26 also have been given, contrary to Heine's intentions. Thus this song is made truly biographical. This "fairy tale" is basically instrumentally conceived; it bears many similarities to the string quartet in A minor. The work's magic harmonies result in greatly varied tonal color. The flickering, flame-like motion of the diminished seventh chord functions as the fundamental idea through which Schumann expresses his intense anger (Example 36).

"Mein Wagen rollet langsam" Opus 142, No. 4, features the imagery of the piano part at the expense of the voice. As was frequently the case, Schumann put more effort and concern into the

Example 36

Example 37

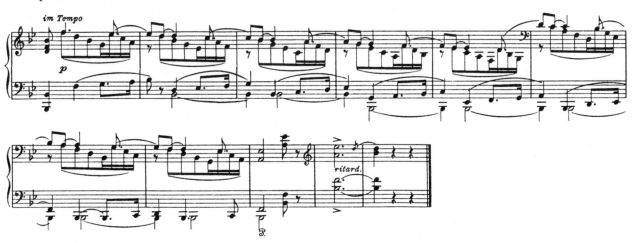

rhythms and patterns of the accompaniment than the vocal line. The piano constantly courts the voice, but is never truly successful.

If the *Lied* were not a distinct genre, the result of both tradition and intentional design, it could be argued that the voice accompanies the piano . . . but after all, what is an "accompaniment"? What matters is not the singer or the player strumming his lute, but rather the composer and his inspiration, whether this be people, life, drama or an instrument. In the lover's dream that is "Mein Wagen rollet langsam," Schumann depends heavily on Heine's underlying parody, using it to conceal feelings of love. But at the end the dream is destroyed. In the interludes and the epilogue the piano meditates, and indeed the entire song is a meditation. The composer-pianist steps up to speak with the poet. It is a strange song, sung mostly by the pianist. The rambling rhythms of the introduction are disjointed by harmonic excursions, but a calm melody is heard above it. Suddenly jeering spirits surround the poet, "quirlen wie Nebel zusammen" (whirling like bits of fog) and then disappearing again. Schumann's ghosts "huschen" (flit about) rather than merely "grüssen" (greet) as they do in Heine's version. The singing ends, and the piano plays on with the same rocking motion used in the opening of the piece, as if falling asleep in a moving coach. The music descends to lower and lower ranges, where the notes can no longer be clearly distinguished, until the last measure, when a humorous, cuckoo-like skip of a third wakes the traveler who may have nodded off (Example 37).

This was Schumann's last composition based on a text by Heine, though two earlier pieces were not published until later. Whoever attacked his friend Mendelssohn also attacked Schumann. So when Heine publicly insulted Mendelssohn, Schumann's devotion to the poet was extinguished, after his poetry had served as a musical beacon for only a matter of months.

Chapter 10

Schumann's great surge of productivity had relegated Wieck's disturbances to the back of his mind. By June of 1 8 4 0, however, Schumann felt that he owed it to himself to put an end to the constant slander: he decided to lodge a complaint of defamation against Wieck. It took until May, 1 8 4 1, to have Wieck sentenced to 1 8 days in prison. "Robert had no other choice," Clara stated in her diary; thus clearly indicating where she stood. With the help of her mother, she now prepared herself for the "difficult task" of "combining, as far as possible, the duties of a performing artist with the work of running a household." She traveled to Leipzig in June in order to celebrate Robert's birthday with him, for the first time. Though she also spent a few weeks with her aunt, proximity to Robert was the main impetus. He was more confident than his bride, who feared that the wedding might be delayed until winter—a worry because until then she would proudly refuse to accept any money from Robert. Yet, as she admitted, her financial situation was "depressing and humiliating."

All the while, Schumann's thoughts were entirely preoccupied with the psychology of women. He turned to composing *Frauenliebe und -Leben* (Woman's Love and Life, Opus 4 2; text by Chamisso) a year after Carl Loewe who had set the same poems as his Opus 6 0.

Long before the present there were those who voiced their objections to Chamisso's antiquated concept of the woman who only found happiness in "giving" herself. As early as 1 8 7 4, Theodor Storm wrote to Paul Heyse about these poems: "Mörike once told me how distasteful all this was to him, and those are exactly my sentiments."—The song cycle has become such a standard item in the Lieder repertory that it seems to have risen above the conventions of time. Yet, the weaknesses of the poems are clearly evident now. Not that Schumann's music stoops to lower middle class idyls or conventions. Its expression is straightforward; the tragic quality of the final parting especially is of lasting significance. The poems in this cycle, more than the others, represent a continuing yet coherent development. The piano postlude symbolically refers back to the opening, reminding us of Beethoven's cycle *An die ferne Geliebte,* Opus 9 8. Schumann had already established such interrelations in Nos. 2 and 1 7 of the *Davidsbündlertänze;* he first applied them to song in Heine's *Liederkreis.* The choice of tonalities indicates that feminine qualities to Schumann suggested the use of flat keys, as had already been the case in Opus 2 5, Nos. 1 and 7. Possibly this goes with the general convention that "sharp" keys are "hard" and flat keys, "soft."

In *Seit ich ihn gesehen* (Since I first saw him) the melody moves, fitfully at first, but with dignity—the reflection of a fateful encounter. Yet the song is but a prelude; it does not provide a vision of things to come. The rhythm at first is hesitating, then gradually assumes shape and moves on—sequentially, calmly. There is some awkwardness in the declamation of the first two stanzas: "heller" receives too little emphasis; "lieber", too much. But this does not interfere with the expression of profound sentiment. It isn't until the end of the cycle that we understand the saraband dance rhythm of the opening—a "dance of death" (Oehlmann). Love and death are intertwined. Schumann, in a way quite typical for him, inserts the wave lines of the accompaniment between the accents of the voice line.

The first phrase approximates canon, a device that was to be important in Schumann's later writing. In the piano part the melodic line reaches its high points in the third and sixth measures, with the voice part following in measures four and seven. At the end the accompaniment adds tension by repeating the motif one step higher.

Er, der herrlichste von allen (He, in all the world the noblest) draws an ardent portrait of the one who is secretly loved. Moreover, it is a piece of "absolute," abstract music, though its rhythm is derived from the poem. The song moves through many keys. Individual words are repeated where musical considerations demand. Some aspects of the song may strike the listener as trivial, but the postlude sets this initial impression at rest. The overall mood is one of confidence that her love is returned, but the following song, *Ich kann's nicht fassen, nicht glauben* (I cannot believe it) is more passionate. Again the melody grows out of the poem's rhythm—tentative at first, reciting over staccato chords. A long postlude begins, only to be interrupted once more by the opening of the text and the refrain, with the final ritardando resolving the tension.

Du Ring an meinem Finger (You ring upon my finger) is more simply conceived, praising the symbol of their union. It exudes a sense of warmth and security. The middle section digresses briefly, but there is no drama or contrast: the basic theme, the symbol of the ring, is always in sight.

Helft mir, ihr Schwestern (Help me, my sisters) is even more markedly dominated by musical considerations. There is a hint of melancholy—the thought of saying farewell to her girlhood years.

The pattern of the accompaniment, rising and falling, is derived from the earlier *Widmung*. Such an accompaniment might express other emotions as well. The poem seems to be superimposed on the music, rather mechanically observing the beginnings of each line. (*Aber* euch Schwestern *Grüss* ich mit Wehmut . . .) The only instances of close text-music relationship occur at the word "Wehmut" (sadness), with a sudden turn to G♭ major, and in the postlude where there is a suggestion of a wedding procession which the bride joins, tearing herself from the girl friends of her youth. Schumann changes Chamisso's text in four places; in two other places he adds words (meas. 13 and 33: "sonst" and "lass").

The style changes in *Süsser Freund, du blickest mich verwundert an* (Dearest one, you look at me). A new, monodic delivery characterizes the voice line, proceeding over static harmonies. Yet this recitative-like style results in one of Schumann's most musical lines, endowing some rather empty words with profound music. This quality of the music demanded the omission of one verse of Chamisso's poem; it would have been too prosaic an utterance (after meas. 21). Following a succession of seventh-chords in the middle section the voice line abandons its earlier free rhythm, only to resume it with the return to the beginning, thus rounding out the three-part form. An upbeat motif dominates the piano postlude. We are reminded of Beethoven when, over the last chord, we once more hear the words "Dein Bildnis!" (Example 38).

The rather tritely conceived text of *An meinem Herzen* (Here on my bosom), expressing the bliss of a young mother, is compensated for by the music, a merry round dance. The sweeping, loving gesture in the piano part's conclusion raises this song to a high level despite Chamisso's text.

Example 38

Suddenly the stark D minor triad at the opening of *Nun hast du mir den ersten Schmerz getan* (The first time you have caused me grief) announces the end of blissful days—a lament above lifeless chords. Words seem to fail the protagonist; the piano—Schumann's piano—speaks instead.

A life has been lived, richer and more eventful than the text could convey: almost a monodrama for piano. Schumann changes "vergangenes" Glück (past) to "verlorenes" Glück (lost) happiness, for he will not compose Chamisso's ninth poem in which the old woman speaks to her grandchild. The Schumann of the 1840s would not undertake giving artistic expression to emotions that could only be distilled from time and experience: he created music out of his own immediate experience. He had no use for Chamisso's conciliatory ending, finding happiness in children and grandchildren; rather he inserted in the piano postlude the theme from *Seit ich ihn gesehen.* The mourning woman finds happiness only in remembering that which is lost. One day this was to be Clara's fate.—Audiences found fault with the ending, which does not seem to invite applause, but in the long run Schumann's arrangement was seen to be right.

The genre of the ballad may have been viewed by Schumann as a preliminary step on the road to writing an opera. The elements of legend and folk style, inherent in ballads, may also have attracted him. But in this genre, too, Schumann remained the lyricist. His three songs to texts by Chamisso, Opus 31, were dedicated to Ernestine von Fricken whose married name was von Zedtwitz. It is to her credit that she came to Schumann's help in his struggle with Wieck. She did not allow herself to be used as a witness to testify about Schumann's irritability or alcoholism; rather she sided with him, knowing full well his feelings of guilt about her. Following the death, soon after their marriage, of her husband, Count von Zedtwitz, Robert and Clara continued their friendship with her.

Die Löwenbraut (The lion's bride, Opus 31, No. 1): Schumann's music rises above the text, a gruesome tale. He begins, no doubt

intentionally, with the archaic time signature as though he wanted to stress the "long ago" quality of the story. The poem is charac-

Three Songs by Adelbert von Chamisso,
for Voice and Pianoforte, Op. 31—
Title page of the First Edition

terized by great intensity of feeling, quite typical of Chamisso's poems written during his last years of ill health, before his death in 1838.

Chamisso was seeking a solution to the dilemma in which he viewed contemporary poetry to be caught. Immermann, who had visited him in Berlin, recalled:

> Chamisso, looking patriarchal with his long, white hair, received me in a room full of tobacco smoke. With the preliminaries out of the way, he soon started complaining about the sorry state of poetry and literature. This kind of talk always infuriates me, and so I shot back: "Just because nothing grows in the sandy soil of your Berlin you proclaim the demise of poetry everywhere." To which he replied, good-naturedly: "It's true, everyone judges the world from within his own four walls."

Schumann undoubtedly felt strongly about this poem. To him the animal, wild and cruel, was Wieck. Critics of the time considered Schumann's setting a failure, as they often did when his works dealt with more than deep emotion. The same critics failed to appreciate the daring chord fragments (at the lion's escape); heavy, ominous sounds that were well ahead of their time. (Example 39).

The form of this ballad is based on the miniature cantatas of Zumsteg and Schubert, frequently-used models for subjects of this kind. In Schumann's setting it is turned into variations on a simple melody. Some recitative-like material frames the heroine's song. It is significant that she repeatedly paraphrases the melody addressed to Clara in *Widmung*. (Example 40).

The solemn mood of the piano's opening and closing sections provides the rhythmic raw material which represents wild passion. A persistently maintained metric pattern gains intensity in the middle section, only to return to the archaic manner of the beginning. Before that, the high point (the lion's attack) is represented by chromatic contrary motions between voice and piano parts. Yet Schumann, as the narrator, preserves a certain detachment, refraining from clouding the action by the introduction of a number of themes, as he occasionally did elsewhere. Instead he relied on the

Example 39

Example 40

PIERRE JEAN
DE BÉRANGER

Together with Gaudy, Chamisso translated several
"songs" by Pierre Jean de Béranger (1780–1857). He was
the son of poor parents and brought up by his grand-
father, a tailor. After the Revolution, the 14-year-old was
apprenticed to a printer. By studying the poems of André
Chenier, which he printed, he acquired his first knowledge of style and versification. In 1797 he returned to his
parents in Paris, full of plans for the future which he was
not able to realize. His father had been ruined by
speculations and involvement in royalist conspiracies.
The family lived in extreme poverty. Young Béranger
was about to join the army and go to Egypt when his
literary efforts attracted the attention of the then Senator
Lucien Bonaparte who turned over to Béranger the
yearly stipend to which he himself was entitled as a
member of the *Institut.*

In 1809, Béranger obtained a well-paid secretarial
position at the University which he retained until 1821.
His first collection of songs, *Chansons morales et autres*
(Paris, 1815) was enthusiastically received. Though he
avoided politics in it, Béranger was reprimanded by his
superiors. This did not keep him from writing, but on the
day his second collection of poems was published he
resigned from his position. His attitude had not changed.
He was not moved by the fall of the Empire in 1814 nor
by the restoration of the monarchy. He declined the position of censor which was offered to him during the
"Hundred Days." But as the forces of reaction increased,
his opposition mounted. The government confiscated
those of his books that remained unsold and sentenced
the poet to three months in prison and a fine. The poems
he subsequently wrote resulted in yet further prosecu-
tion leading to nine months in prison. There he continued to write against "the enemies of progress and
freedom." His fourth volume of poems clearly shows
how his writings paved the way for the July Revolution.
When, later, he was offered various positions and honors
he steadfastly declined them. He sold his works to a publisher for a life pension, retired to the country in 1833
and returned to Paris only in the last years of his life.
Though he had wished for a pauper's funeral it was
denied him and he was honored with a state funeral.

Béranger composed melodies for some of his poems
which appeared in print. Chamisso was but one of many
who translated his works into German. Many of his songs
still survive in France as folk songs. His poem *The Two
Grenadiers* served as the model for Heine's ballad.

effectiveness and evocative power of the ritornello (Example 41)
that conveys well the flavor of a legend.

For *Die Kartenlegerin* (The fortune teller, Opus 31, No. 2;
originally *Les cartes ou l'horoscope*) Schumann did not compose the
sixth stanza. To compare the opening measures of this song with
those of *Die Löwenbraut* is to realize Schumann's extraordinary ver-
satility. Here a few brief staccato chords, suggesting woodwind
accents, suffice for the accompaniment, while an ominous mood is
established with sweeping lines. Subtle nuances of declamation are

Example 41

93

handled with ease, almost too easily. A casual, clownish manner characterizes the girl who asks to have her fortune told; this is handled in a rather routine way. The ballad, here in the form of a monologue, may seem too facile in its conventional humor together with its "cute" piano part containing playful phrases reminiscent of an earlier, *galant* period.

The composer made some changes in the text, substituting the line "kommt das dumme Frau'ngesicht" and omitting the line "legen will ich mir die Karten." The repetitions at the end are also Schumann's.

Chamisso's translation of Béranger's *Jeanne de Russe, ou la Femme du Braconnier* is intentionally naive. For his song *Die rote Hanne* (Red Hanna; Opus 31, No. 3) Schumann appropriately chooses the form of a traditional round with choral refrain. The pseudo-serious tale of the wife of a poacher who has been caught red-handed is told in musical stanzas, almost all alike save for a few welcome variants. Such sad tales, told in many verses to repetitive music, barrel-organ-like, seemingly ignoring the story's mood, remind us of some folk singers of our day. Schumann revived and gave new meaning to the genre.

Chapter 11

After filing a suit against Wieck, Schumann indicated to Clara his confidence in the outcome by having a grand piano, decorated with flowers, installed in her room. She was away at the time, but touched as she was by his gesture, on her return she found little time for the piano. Robert was able to surprise her with the news that Wieck had withdrawn his action to establish legal proof of Robert's alcoholism. His imminent consent to their marriage was anticipated by both of them, so they undertook a search for an apartment, and when the consent appeared on August 1 they already had found lodgings on Inselstrasse. The Danish poet Hans Christian Andersen was one of their first visitors to read them his manuscript *Die Blume des Glücks.* Schumann, all enthusiastic, immediately offered to use the fairy tale for an opera, but Andersen already had conveyed music rights to a Danish composer.

However some of Andersen's other poems inspired Schumann to compose some superb songs. He discovered them, in the same collection in which he had found *Frauenliebe,* translated by Chamisso. He sent a copy of these songs, Opus 40, to the poet—a token of thanks, accompanied by a letter containing a significant passage: "I did not want to come to you empty-handed, though I know fully well that I really am only returning something I had received from you. I hope you will accord a favorable reception to these settings of your poetry. Perhaps they will seem strange at first, which is how your poems impressed me when I first read them. As I immersed myself in them, I came up with music that also seemed strange—so the fault is yours! One cannot write music for Andersen's poems the way one might set *Blühe, liebes Veilchen.*"

Schumann's Opus 40 songs, four of which are settings of Andersen's poems and are dedicated to him, display a naturalness of expression and have an easy, direct appeal, whether they depict mysterious moods or alternate between the light and the serious. In their demonic or grotesque, yet folk-like qualities, they point to later songs by Gustav Mahler.

A pleasant, amiable mood reigns in *Märzveilchen,* Opus 40, No. 1; there is no harshness, no heavy accentuation. As in earlier songs, syncopations provide an unsteady, floating, rhythmic quality. The title of this series as well as others remind us that young Schumann had sought to find a musical "language of flowers." The concept was inspired by the title of a Schubert song, *Der Blumen Sprache.* He intended to pursue this idea further, even concluding for a time that this was the real objective of his new approach to composing. Though he eventually lost sight of this objective, the result of composing fugues and a toccata under Dorn's tutelage, he continued to be attracted to flowery expression in both text and music.

Muttertraum (Mother's Dream, Opus 40, No. 2), a very intense song, might well be considered a Bach study. It invites comparison with *Zwielicht,* from the Eichendorff cycle, both in its thematic material and the prevailing, dusk-like mood. As in all of Schumann's most inspired songs, the voice line is quite independent of the accompaniment, the thin texture of which suggests barrenness and sadness. The intertwining lines, in tired, trembling sounds, convey the sense of fear and uncertitude.

Der Soldat (The Soldier, Opus 40, No. 3), a gripping, balladlike song, brings to mind Mahler's soldier songs and symphonic march

HANS CHRISTIAN
ANDERSEN

Hans Christian Andersen first made his reputation with
his fantastic satires and vaudevilles [light comedy songs—
ed.], only turning later to the soulful poetry for which he
is remembered. He was born in Odense in 1805, the son
of a shoemaker. Loneliness and poverty marked his early
years; only puppets and books provided an escape to an
imaginary world. At the age of 14 he started singing in a
Copenhagen theater. His talent led to a royal scholarship which enabled him to obtain not only further education but to undertake a trip to Italy. These years saw the
writing of fairy tales, poems, travel diaries and his novel
Der Improvisator.

Travel occupied much of Andersen's life and
inspired, above all, his fairy tales—world famous,
profound, full of humor and imagination, beloved by
young and old alike. He died in Copenhagen in 1875.

Der Spielmann (The Fiddler, Opus 40, No. 4), a ghostly ballad,
is the high point in the small group of Andersen songs. Schumann's
interpretation of the setting and of the protagonist's feelings is
every bit as intense as the poet's: there are the fiddles, sounding
"mistuned" with their diminished fifths; there are waltz strains,
again and again interrupted by cadential measures. A mood of
collapse, doom, and threatening madness characterizes this music in
a way that is rare for the composer. The conclusion is frightening,
with its autobiographical implications, praying to God for protec-
tion "that no one be overcome by madness." Dance rhythms,
dissonance, and dismembered melodic lines characterize the song.
Within its contained dimensions it tells of a tragedy—Schumann's
own. The quiet conclusion in G major is deceptive as the melody
vanishes into lowest registers. The listener is strangely reminded of
the veiled aspects of Schumann's own wedding when a phrase from
the *Lied im Walde* is transformed into the grimacing theme of the
fiddler, which then (eight measures before the *Langsamer* section)
becomes a fanfare, taken from *Papillons* (Examples 42 and 43). This
song is a devastating personal confession, made all the more
poignant since the piece is related within the formal scheme of
triple rhythm and the persistent fiddle tune.

Example 42

Er streichet die Geige, sein Haar ergraut,

Example 43

Es zog ei - ne Hoch-zeit den Berg ent-lang,

movements by virtue of its orchestral effects, and more notably its
relentless, steady rhythm. At the words "Ich aber," the high point,
Schumann abandons the basic pattern, in which accompaniment
rather than text has dominated, and turns to recitative. The song
ends on the dominant, on the unanswered question as to how the
soldier will cope with his grief. This contrasting ending greatly adds
to the song's effectiveness: after the persistent drum sounds,
Schumann "composes" four measures of silence. He never permits
the text's inherent sentimentality to emerge.

For the last song in Opus 40, Schumann chose an anonymous
poem in modern Greek, translated by Chamisso. According to
Sams, it was taken from the *Chants populaires de la Grèce moderne* by
Fauriel (1825). *Verratene Liebe* (The Tell-Tales, Opus 40, No. 5) is a
surprisingly amiable conclusion, following such an emotionally

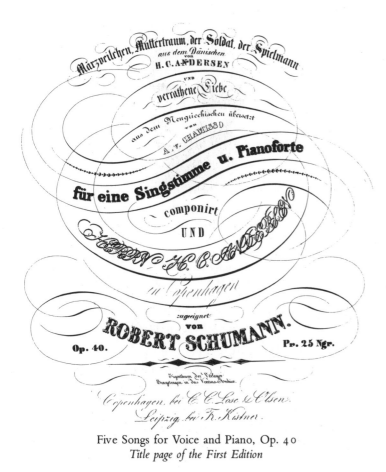

Five Songs for Voice and Piano, Op. 40
Title page of the First Edition

stormy series of songs. With its playful, jolly finish, including the coquettish flourish in the piano, it was no doubt intended to restore emotional balance.

Before turning to a group of six poems by his friend Robert Reinick, Schumann wrote the *Four Duets, Opus 34,* the first of which also is based on a text by Reinick. For the second and third duets the composer again turned to Robert Burns. *Liebhabers Ständchen* (The Lover's Serenade) consists of two poems which the composer combined, giving the first to the tenor, the second to the soprano. The lively No. 4, *Unterm Fenster* (Under the Window) calls upon the interpreter to locate the passages calling for a ritardando, followed

by an "a tempo," as they are not indicated in the music.

The Schumann literature is replete with unfortunate assessments that the later song cycles lack cohesion and overall formal organization. Actually, the true cycles are limited to those stemming from the "wonderful month of May" in 1840, i.e., *Dichterliebe* and *Frauenliebe.* In all the song collections following these the terms "Liederspiel" or (Schumann's own term) "Liederreihe" are more appropriate. This observation is particularly relevant to the group of six songs *Aus dem Liederbuch eines Malers,* (From the Songbook of the Artist, Opus 36) to texts by Reinick. Though the connection between the songs is but tenuous, the impression of an organic whole is created by their truly folk-like flavor. No great depths are probed; they exude *joie de vivre* though they do include contemplative moments.

Sonntags am Rhein (Sunday on the Rhine, Opus 36, No. 1) shows the great pains Schumann took to transform a weak poem into beautiful music. He established a dream-like mood with the distant sounds of an organ and a solemn procession. The song displays inventiveness but remains simple, as does the treatment of the piano accompaniment. In this, more than in his vocal writing, Schumann's song style differs from that of Schubert. In *Sonntags am Rhein* the composer was once more under the spell of Schubert, but this example is now an exception. The range of the voice part is unusually wide, which may be one reason why the song is seldom performed. The very low register at "da singt und jubelt's drein" is typical of Schumann's understated approach to vocal writing. Like Mozart he sometimes intentionally "held back," regardless of the difficulties this may create for the performer. Patriotic feelings also occur in *Sonntags am Rhein:* pained by political suppression and frustration, the singer dreams of the "good old days." Aside from such thoughts, we are immersed in a country scene with church bells, processional hymns, with castles, mountains and forests. The attractive postlude suggests the sound of footsteps disappearing in the distance.

Ständchen (Serenade, Opus 36, No. 2) appeals, thanks to the moods created, entreating and tender. Why is it that this elegant little jewel among Romantic serenades is so seldom performed? Schumann was wise not to compose the last two verses of Reinick's

97

poem with their awkward, forced rhymes. A comparison with Hugo Wolf's early (but more profound and complex) setting is revealing. In the accompaniment Schumann does little more than suggest the strumming and playing of a group of serenaders.

Even Schumann could not rise above the trivial text of *Nichts Schöneres* (Nothing Fairer, Opus 36, No. 3). The shape of the melody suggests one of his imitators rather than the master himself. Still, he succeeded in creating a song in the spirit of simple, sincere folk music.

Under the influence of Romantic verse, Schumann's songs represent a fusion of North German elements with those of Schubert's Austria. The rediscovery of folk song by the Romantics had inspired composers of the "Berlin School," including Zelter and Fasch. How strongly this rediscovery (or new appreciation) of folk song affected Schumann is clear in his setting of Reinick's *An den Sonnenschein* (To Sunshine, Opus 36, No. 4). The song's great and lasting popularity was in part due to the fact that Jenny Lind often included it in her recitals. Such successes invited imitation by other composers. *Weltschmerz* and melancholy are absent; Schumann's only indication for its performance is *Im Volkston* (In the manner of a folk song). Such homophonic vocal writing has not infrequently led critics to accuse Schumann of sentimentality, and indeed some of his compositions closely skirt it. In all such instances, however, the obvious sincerity of feeling overcomes these shortcomings, making Schumann stand above much of the mediocrity of his time.

Dichters Genesung (Poet's Recovery, Opus 36, No. 5) continues in a similar vein, its dreamy mood giving way to the ironic realization that the poet has been deceived. There may be traces of some of Mendelssohn's spooky sounds, but it is possible that Schumann meant to poke fun, subtly, at the "head-in-the-clouds" kind of Romanticism of his day. If this was his intention, the absence of a "concept" or of "depth," for which some critics chided him, seems quite in order. Schumann's facility in finding a folk-like style, very much his own artistic expression, forceful and inventive, is evident in this song. He made seven changes in Reinick's text.

Another separation from Clara occasioned the next song. Though their marriage had been officially sanctioned, the couple

ROBERT
REINICK

Robert Reinick, painter and poet, was born in 1805 in Danzig. He studied under Reinhold Begas in Berlin. After visiting Düsseldorf and Italy he settled in Dresden where he lived until his death in 1852. His first published work was *Drei Umrisse von Holzschnitten von Dürer mit erläuterndem Text und Gesängen* (Three Sketches of Woodcuts by Dürer with Explanations and Songs, Berlin, 1830). Later he collaborated with Kugler on a *Liederbuch für deutsche Künstler* (Song Collection for German Artists; with engravings). His reputation was established with his *Lieder eines Malers mit Randzeichnungen seiner Freunde* (Songs of a Painter, with Marginal Drawings by his Friends, Düsseldorf, 1838) which went through many editions. Together with Ludwig Richter he published Hebel's *Alemanische Gedichte* (Alemanic Poems) which he had translated into modern German. He also wrote a commentary on Alfred Rethel's *Totentanz* (Dance of Death). His collected *Lieder* appeared in 1844.

Reinick's style was unaffected and child-like. His appeal to young people was reflected in his *Illustriertes ABC-Buch* (Illustrated Abecedarium), the *Deutsche Jugendkalender* (German Youth Almanac), and his fairy tale *Die Wurzelprinzessin* (The Princess of the Roots). As late as 1905 his *Märchen-, Lieder- und Geschichtenbuch* (Book of Fairy Tales, Songs, and Stories) appeared in a 14th printing.

Ludwig Richter: Ständchen

could not yet breathe easily, for Wieck had ten days during which he could appeal the judgment. Schumann wisely suggested that Clara undertake a short concert tour through Thuringia, believing that this would distract her during this period. Accompanied by her aunt, she traveled to Jena, Weimar, Altenstein, Liebenstein, Gotha and Erfurt. About *Liebesbotschaft* (Message of Love, Opus 36, No. 6), one of his most profound Adagio melodies, Schumann wrote on August 24: "I wanted to write today, but there were endless interruptions, and here it already is four o'clock. But you will soon receive another *Liebesbotschaft,* maybe a musical one, which came to me yesterday and which I composed for you." The opening melody is taken from Clara's own song, *Liebeszauber* (Magic of Love; her Opus 13); thus Robert and Clara jointly contributed the conclusion to this group of songs, providing an ending that is of a higher calibre than the rest of this modest group of songs. One of Reinick's verses (after the word "prangen") was not set by Schumann. Carl Reinecke, with Schumann's consent, arranged several songs from Opus 36 for piano or as duets for two sopranos, just as he had done with eight songs from *Myrten.*

Emanuel Geibel's poetry occupied Schumann during August of 1840. *Ländliches Lied* (Rustic Song) is the first of *Three Duets,* Opus 29. Actually, this is the title of the Geibel collection; the correct title for the first song being *Frühling* (Spring). *Three Poems* by Geibel, Opus 30, are more significant. They involve three male characters; perhaps reflecting a desire on Schumann's part to create a counterpart to Chamisso's three female portraits. A more friendly mood, of chivalry and romance, speaks from these Geibel songs. The title of *Der Knabe mit dem Wunderhorn* (The Youth, Opus 30, No. 1) stems from Arnim and Brentano's collection of folk poetry. It is the song of a carefree wanderer, full of exaltation and bliss, a mood that Schumann could express far better than his contemporaries. In *Der Page* (The Page, Opus 30, No. 2), a *parlando* style serves to relate a confession of secret love; the piano providing only minimal support. The page's humility and devotion are most delicately expressed.

Der Hidalgo, Opus 30, No. 3, assumes special importance among the Geibel settings. On the margin of his manuscript Schumann noted: "composed on the day of the consent," i.e., August 1, 1840, when Clara received the court's permission to marry Robert despite her father's protests. Schumann here expresses in music both facets of his personality: the lyrical Eusebius and the forceful Florestan. Perhaps, by the exaggerated portrayal of both, he was trying to stabilize his own mental equilibrium. The humor of the beginning is subtle; Schumann expresses it through the concise motif of the Bolero rhythm. To insure its proper interpretation he marks this beginning "Etwas kokett" (Example 44). There is not much concern with the subtleties of the meaning of the text. Two strong, lively stanzas frame a lyrical, sly one. Ebullience and bravado characterize the Hidalgo's music, always tied to the basic rhythm. The end of the song is flashy—something truly exceptional for Schumann. Again the composer made several changes and introduced word repetitions not found in Geibel's poem.

On August 9, while on her Thuringian tour, Clara again was told of new songs. "There is *one* song that I think will really please you. It is written in a special, ingenious way." This description fits *Sehnsucht* (Longing, Opus 51, No. 1, text by Geibel) extraordinarily well. Only prelude and postlude express impatient longing, using 32d-note figuration; the vocal stanzas convey only feelings of melancholy. By contrast they seem "passive," a quality to which some critics objected. The surging beginning and end recall the piano etudes of the previous year; they still impress us today by their daring. Though the melody seems characteristic of Schumann, it also owes something to Schubert. When, in the raw, northern climate, the singer yearns for the sunny south, there is a hint of Schubert's *Aus Heliopolis I*. The complaint, fading away, "kann nicht hin" (I cannot go there), seems to reply to the question "immer wo?" asked by the *Wanderer* (Examples 45 and 46). Spohr's Opus 103 includes a setting of the same poem.

Example 44

Example 45

und im _ mer fragt der Seuf _ zer wo? im _ mer wo?

Example 46

und ich kann___ nicht hin,　　kann nicht hin!

Chapter 12

Myrten, Op. 25 : Dedication

The court decision took effect on August 12; four days later the banns were published. The couple set the wedding for September 12, on which day it took place, very quietly, in Schönefeld near Leipzig. One of Robert's school friends, Pastor Wildenhahn, spoke, "From the heart, going to the heart." Robert's wedding gift to his bride was the beautifully bound volume of *Myrten*. On the title page the dedication "To my beloved bride" was framed by a wreath of myrtle. Clara's diary records: "In the morning, on our way to the wedding, the sun appeared, after hiding behind clouds for days, as though it wanted to bless our union."

In this new diary, planned as a joint volume but largely maintained by Clara, she recorded her concept of what a German Lied should be. Her friend Emilie List had sung some of Robert's songs, but not to Clara's satisfaction. She had begun with a brilliant Rossini aria; for once Clara was captivated by this kind of music. But, she observed, "She doesn't really have the right feeling for German song. I can't quite put my finger on it, but she lacks real comprehension of the text. Once, when I heard Pauline Garcia sing Schubert's *Gretchen,* I had the same feeling. She seemed to be more concerned with striving for effect, not with conveying the glowing emotion so eloquently expressed by the text and Schubert's music."

Robert wished to present a private song recital, featuring his bride. Quite likely he had the timbre of Clara's voice in mind during the months when working on these songs. She had voice lessons with Nieksch and Banck. The outcome was not particularly impressive, for she confesses in her diary of 1840 that she "blushed at the very thought of singing such a recital for you! That requires good diction! I might be able to produce a musical sound, as long as no words are involved. You have no idea how rusty my voice is. The two years during which I hardly ever sang are to blame!" Schumann had asked her to sing "quietly and simply; just as you are" (February 1840). His words give us an idea of Clara's singing abilities and also of his concept of vocal timbre. About half of his songs are merely marked *p* or *pp;* occasionally the words "leise" or "zart" ("soft," "tenderly") replace tempo indications. It is possible that this concept is related to his habit, when deep in thought, of pursing his lips, as if he were about to whistle. His manner of speech also tended to be subdued and halting.

Some of the composer's greatest works took shape during the years that followed. In Clara he had found the interpreter of his music, the mother of his children and a partner ever ready, despite sacrifices, to join in musical undertakings. Their marriage was not without complications. Unintentionally Clara could be a rival, her own ambitions driving Robert to over-exertion. He was still little known as a composer, nor was he the best interpreter of his own music. He was not wise to the ways of the world, depending upon Clara in many ways.

During Schumann's years of study, Albert Theodor Töpken, a childhood friend, was the recipient of letters full of delightful musings. Now the composer sent him, along with news of the wedding, a sheaf of new songs. He asked his friend, who had settled in Bremen as a lawyer: "Do you like my new songs? I should hope that some of them would move you, too. Recently I have written so many songs, very different ones—you would be amazed if you saw the whole stack. I've become addicted to song writing."

Indeed, vocal music now became Schumann's preoccupation. What had been literary concepts embellished by music now gave way to the dominance of melody. Bach and Mendelssohn became the composer's chief models. Marriage brought with it a more solid, regular life style, as shown by Robert's diary entries. Marriage also led to increased concentration on his real life work: creating music. Life could now hold few distractions from composing, and writing reviews for the *Zeitschrift* was not one of them. Being a daily witness to Robert's artistic activity and agile mind, Clara became aware of her own lack of intellectual training. So together they read Jean

JOHANN GABRIEL SEIDL,
1804–1875

Seidl was an Austrian poet, famous for having written the text for the Austrian hymn, *Gott erhalte Franz, den Kaiser.* [The later version; the original text was by L. L. Haschka, 1797.—ed.] He belonged to the circle of friends around Schubert and composed the text for many of his songs. Seidl also wrote *Singspiel* texts, short stories, and poems in the dialect of Lower Austria. At various times he was active as a lawyer, secondary school teacher, curator, book censor, court appraiser and councillor. He did editorial work for various journals and wrote plays for the Burgtheater. Little of his poetry became known outside of Austria, nor did it last there beyond his time.

Paul and especially Shakespeare. Clara kept a notebook for Robert in which she recorded Shakespeare lines that dealt with music—a practice that she continued throughout Robert's active life. Since writing his dissertation, the idea of writing an essay on Shakespeare and music was never far from his mind. "No one has commented on music as beautifully and meaningfully; and that at a time when music was still in its infancy."

In spite of worries and some physical ailments that Clara experienced during her first year of marriage, this was a period of happiness heretofore unknown to her. She felt sorry for "those who did not know such domestic bliss," whose lives were only half fulfilled. Actually, the foundations of their life together were shaky from the beginning. Robert instinctively knew that good health and an ordered life were necessary for his creative work—a life that included good food and drink, a responsible position in society, and a happy family life. But such an ordinary life proved to be a delusion, a mirage. Troubles surfaced as soon as the initial state of bliss began to fade.

The biographer must see the fall of 1840 as the watershed, the dividing line in Schumann's life. Till then everything seemed to be moving onward and upward, propelled by youthful exuberance. From 1840 on, however, Robert's interest in other people in other walks of life diminished, despite Clara's efforts to broaden his horizons. Having become used to success herself, she tried to smooth Robert's way, to introduce him, where possible, to members of high society. Schumann's health steadily declined. He gained weight and within a few years changed from a vigorous young man to someone "getting on in years." His marriage marked the caesura between easy artistic productivity and a growing battle with illness.

Aside from composing, Schumann wrote countless letters. With some he sought to interest musicians abroad in his work. He sent a copy of *Myrten* to Georg Kastner in Paris: "These songs are reflections of the time when I composed them—a time of many sorrows but also of joys. Please give them a few hours' attention, and pass them on to my musical friends in Paris, especially Berlioz and Chopin. I would be most obliged to you. These songs are beginning to be well known in Germany." He urged Franz Liszt, who was giving concerts in Hamburg, to take an interest in his Chamisso songs, Opus 31: "I have been industrious since you left, though less so in the field of piano music. Please talk to Cranz [the publisher—ed.] about my songs; he doesn't know anything about them, and I only wish he were convinced of their worth as he sends them out into the world."

Schumann was now at work on the first of the *Balladen und Romanzen,* Opus 53. Their folklike flavor is that of *Orpheus,* the Viennese almanach, for which Schubert's friend Seidl had written the poem *Blondels Lied.* This flavor also seemed right for the informal kind of music-making in the home for which it was intended. Schumann notes that the first song was greatly enjoyed in such a setting.

Robert Schumann, 1841

This ballad tells of a minstrel who, by his song, succeeded in freeing his king, imprisoned in Dürnstein castle. Schumann casts it in strict strophic form with an accompaniment that conveys an archaic flavor through the occasional use of pentatonic harmony. There are two melodies: one serves for the outer verses, the other for those in the middle. A refrain, "Suche treu, so findest du" (Search faithfully, and you will find), concludes each stanza and serves to unify the song which conveys the mood of an ancient *Romanze.* Special treatment is given to the passage describing the moment when King Richard Lionheart hears his minstrel Blondel and answers him in song. Schumann omitted Seidl's third verse.

Schumann's balladesque style is most characteristically used in the two Eichendorff ballads (autumn, 1840) and in *Abends am Strand.* The latter was added to the Opus 45 collection; it probably was written in April of the same year. As a composer of ballads

Schumann did not consider himself the equal of his contemporary, Carl Loewe, nor did he expect these works to prove great successes on the concert stage. Their many subtleties, however, belie this expectation—effects that are not readily apparent on first hearing.

There is an old recording of *Der Schatzgräber* (The Treasure Digger, Opus 45, No. 1; text by Eichendorff) by Therese Behr, accompanied by her husband, Arthur Schnabel. The keyboard part is performed with the vitality that is essential to this song. Rendered in this fashion, it demonstrates Schumann's penchant for the demonic and bizarre, quite different from the stereotype of Schumann, the sentimentalist. The "digging" is graphically expressed by the rising figures at the beginning (Example 47); which are at the end of the song replaced by staccato chords, musically representing the "wild, derisive laughter" to which the text refers. Such tone painting is rare in Schumann's music. Once more Eichendorff inspired him to give musical expression to the relationship of man to nature. The song is rarely performed; it deserves to be revived.

Frühlingsfahrt (Spring Journey, Opus 45, No. 2) is the title Schumann chose for Eichendorff's poem. In many editions it is called *Die beiden Gesellen* (The Two Journeymen). The journey's beginning is stormy, though the melody is simple. More mysterious sounds describe the other traveler. These sounds, as shown by the manuscript, also do duty for the second verse; the composer does not save them simply for the description of the deep water. When Eichendorff concludes with the story's moral or meaning, Schumann, somewhat unconvincingly, returns to the opening motive, but this vanishes during the instrumental postlude which evokes different thoughts. From its impetuous opening to the mourning for lost happiness at the close, the song appears to be longer than it actually is. In order to accommodate his melodic line (measures 47–50), Schumann substitutes "in der Wogen farbig klingenden Schlund" for the poet's original wording. Slight changes are made in three other places as well.

As remarked earlier: Eichendorff was fond of the subject of wandering, wayfaring, journeying, which almost always had undertones of longing, both for places far away and for the return to home. *Die beiden Gesellen* is a case in point, containing a good deal of symbolism as well. Two young men set out on life's journey. The

Example 47

Example 48

first's curiosity about the world is soon satisfied and he settles down to become a "Philistine." The other loses his way and falls into the abyss of life, into "der Wogen farbigen Schlund" (the deep, dark waves). The two extremes: "the narrow confines of Philistine existence" and "the absence of any confines, leading to loss of identity" (Seidlin)—are the dangers confronting every life; they define the human condition. How Eichendorff comes to terms with this contradiction is expressed in the last stanza: "Ach Gott, führ' uns liebreich zu Dir" (Dear Lord, lovingly lead us to Thee). Another subject closely tied to that of travel in Eichendorff's view is that of the double. For Schumann this preoccupation may have been the poem's chief attraction. One can view the two wanderers as representing *one* person, as Eichendorff suggests, leading to the ominous interpretation of a dual personality. Quite understandably Schumann chose strange, remote keys and progressions to represent doubt and despair. The drowning of the second wanderer is vividly expressed by the gradually descending motion in the accompaniment (Example 48).

Zimmermann gave the title *Distichon* to his *Nur ein lächelnder Blick* (Only One Smiling Glance, Opus 27, No. 5). In composing it Schumann paid little attention to the poem's rhythm. The listener gathers the impression that the composer made use of one of his piano pieces to which text was added. When the song was first published (as a supplement to the *Neue Zeitschrift für Musik*), two additional keyboard interludes were included. Nevertheless, Schumann found a felicitous solution to a problem that must have seemed difficult at the time: to set to music a text employing both hexameter and pentameter. We are here witnessing a new esthetic of song writing; the delicate emotions of the text are convincingly expressed. The music readily shows that the vocal line, rising chromatically, is not self-sufficient. Without the underlying harmonies it is meaningless; it can be understood only as forming part of the sequentially rising seventh-chords that extend and enhance the emotional message. Longing is expressed through the dissonances which continue, unconcerned about resolutions, leading to further tension. Having reached a high point the motion gradually subsides, giving way to calm and tenderness. One thinks here of Beethoven, as one who prepared the way for Romanticism.

GEORG WILHELM
ZIMMERMANN

The *Gedichte* (Poems) of Georg Wilhelm Zimmermann (1807–1878), poet and prose writer, had attracted Schumann's attention as early as 1832. After studying theology Zimmermann settled in Stuttgart, pursuing a variety of studies. He then became a parson in Urach and taught at the polytechnical school in Stuttgart from 1847 to 1850 when he was dismissed for political reasons. Save for the one Schumann song, the only work that outlived the author was a history of the Peasant Wars. During the last years of his life he again served as a clergyman, first in Leobrunn, then in Owen.

His creative life, like Goethe's, included periods of differing outlooks and purposes, giving tentative shape to what was to become a more defined style. Thus there is an affinity between this song and the first movement of Beethoven's Sonata, Opus 101, among others; less in its tempo than in the way melodic lines are shaped, in the choice of harmonies, phrasing, and underlying rhythms, and especially in its delicacy and transparency (Examples 49 and 50).

Example 49

Example 50

Clara Schumann

The text for *Die Nonne* (The Nun, Opus 49, No. 3) is found among the fables of Abraham Fröhlich (see footnote). One doubts that Schumann was attracted by the poem as such; rather perhaps he

felt intrigued by the challenge of expressing, through music, the symbolic aspects of such an isolated human being. His music leads us to overlook the cloying qualities of the poem, especially the Adagio ending, organ-like, with an unanswered question. Over a half cadence on the dominant the question is asked, timidly, why this woman, "deprived of happiness," must fade away amidst red roses. To this the wedding music of the song's middle section forms an effective contrast. A later song, a setting of Kerner's *Stirb, Lieb und Freud* (I Loved Her So, Opus 35, No. 2), also has a nun as its central figure. The present song, shorter and generally less significant,

---

Abraham Fröhlich (1796–1865) studied theology in Zürich. In 1827 he was appointed Professor of German at the cantonal school in Aarau; in 1835 he became the director of a district school there and also a deacon. The second edition of his *Fables* appeared in 1829. His poems deal with both Swiss and theological subjects. He also published essays that were strictly conservative in orientation. He was interested in sacred song, writing several essays on the subject.

Example 51 [Kerner]

Example 52 [Fröhlich]

begins with a motif related to one in Kerner's song (Examples 51 and 52).

Perhaps there is some connection between this song and the fact that Clara (and later her daughters) always wore black—a custom that may have bothered Robert. To the end of her life Clara never wore any other color, leading her neighbor in Baden-Baden, Pauline Viardot-Garcia, to ridicule her. She thought it peculiar that Clara should be perpetually in mourning, and that Clara's pupils also wore black. Moreover, the teacher personally made sure that their garments were suitably modest.

According to Paula and Walter Rehberg, the text of *Mädchen—Schwermut* (A Girl's Melancholy, Opus 142, No. 3) was by Lily Bernhard, one of Clara's friends. Except for an unusual dissonance at the word "Himmelszelt" (firmament) the song contains nothing of interest. It was understandable that it was not published during Schumann's lifetime.

The apparent peace and calm of the couple's life in Leipzig (second floor, Inselstrasse 5) was deceiving. Every day brought its problems and tensions developed between the two artists. Only one of the two grand pianos was to be used at one time. Clara, the housewife, complains in her diary: "My own playing has to take a back seat whenever Robert composes. Not a single hour of the day is set aside for me! I worry about falling far behind!" When the couple were not otherwise engaged and were together Clara felt that Robert was "cold" and preoccupied. "There may be a good reason for this. No one could be more sincerely interested in whatever he undertakes than I am. Still, I am at times hurt by this coldness; I am the last one to deserve it."

Chapter 13

The struggle to win Clara's hand had not only challenged Robert to use all his ingenuity, but also inflicted wounds that were never to heal—that drained him of his noblest qualities, until death brought deliverance. Further, the rapid political and social changes of the times also troubled him. Artistic creation now meant putting public success ahead of the intrinsic merit of his art. His responsibilities as husband and father demanded expanded activities. "It never mattered to me whether or not the public took an interest in me. But with a wife and children all this changes. One must plan for the future, one wants to harvest the fruits of one's labors—not the artistic rewards but the material ones which lead to a better life. To achieve this one must be widely known." He advised the composer Koszmaly: "Concentrate on the large orchestral forms—that way you can make a name for yourself and you will gain the respect of the publishers. Compose large works: symphonies, operas. It's hard to reach the top with short pieces." It is as though Schumann were talking to himself.

Robert was not happy with his musical productivity. He realized that it was achieved at Clara's expense, that "the price she had to pay for my songs was frequent silence and inaccessibility on my part." He often was given to depressions and haunted by feelings of being a failure. Clara did not know of these feelings, and so believed she was the cause of his moodiness. Nevertheless, she was pleased by his industry. "Robert has written three more magnificent songs. The texts are by Justinus Kerner: *Lust der Sturmnacht; Stirb, Lieb' und Freud'!*, and *Trost im Gesang*. He thoroughly absorbs the meaning of the texts; more profoundly than any other

composer I know. No one else has his sensitivity!" *Sehnsucht nach der Waldgegend* (Longing for the Woods, Opus 35, No. 3) was written early in January of 1841, though Schumann's manuscript copy carries the date 10–24 November, 1840.

One discovers from these Kerner songs that Schumann looked for more in a poem than attractive formal design. None of these poems speak of joy or contentment but rather with dramatic force of sadness, loneliness, sacrifice and madness. But even as the voice rises to express intense emotion, a feeling of failure, of not knowing what to do, intervenes.

These Opus 35 songs are a unit, a fact that has escaped many students and singers because they were published in two different volumes of the three-volume Peters Edition. *Wanderlied* and *Erstes Grün* (Green of Spring, Opus 35, No. 4) were considered "famous" and were therefore given a prominent place in the first volume. In the first edition by C. A. Klemm the title is *12 Poems by Justinus Kerner*. H. J. Moser has shown that the songs are organized harmonically around A♭ major; he recommends that this relationship be retained when the songs are performed in transposition, preferably no more than a minor third. Schumann managed to combine Kerner's individual poems into a unified whole. The indication "Novelle" [a continuous story—ed.] may have guided the composer. Realizing that the songs were related to each other in subtle ways, Schumann referred to them as *Liederreihe* (group) rather than *Liederkreis* (cycle).

These songs are a breed apart, unlikely to reveal their beauties on a first hearing. They do display one weakness common to

Schumann's songs: the piano part too often doubles the voice line, in unison or at the octave. It is an odd mannerism, for in all other ways Schumann treats the piano as an equal partner.

In *Lust der Sturmnacht* (Joy on a Stormy Night, Opus 35, No. 1), in the minor mode, Schumann does not use the key signature of the relative major; instead he provides individual accidentals where required. He pictures musically the emotional gambit, from tense feelings and pulsating exuberance in the face of the storm to the return of calmness.

The following song reminds us that Bach, even by way of his keyboard style, influenced Schumann who marvelled at the "complexity, poetry and humor" of Bach's language, together with his "wonderful ability to weave a fabric of sound." In *Stirb, Lieb' und Freud'* (I Loved Her So, Opus 35, No. 2) Bach's style is evoked in the polyphonic "organ prelude;" it symbolizes the large cathedral in which the anguished outcry of the nun loses itself. High tessitura suggests a child's voice. The instruction "Preferably for tenor" is appropriate, for a baritone would experience difficulty in producing the highest notes softly, unless he has a good command of head tones. A sequence of descending steps for the nun's exclamation is based on the final chorus from Bach's *St. John Passion,* "Herr Jesu Christ, erhöre mich." Schumann had heard the work for the first time in 1840. The final appoggiatura on the word "trag'" shows how one single note can add greatly to the effect of a song. Here, too, we find the archaic time signature ₵₵ which also stands at the beginning of the "Chorus mysticus" in the *Scenes from Faust.* Perhaps it is meant to convey something of the flavor of a medieval town, seen through Romantic eyes.

Wanderlied expresses the fondness for student life, so often encountered in Schumann's songs, and not always in particularly inspired ways. Here it did result in one of his most popular songs: "Wohlauf, noch getrunken den funkelnden Wein" (Fill up your glasses!). The principal theme may return too often, and the music in general may not be of the highest order, but the middle section is irresistible, and the transition to the last stanza is startling. From its opening fanfare to the contemplative middle section in G♭ major to the buoyant conclusion and lively postlude, this "Florestan" song continues to make its mark.

Wieck's charges relative to Schumann's drinking problem proved not to be exaggerated. Alcohol apparently had become a necessity for him. Eventually he gave up wine: beer was cheaper. But its excessive consumption was detrimental to his health. There is clear evidence that in his later years diabetes and high blood pressure contributed to his apathy, resignation, and collapse.

Schumann substituted the title *Erstes Grün* for Kerner's original title, *Frühlingskur* (Taking the Spring Cure)—not necessarily because Schumann was a hypochondriac, as is suggested by Sams, but merely in order to avoid the medical implications of the word "cure." The piano interludes are the most characteristic feature of the song, providing contrast to the text and to the minor mode of the vocal stanzas. At the end the piano dispels any doubt that the "first signs of spring" can cure the ailing soul (Example 53). Schubert seems to speak to us in the G minor melody, quiet and resigned. The ritardando markings are quite typical of Romantic music, so fond of rubato effects. Kerner's last stanza recalls an early Schumann letter to Gisbert Rosen: "What is this world with all its

Example 53

humanity but an immense cemetery of buried dreams, a garden with cypress trees [traditionally found in cemeteries—ed.] and weeping willows—a silent drama populated with weeping figures."

In *Sehnsucht nach der Waldgegend* (Longing for the Woods, Opus 35, No. 5) Kerner alludes to his change of domicile from Welzheim to the "crowded" Gaildorf. The song is quite different from the one it follows, as is indicated by Schumann's instruction "innig, phantastisch" (with tenderness and imagination). His effort to give an *arioso* quality to the vocal line resulted in some awkwardly accented words, such as "Wo in *euren* Dämmerungen; ist auch *manches* Lied entsprungen," "Eure *Melo*dien alle." But the song's appeal stems not only from the way it ends, fading away into nothing, but chiefly in its elusive harmonies that skirt the basic tonality. Both Clara and Brahms had a special affection for the song. Brahms seems to have had it in mind when he wrote *Alte Liebe*.

There is something magical in Kerner's poem *Auf das Trinkglas eines verstorbenen Freundes* (To the Goblet of a Dead Friend, Opus 35, No. 6) which may be the quality that attracted Schumann to it. Some of this magic permeates the entire group of songs. Here it is a meditation about the friend who has passed away. For Kerner this was Stierlein von Lorch; for Schumann it may have been Ludwig Schuncke, a companion whom he had lost several years previously. With his music he lifted this student song to a higher, more idealistic plane, giving it a mystic flavor. It became a favorite song of Hugo Wolf, which is consistent with the opinion of it still held today, and it incorporates many qualities of Schumann, the song writer, including his search, late in life, for an eloquent simplicity that was also strikingly new. After a serious and unpretentious opening, the modulations at the words "nicht gewöhnlichen zu nennen" anticipate the announcement of death in Act II of Wagner's *Die Walküre*. The retards and fermatas are already implied in the music and should not be exaggerated in performance. An effect of feverish pain can be achieved simply by pausing to breathe, while the phrase endings suggest the mood of someone lost in thought.

The description of midnight takes exactly 12 measures, though we do not hear the striking of the hour. The mood of that time of night is suggested by four successive, floating seventh chords.

Moonlight illuminates this poetic scene, while the song in praise of friendship is heard. The piano's conclusion alludes to the line "Du liebst mich wie ich dich" from the duet *So wahr die Sonne scheinet*.

Following such depth of feeling, *Wanderung* (Wandering, Opus 35, No. 7) conveys a less pretentious sentiment. The changing moods at parting of the opening must be expressed by subtle gradations of tempo. Every retard must quickly lead back to the basic tempo which should not be too fast or the acceleration in the last stanza will lose its effect. The horn call in the piano part should sound distant—hence Schumann's indication "the accompaniment should be light and delicate."

The musical treatment of *Stille Liebe* (Silent Love, Opus 35, No. 8) invites comparison with *Ich will meine Seele tauchen* from *Dichterliebe*. Here, too, there is mention of singing that has not yet occurred. To achieve this sense Schumann resorts to declamation lacking any melodic substance, while the keyboard part contrasts with eloquent "speaking." We hear sighs, barely suggested by fermatas on weak beats; sighs that recur several times in new harmonic guises. At the end the monologue turns into a vanishing melodic arabesque. In the first two stanzas the melodic line of the accompaniment anticipates the vocal line; in the third stanza it is supported by quintuplets that produce a veiled effect. Drawn out 16th-note quintuplets in the last stanza are a free variation of the chords in measure five (ritardando) of the introduction.

Schumann took great care to render the meaning of the following song, *Frage* (Question, Opus 35, No. 9). He made a new copy of the song in 1847, as a gift for Pauline Viardot-Garcia when the Schumanns were in Berlin attending a performance of the oratorio *Das Paradies und die Peri*. On this and other occasions he revised the printed version slightly. *Frage* is to be sung "langsam, innig" (slowly, with tender feeling). But there is no implication that a discouraging "Nothing" is the answer to the question. That theory has been advanced because Schumann ends the song with a half-cadence to the dominant of the relative minor, a progression already used by Handel, and later also by Wagner (Example 54). There is a good explanation for this ending: it leads into *Stille Tränen* (Silent Tears, Opus 35, No. 10), to be sung with strong emotion. It deals with a state of intoxication, brought on by one's own sorrow;

Example 54

with solitude both desired and regretted. A true "singer's song" it offers great opportunities to the interpreter: sweeping melodies in which the use of portamento is not only permissible but necessary, especially at the ends of phrases. The composer must have considered *Stille Tränen* among his best, for he soon published it as a supplement to the *Neue Zeitschrift für Musik* of 1841. There are few other Schumann songs with such opportunities for expansive singing, nor are there many others based on a single motif. The end is thoroughly Romantic with its interweaving of lines and themes. We are in Chopin's proximity. Schumann recalled this ending (Example 55) when he set Lenau's *Meine Rose*.

The last two songs of the Kerner group are identical save for the introductions; something no previous composer had done. Kerner did not conceive the poems as belonging together, but since they flow in the same meter this treatment became possible. To bring them together Schumann omitted the last stanza of *Wer machte dich so krank?* (Who made you so ill? Opus 35, No. 11). This group of songs was practically unknown until Hans Joachim Moser brought them to light. Their obscurity may have been due to the complete absence of a traditional, effective ending, yet this *pianissimo* conclusion of *Alte Laute* (Dejections, Opus 35, No. 12) is not all that different from *Leiermann* which concludes Schubert's *Winterreise*.

The brief transition from *Wer machte dich so krank?* to *Alte Laute* suggests the introductory measures of the second *Kreisleriana* Phantasy. But the two songs were not intended to create a dramatic effect. Schumann established a connection that was sufficiently gentle to make possible the "Noch langsamer und leiser" (even slower and more softly) of *Alte Laute*. D. Conrad detected the singing of birds in this interlude, an acceptable interpretation if one keeps in mind that the implication provides an answer in the negative to the question: can nature bring solace to the heavy heart (Example 56)?

Example 55

Example 56

Nothing could be more delicate than this "double song" which never stoops to sentimentality. Its inner glow is hidden under a deceptively cold surface. Schumann's longing for a world full of light and happiness finds expression here—painful longing, for such a world was moving farther and farther beyond his reach. Such emotions account for new stylistic qualities in his music: frequent use of altered chords, chromatic lines, and passages with long, insistent crescendos. These may seem daring to the unprepared listener, but they are musical manifestations of the composer's inner life. His harmonies suggest fear; drawn out suspensions tend to cloud the voice leading. Such tense harmonies remind one of a face distorted by pain. Lonesome and from a distance the composer gazes upon the busy world.

Schumann was wise to give up an earlier plan to add another song, *Sängers Trost* (The Singer's Consolation, Opus 127, No. 1) as a kind of happy end. It is unlikely that the rather pedantic poem would have resulted in anything but third-rate music. Sketched in 1840, the song was not published until 1854. Some early editions assign the wrong date to it, possibly because of the high opus number.

Three two-part songs constituting Opus 43, mark the end of the "Year of Songs": *Herbstlied,* the setting of a poem by August Mahlmann, and *Schön Blümelein,* by Robert Reinick, are preceded by *Wenn ich ein Vöglein wär,* the most interesting of the three. In 1847, Schumann used half of it in his opera *Genoveva.* The text (author unknown) is found in Herder's collection of folk songs (Leipzig, 1787) where it is entitled *Der Flug der Liebe.* Beethoven's setting is based on a different version of the poem by Treitschke. Schumann's song is short; both voice parts lie quite low. The music does not seem to express the singer's longing for his distant love, but rather his wish to escape from a confining situation.

Before we leave the year 1840 we must look at the Heine trilogy *Tragödie* (Tragedy, Opus 64) which is not dated but was probably composed before *Es leuchtet meine Liebe.* This is a three-part miniature; both Heine and Schumann considered the middle song to be the most significant. The poet thought of it as a folk song and the composer wanted it to be sung in that way. It follows the tempestuous *Entflieh mit mir und sei mein Weib* (Come, Flee With Me

and Be My Wife), but already in the conclusion of that song the storm vanishes and the mood changes, as if in preparation for the subdued, sad story about to be told. This is the only Heine text set by Schumann that was not taken from the *Buch der Lieder* but from a *Taschenbuch für Damen* (Ladies' Almanac) of 1821. Clara had turned to the same source for her own composition of the poem which was a Christmas present for Robert in 1840. Heine's poetry draws on a folk song dealing with this subject. Anton Zuccalmaglio, a friend of the Schumanns and a specialist in folk (or pseudo-folk) lyrics, had also prepared a version of this little ballad and invited Schumann to set it to music, but the composer never took him up on it. This song, the second of the three, *Es fiel ein Reif in der Frühlingsnacht* (One April Morning the Hoarfrost Fell), calls for minimal accompaniment. The end is halting. A brief phrase, sounding like two French horns, serves as beginning and conclusion for this touching and fragile song.

Schumann's manuscript reveals that the third song, *Auf ihrem Grab, da steht eine Linde* (A linden tree was planted on her grave), had originally been planned for chorus. Unfortunately, this plan was not carried out. For no particular reason it became a duet instead, in which the second voice, mostly doubled by the piano, really is superfluous. Again Schumann reintroduces material from the first song, for reasons that relate to the text and story. Intervals of a fourth, used dramatically at the opening of the first song, now reappear, distorted. The reason for weeping thus is starkly revealed; the change is emphasized by the indication "more slowly."

In this instance Schumann paid no attention to the slight irony found in so much of Heine's poetry. Mendelssohn also composed these three poems, for a quartet of mixed voices, to the dislike of his sister Fanny who believed that Heine here treated sincere feeling in a frivolous manner. Mendelssohn's lighter interpretation reveals a greater awareness of Heine's irony, while Schumann seems only genuinely moved by the poems. In 1841, at about the time of the unfinished "little" C minor symphony, Schumann for the first time tried his hand at writing for voice and orchestra. He began an orchestration of *Tragödie.* The manuscript bears the notation "not yet finished;" Schumann never returned to it.

Another group of choruses from 1840 should be mentioned

NIKOLAUS BECKER
(1809–1845)

Becker was the son of a merchant. After studying law in Bonn he held a position in the civil court in Cologne. For a time his "Rhine Song" led many to regard him as *the* German patriotic writer, though he produced nothing of literary merit.

Sie sollen ihn nicht haben, den freien deutschen Rhein (They [i.e., the French] shall not have it, our free German River Rhine) is one of the countless patriotic poems that flooded Germany at the time. Protests from France were not long in coming—both Lamartine and de Musset replying with "counter poems"; the enraged Lamartine began his with the line: "Nous l'avons eu, votre Rhin allemand" (We *did* have it, your German Rhine).

here if only because their high opus number resulted in their erroneous placement among the songs of 1849. They were, however, composed during this "Year of Songs," proving that Schumann had developed a sure and advanced choral style at this early date. The *Romanzen und Balladen,* Opus 67 (*Der König in Thule, Schön Rohtraut, Haidenröslein, Ungewitter, John Anderson*) clearly show how elements of the ballad were effectively incorporated in choral settings through telling harmonies rather than tone painting.

Schumann wrote *Der deutsche Rhein* (The German Rhine, without opus number) for solo voice, chorus and piano accompaniment to a text by Nikolaus Becker. The occasion was a competition, but the work did not win a prize. That it was ultimately successful is due to the catching melody rather than political considerations (Example 57). Indeed, the intense patriotism displayed in the text caused the song to fall into oblivion, probably forever. At the time, the hymn was such a "hit" that within a month 1,500 copies were sold, followed by many additional printings.

Example 57

Chapter 14

Schumann's gloomy mood during the last months of this "Year of Songs" may be related to his attempts to come to terms with symphonic forms. His gloom was relieved for a short time however by the stimulus provided by a Christmas gift from Clara: "The idea of publishing a collection of songs together with Clara kindled my enthusiasm for work. From one Monday to the next, nine songs on Rückert's *Liebesfrühling* were completed." While committing these to paper Clara, the composer, was troubled by a lack of self confidence. "I have tried repeatedly to compose these Rückert poems which Robert wrote down for me, but I can't get anywhere with them. I simply have no talent for composing." Not long before in looking over several songs by Mendelssohn's sister, Fanny, she declared "a woman composer can always be recognized as such; that's true of me and others."

The Christmas gift consisted of *Am Strande* (Musing on the roaring Ocean), text by Burns, beginning with the line "Traurig schau ich von der Klippe auf die Flut, die uns getrennt." (Musing on the roaring ocean / Which divides my Love and me.) Quite likely these words reflected her recurring sense of loneliness during the first months of their marriage. *Ihr Bildnis* (Her picture) by Heine followed, which was eventually included in her *Six Songs With Accompaniment of the Pianoforte, Dedicated to Her Majesty, Queen Caroline Amalie of Denmark,* published as Opus 13 by Breitkopf & Härtel. She included Heine's *Volkslied,* "Es fiel ein Reif," which Robert was to compose more convincingly subsequently. Her setting of Geibel's *Die stille Lotosblume* (The Silent Lotus Flower) completes the group. She shows herself to be Robert's pupil, particu-

larly in the way the question "Kannst du das Lied verstehen?" remains unanswered. Clara's songs are charming and simple, displaying a good sense of form. They all express similar feelings and are set in flat keys, the last three in A♭ major.

Among the *Liebesfrühling* songs, Nos. 2, 4, and 11 sound so much like those of Robert that one might think he provided some help. On the other hand, the statement that they were "written jointly" could also mean that Clara contributed her share of ideas to songs written by her husband. This collection of songs by both of them thus might represent a repetition of an earlier joint undertaking, when Robert incorporated some of Clara's themes in his own piano works. There is a parallel here to the way in which Felix and Fanny Mendelssohn collaborated on some songs—a practice which at first they did not divulge.

The *Liebesfrühling* songs speak in a calm, sensitive, introverted language, possibly because of Robert's preoccupation at the time with matters of symphonic form. They seem pale even when there is a hint of exuberance. Rückert, to be sure, did not make things easy for Schumann, being "so musical in his language and thoughts that a composer was hard put to add anything." Marital bliss, a happy home, things that Schumann mentions with ardor in his letters are evoked here, especially in the final duet. Though there is contentment and simplicity, the manner in which these moods are expressed somehow does not touch the listener. One thinks of the couple's anticipation of peace and quiet in their wedded life, and the coming unpleasant surprises.

Der Himmel hat eine Träne geweint (From Heaven Once Fell a

Example 58

Einfach *p*

Der Him - mel hat ei - ne Trä - ne ge-weint,

Example 59

Einfach
(Sopran)

So wahr die Son-ne schei-net,
(Tenor oder Bariton)

So wahr die Son-ne schei-net,
Einfach

Tear, Opus 37, No. 1) opens with a motif of Clara's invention (Example 58). It is identical with the beginning of the duet, *So wahr die Sonne scheinet* (As surely as the Sun is Shining) that concludes the cycle (Example 59).

In *Er ist gekommen* (Through Storm and Tempest He Came, Opus 37, No. 2) Clara captured the sound if not the emotional essence found in much of Robert's piano writing. She also emphasizes important lines of the poem by repeating them. Perhaps the awkward rhymes found in *O ihr Herren* (Oh, Ye Gentlemen, Opus 37, No. 3) caused Robert to write melodies that overlap the line ends of the poem, so that one is hardly aware of them: ("werten—Gärten," "stilles—will es"). Yet we tend to admire the simplicity of these melodic lines all the more. Clara's *Liebst du um Schönheit* (Love You but Beauty), Opus 37, No. 4) is her declaration of love. The music speaks with a calm assurance of affection easily grasped by the listener.

Schubert was the first composer to discover Rückert as a source for songs. His plan to set *Ich hab in mich gesogen* for male quintet was never realized. Schumann's own skilful composition of this text (The Spring is With Me Always, Opus 37, No. 5) employs extensive chromaticism which lifts the song above the general level of the

cycle. Intricate three-part writing gives life to a motif that returns again and again. Later on, complex harmonic motion unfolds over a pedal point on the note C. The interval of a fifth, lying above the ostinato motif, gives unity to the song as a whole. A garland-like motion characterizes the accompaniment whenever the voice pauses for breath, displaying great energy of its own.

In the duet *Liebste, was kann denn uns scheiden* (Dearest, is There Aught Can Part Us, Opus 37, No. 6) the tenor displays such fervor that the soprano is given few opportunities to respond. The 7th and 12th songs are also duets. Canonic writing is found in *Schön ist das Fest des Lenzes* (Beautiful is the Celebration of Spring, Opus 37, No. 7), using imaginative, vigorous melodies. Again the second voice is doubled by the piano, reducing the independence of voice leading.

Clara may indeed have supplied the opening phrase of *Flügel! Flügel!* (Wings! ah, wings! Opus 37, No. 8), as has been claimed. But for the rest, Robert, inspired by the poem that is a cut above the others, composed a scherzo of great originality. While the middle section is subdued and withdrawn, the piano part regains momentum as it races towards the end. A vision of Icarus's crashing fall brings the song's climax: "Der Sinne Brausen wälzt über'm Geist sich her" (The roar of earthly bedlam surges over me). This was a fear that plagued both the composer and the poet. How closely Schumann related to this passage is shown by his many modifications of the text in order to modernize Rückert's quaint, old-fashioned language.

Rose, Meer und Sonne (Sun and Sea and Roses, Opus 37, No. 9) fascinates by the gradual buildup of intensity. Schumann avoids the temptation of succumbing to the emotional excesses of the text by supplying music with steady rhythm and consistent melodic gesture, an approach that in other cases could have led to monotony. The instrumental conclusion is independent (recalling *Dichterliebe*), introducing a new theme, set off from the song with all its splendor.

O Sonn', O Meer, O Rose (O Sun, O Rose, O Ocean, Opus 37, No. 10) is related in content to the preceding song—a way of examining a subject from several angles that Hugo Wolf also frequently used. The song opens with a somewhat banal musical idea, possibly by Clara, which tends to weaken the impact of the entire piece. Though suggested by the text, the increasing musical tension seems artificial. The following song is Clara's *Warum willst du andre fragen?* (Why Inquire of Other People, Opus 37, No. 11). Quite fiery, it serves to interrupt the contemplative mood of the cycle which closes with *So wahr die Sonne scheinet,* Opus 37, No. 12, a song that achieved great popularity. All in all, one gains the impression that Robert wanted Clara to have a place in the limelight.

Schumann first tried to sell *Liebesfrühling* to Kistner. "Some time ago a thought came to me which might interest you. My wife has composed several attractive songs. These in turn inspired me to set some additional ones from Rückert's *Liebesfrühling.* Altogether, it turned out to be a rather nice set; we would like to issue it as *one* publication. . . . If you should be inclined to bring it out in an attractive format (on 20–22 plates) by September, it would greatly please us." Kistner showed no interest, but given the enterprising spirit of publishers at the time, Breitkopf & Härtel managed to publish the volume by the requested date. Schumann had written to them: "My wife's birthday comes in mid-September; I should like to surprise her with the following: together we composed a number of Rückert songs that are related to each other, like a series of questions. It would be wonderful to present her on that day with a printed copy. Would it be possible for you to have the volume ready by that time? I should think that there would be demand for these songs: most of them are simple, easy to sing and play. Composing them gave much pleasure to both of us."

The Schumanns received no fee for these. Instead the publisher supplied them with a large quantity of sheet music which both Clara and Robert needed. Thus both parties were satisfied.

In spite of his busy work schedule Robert set aside time for he and Clara to study together. He gave Clara much reading material, and they often read to each other: Goethe's *Dichtung und Wahrheit,* poetry, Shakespeare's writings, Byron, and Jean Paul. Together they examined Bach's *Well-Tempered Clavier* in detail. Robert also trained Clara in the niceties of preparing piano scores, so that she would be able to assist him with proofreading and making arrangements for piano. The vocal score of *Genoveva* was her work, for example.

Title page of the First Edition of Liebesfrühling, *Op. 37*

The Schumanns had eight children. Their sixteen years of marriage produced four daughters. Marie was born in 1841. Elise, born 1843, died in 1911, the wife of a businessman named Sommerhof. Some grandchildren now live in America. Julie (born in 1845), having been secretly engaged to Johannes Brahms, became a Countess Marmorito and moved to Turin where she died shortly thereafter. Marie and Eugenie (born 1851) both became piano teachers, at first for their mother at the Hoch Conservatory in Frankfurt-on-the-Main. After Clara's death they lived in England and Switzerland, chiefly in Interlaken. Both lived to be almost 90 years old. The first son, Emil, born in 1846, died within a year. Ludwig, born in 1848, was confined to an asylum when he had reached the age of 22; the stated reason "melancholy." He spent the remaining 27 years of his life there, "buried alive," according to his grieving mother. Ferdinand, born 1849, was a bank employee. During the Franco-Prussian War (1870–71) he contracted rheumatism, the cause of his death 20 years later. Felix, born 1854, showed promise both as a poet and musician but died of tuberculosis at the age of 24.

Schumann had completed a draft of his Symphony in B♭ major during five days in January of 1841, "in a happy working mood while yearning for spring." Having completed *So wahr die Sonne scheinet* a few days before, the work on the symphony's scoring was now a pleasure and release for him. The instrumentation was completed on February 20, after which Mendelssohn immediately rehearsed the work "with great love and care," so that by March 31 its triumphal first performance could take place. The occasion was a benefit concert for the orchestra arranged by Clara, with Robert conducting. Aside from the symphony the program included *Die Löwenbraut* and *Widmung,* sung by Sophie Schloss with Clara as accompanist. Such variety on a concert program was still customary then. According to a letter by Clara to Emilie List, everything went "quite nicely." *Widmung* had to be repeated; Clara's own *Am Strande* was also on the program.

On September 1, after a long labor, Clara gave birth to their first child, Marie. The girl was christened on Clara's birthday, on which occasion Robert surprised the young mother with the manuscript to what was to become his fourth symphony, in D minor. He had "completed it unknown to anyone else." Another birthday gift was the volume containing their songs, *Twelve Poems from Rückert's Liebesfrühling* and whose subtitle stated "For piano and voice, by Clara and Robert Schumann." Listing the piano first served to indicate what importance and independence Schumann attributed to the keyboard part. His high opinion of the cycle comes to light in a letter of May 2, 1842, in answer to one from Kahlert who had provided comments on the B♭ major symphony. "I wish you could take a close look at my songs; they say something about my musical future. I can't promise that I'll ever accomplish anything better, and I am quite satisfied with that."—Does Schumann speak of a musical future that is based on a philosophy of art as expressed, for instance, by Flaubert in his *L'éducation sentimentale,* according to which art must remain impersonal and not represent the author? Traces of such a viewpoint can already be detected in *Liebesfrühling* and recurs in the late choral works, the Mass and the Requiem. Beauty and truth must be inseparable as must form and substance. Schumann had assimilated the essence of realism, quite different from his outlook at the time of the early piano works. Now he was convinced that there was only one kind of beauty which was the same everywhere and which paid no heed to the person of its creator.

Schumann's first symphony attracted a good deal of attention, the *Blätter für Musik und Literatur* soon after hailing him as "the prophet of a new kind of German song." It is odd that at this very time he should have become increasingly distracted from song writing, setting out instead to master musical genre in which he had not yet proved himself. A request from Weimar for a concert featuring an orchestral work by Robert and a piano performance by Clara led to another benefit concert for the orchestra. Clara played before the intermission; the symphony followed. On November 2 5, Clara accompanied several songs by Schumann. An added plus was a meeting with Liszt who insisted that they stay an extra day in Weimar and who announced that he would appear in Clara's concert in Leipzig on December 6. Schumann expressed satisfaction with this, their first joint tour.

During the last months of 1 8 4 1, however, a number of problems arose which detracted Schumann from composing. The Leipzig concert was one. The program included the first performance of the Symphony in D Minor in its first version, together with *Overture, Scherzo and Finale* which then was still named *Symphonette.* But the concert was only moderately successful. Clara was unhappy to have to perform Liszt's *Hexameron,* with the composer—"a frightfully brilliant piece," just as unsuitable for her as Liszt's Fantasy on *Lucia di Lammermoor* which she also played. Schumann's *The Two Grenadiers* was insufficient to save the evening. These joint public appearances put an end to the peaceful life of their first married year.

In mid-February 1 8 4 2 Schumann took a few weeks off from composing and from work on the *Zeitschrift* in order to accompany Clara to several North German cities. While the symphony in B♭ major was mildly successful, Clara impressed audiences with brilliant performances of Weber and Mendelssohn. She also presented matinees in Hamburg and Oldenburg which included parts of *Liebesfrühling.* Robert was hurt because only Clara was received at the Oldenburg court, and especially so since she returned having greatly enjoyed the occasion. During their stay in Hamburg (which Schumann barely mentions in his diary, his nose

having been out of joint) everyone advised them to take a side trip to Copenhagen. Clara was pleased to return to public performing, which also improved the family finances. They separated at this point, causing some talk about a rift.

Schumann's diary for March 1 4 clarifies his reasons for returning home to Leipzig. "This separation drove home to me painfully the difficulty of my situation. Should I neglect my talent in order to accompany you on your journey? Is it right for you to neglect your own talent because I must work for the *Zeitschrift* and compose at the piano? Now, while you are young and energetic? We found a solution: you found a woman to travel with you while I returned to our child and to my work. What will people say? I do worry about these things, but it is essential to find a way for *both* of us to make the best use of our abilities."

In their account book there are repeated references to Robert's "dizzy spells" and "nervous exhaustion." Clara, for her part, cancelled a concert in Kiel, the first stop on her tour, because her mood was such that she did not feel up to it. Though Schumann's name and the *Zeitschrift* were known in Copenhagen, hardly any of his music had been heard there, nor did Clara do much to change this: *Widmung* and one of the *Novelletten* were the only works she had programmed. Financially the tour was a success; it also provided new contacts and other stimuli. Clara was fascinated by once more meeting Hans Christian Andersen. He complained to Clara about the lack of recognition he received in his own country which she attributed to his gruff personality. Nevertheless, she was again greatly impressed by the tall, haggard man with his large nose, recessed eyes and brooding, sentimental expression. The meeting was recalled in Schumann's dedication of his Five Songs, Opus 4 0 to him. They were published in Copenhagen. Her tour also resulted in Clara's subsequent dedication of her own songs, Opus 1 3, to the Danish queen, an expression of thanks for her "benevolent support."

Robert regained his mental equilibrium soon after Clara returned home. He had taken a brief vacation in the mountains of Saxony. After this, still in June, he composed three string quartets in quick succession. They were first performed at one of the frequent chamber music matinees at their apartment.

Although Schumann lacked experience with string instruments, which caused problems, his musical personality was well suited to the medium: a fondness for subtle treatment of details, and a generally contemplative approach. But when he added the piano, the road was clear for the creation of a masterwork, such as the Piano Quintet, Opus 44, the first major work in that genre since Schubert. It displays a higher dramatic tension, when compared to the piano quintets with wind instruments by Mozart and Beethoven. Schumann seems to have been determined to avoid any of the routine passage work that was so common in works by his contemporaries.

Schumann's diary notes: "On the 15th [of June] we experienced great joy. We had sent our songs to Rückert who now responded with a superb poem." Rückert had written: "Friedrich Rückert to Robert and Clara Schumann in Leipzig, with many thanks for their settings of my *Liebesfrühling*. Neusess near Coburg, June 1842."

Lang ist's, lang
Seit ich meinen Liebesfrühling sang,
Aus Herzensdrang,
Wie er entsprang,
Verklang in Einsamkeit der Klang.

Zwanzig Jahr
Wurden's, da hört ich hier und dar
Der Vogelschar
Einen, der klar
Pfiff einen Ton, der dorther war.

Und nun gar
Kommt im einundzwanzigsten Jahr
Ein Vogelpaar,
Macht erst mir klar,
Dass nicht ein Ton verloren war.

Meine Lieder
Singt ihr wieder,
Mein Empfinden klingt ihr wieder,
Mein Gefühl
Beschwingt ihr wieder,
Meinen Frühling
Bringt ihr wieder,
Mich, wie schön,
Verjüngt ihr wieder:

Nehmt meinen Dank,
Wenn auch die Welt,
Wie mir einst, ihren vorenthält!

Und werdet ihr den Dank erlangen,
So hab ich meinen mit empfangen.

As far as is known, Rückert and Eichendorff were the only poets who extended their appreciation to Schumann, so the couple was understandably particularly delighted with Rückert's verses—well meant, if not literary masterpieces. They moved Clara to continue her composing. Except for a sonatina she only wrote songs during 1842–43. Her *Liebeszauber* (text by Geibel) and *Sie liebten sich beide* (Heine) were birthday presents for Robert, who considered them "the very best she has composed so far." Heine's *Loreley* and two further Rückert settings followed in the summer of 1843.

Schumann's unbalanced state of mind increasingly affected his work. For some months he suffered from insomnia, and by October of 1842 he was in such a state that Clara feared a "nervous inflammation" (*Nervenfieber*). And yet the growing family needed new sources of income. The founding around Easter, 1843, of the Leipzig Conservatory under Mendelssohn's direction, was particularly welcome. Part-time teaching seemed to assure Schumann of income during periods when his productivity as a composer declined. A period of depression early in 1843 was cause for concern. The absence of diary entries from those months are indicative of the problem, but there now seemed to be a solution. "The conservatory causes all of us much work and concern, but it is a satisfaction as well. For the time being I am teaching piano; eventually I want to create a different position for myself. As of now there are forty pupils." He was determined to avoid those practices in teaching that he had criticized in his own teachers and in particular a rigid imposition of his own ideas. Soon he was asked to teach composition and score reading as well. The request pleased him but he found the assignment of only limited interest.

At that time musical instruction in general had not yet acquired the high standards which we take for granted today. Anyone wishing to make music a career looked for a master who would take him on. Thus Spohr and Moritz Hauptmann taught students who stayed in Kassel all year. Such master teachers were not directing conservatories or academies in our sense. Fees for lessons were generally low, which did not help Schumann. It was largely due to Mendelssohn's initiative that conservatories came to be founded in nearly every German city.

Schumann's teaching career might have been successful had he been more communicative. He would in most cases play a student's composition assignment through but fail to offer any comments or suggestions. If he disliked a composition, only disapproving glances were made, after which he would play his own corrected or improved version, again silently. On the positive side it should be noted that musical education was not without interest to Schumann, in the area of both theory and pedagogy, and in the plan to publish a complete edition of Bach's works.

The old Leipzig Conservatory, ca. 1845

Chapter 15

In May, 1843 Schumann was deeply engrossed in putting the finishing touches on his oratorio *Das Paradies und die Peri*. In 1841, soon after his marriage, Schumann had been visited by Emil Flechsig, who wanted to show him an arrangement of some poetry by Thomas Moore. In his unpublished memoirs Flechsig writes: "I found Schumann in extremely good spirits. . . . He enthusiastically exclaimed: 'right now I am all in the mood for composing, and I wish I could come up with something really out of the ordinary. I am so attracted to the East, to the rose gardens of Persia, to the palm groves of India. I have a feeling that someone will bring me a subject that would lead me there!'" Flechsig was stunned, for it seemed incredible how closely Schumann's remarks described the writings which he had brought along and was about to present to the composer. "The whole episode is a miracle—a manifestation of a sixth sense that detects invisible things in our proximity."

The very qualities of the text that attracted Schumann work against its acceptance today. A succession of lyrical, idyllic and elegiac moods results in monotony: there are no contrasts, no forward movement. Beautiful as the music may be it cannot overcome this handicap. Schumann began work on the score in February, 1843. Fully absorbed in it, he found all other responsibilities burdensome. According to the title page the work was completed on "Ascension Day, May 25, 1843."

Contrary to some claims, Schumann did not "invent" the secular oratorio, but his contributions to the genre, together with Mendelssohn's *Erste Walpurgisnacht* are the most significant. Their popularity, however, has not lasted, and conductors are reluctant to program them today.

In the case of *Das Paradies und die Peri,* the designation "oratorio" is questionable. Schumann intentionally avoided any classification and simply wrote the word "Dichtung" under the title. One can agree with his remark that the work "represents a rather new genre." Even before Handel, there were both sacred and secular oratorios. Subjects from classical mythology served the Baroque oratorio; a greater variety of subjects is found in Romantic oratorios, including fantastic themes as in Mendelssohn's *Walpurgisnacht*.

In a letter dated May, 1843 Schumann reveals his sense that he was exploring new territory: "I am presently involved in a major work—indeed the largest I have ever tackled. It is not an opera; I rather consider it a new genre for the concert stage." The language clearly indicates that at the time the term "oratorio" normally referred to church music, especially Protestant church music incidental to the rediscovery of Bach's *St. Matthew Passion*. Another form is represented by Handel's *Messiah,* heralding the move of the genre away from Italy, the land of its origin. While the Italian oratorio was essentially soloistic and consisted of two parts, *Messiah* stresses choral writing and features a three-part arrangement, characteristics of style also used by Schumann. All the great oratorios with which he could acquaint himself were of this sacred, mostly Protestant variety: works by Bernhard Klein, Ferdinand Ries, Louis Spohr and Carl Loewe, as well as Mendelssohn's *St. Paul,* first performed in 1836. They were in all likelihood relatively unattractive to Schumann, for he was the only composer of his

Title page of The Paradise and the Peri

in 1843, brings to an end the creative period in which Schumann harbored few doubts as to his abilities.

Critics of his choral and operatic works occasionally have claimed that they lack tension and profile. By nature somewhat feminine, Schumann related more readily to the emotional life of women. This side of his personality found early expression in the cycle *Frauenliebe und -Leben.* Such feminine leanings did not hinder the dramatic impetus of his works but tended to rob them of vigor. On the other hand, the beauty of the intimate inspired his late works, an inspiration that always aimed for simplicity. Stylistically the oratorio is related to the composer's songs. This is not merely a matter of chronology. The work, as was mentioned above, was already on Schumann's mind in August, 1841 and actually begun the following January. If his first impression was that the subject "simply called for music" it was reconfirmed by *Peri's* lyrical qualities, equalling the best of the 1840 songs. Unflagging inspiration distinguishes the work. Schumann paid loving attention to every detail of the text, so sensitively formulated by the librettist. As a result the figure of Peri emerges with great delicacy, much admired at the time. She personifies those lofty, desirable qualities of earthly life that Schumann would have loved to have possessed himself.

The prelude shows how successfully Schumann could combine traditional elements of form with new principles of Romantic style. He wrote in 1845: "I think it is strange and remarkable that every musical motif that takes shape within me has the potential for all kinds of contrapuntal treatment, even though I haven't the slightest intention of devising themes that can be treated in the strict style. It just seems to happen that way, quite naturally and without my thinking about it."

In order to set the mood for the action of the work's opening, Schumann chose the form of the prelude rather than an overture, following the preferences of Haydn and Weber in entr'actes. Wagner especially was fond of it. The principal motif of the prelude (Example 60) clearly describes Peri's secret longing and is used throughout the entire first scene in the manner of a leitmotif. At first glance the harmonic structure seems advanced, but it moves within the bounds of traditional rules. Though E major is the basic key, it is avoided until the end. Rather there are modulations in both

generation who tended towards mysticism and Catholicism, a tendency rooted in the poetry of that time, especially that of Novalis. Thus Schumann, a Protestant involved in literary activities, wrote no Protestant church music yet near the end of his life, living in Catholic Düsseldorf, composed a Mass and a Requiem.

Peri, the work he had undertaken, was unconventional: the music's content, style and form were not based on any previous model. Further it was Schumann's first try at writing a large vocal work accompanied by symphony orchestra. Following the "Year of Songs," the "Symphony Year" and the year of chamber music, *Peri,* directions on the "circle of fifths," even to the remote D-sharp minor. One might say that the prelude amounts to a tense progression to E major, much instability characterizing its introductory function as well as expressing the underlying mood of longing.

Schumann's songs and symphonies prepared him for combining large-scale vocal and instrumental forces. In the back of the composer's mind, *Peri* undoubtedly served as preparation for writing an opera. Operatic plans clearly occupied him during 1842–43, as is evidenced by his remark: "As an artist I pray every morning and evening for one thing: German opera. There is much to be accomplished." In *Peri,* as in the later stage works, he discards traditional aria form. Without resorting precisely to Wagner's technique of using themes to bring specific associations back to the listener's mind, Schumann regularly employed musical symbols. As principal themes they serve to connect the main situations of the plot. They are entities lacking concrete, verbal meanings. Schumann's work in this form relates to the original, sacred nature of oratorio in its epic, lyrical qualities as well as in the use of the typical fugal ending.

Both sacred and secular characteristics are found in the music, which relate to similar dualities in the texts chosen. Their piety in some instances is poetic in nature, in others it is based on points of faith. Such dualism, in Schumann's view, characterized the subtle aspects of Romantic opera. Writing an oratorio was a proving ground, but did not require the same kind of dramatic cohesion. This lack of cohesion was to account for the failure of *Genoveva.* Oratorio is drama depending upon an imaginary stage. The action, therefore, takes place at a mental level—music's real domain. The poetic picture communicated by the text serves as a point of departure, while the imagination of the listener easily supplies appropriate moods and recreates the action.

Schumann knew how to maintain a sustained delicate atmosphere as demonstrated in *Peri,* where he created a work possessing greater coherence than was typical of earlier Romantic compositions. He deemphasized the overly sentimental qualities of the text and concentrated on musical expressivity. Yet from time to time he brings Peri down to earth, providing a contrast that is musically intensified by Oriental color. As a result of this subtle and masterful musical treatment, the work acquired a certain magic, which explains the effect it still has on sensitive people whose receptivity has not been dulled by today's loud and blatant stimuli.

This major work by Moore is set in the Orient. It consists of four tales told by a disguised Persian prince to his bride-to-be as they travel to his palace. With these tales he hopes to win her love. They are related in rich, colorful language derived from Moore's intense and sustained study of Persia which provided the background and ideas for the text. The Peris were legendary creatures of

Example 60

the air, driven with the fallen angels of the Christian tradition from paradise by their wrongdoing. The poet tracing the legend of one of these beings reveals that grace and forgiveness may be received even when all hope seems to have fled. Sinful Peri, according to the touching story, will be permitted to re-enter paradise if she can bring back with her "heaven's most precious gift." After two unsuccessful attempts the heroine succeeds, returning with the tears of a repentant sinner, the blood of a hero, and the sigh of love. We are not far here from Wagner's favorite subject: salvation through repentance and love. The successful expression of all this through music challenged the composer's resources: "It was a great effort. I came to appreciate what it takes to write many works of this kind, such as Mozart did in a short time. With gratitude to God who gave me strength to complete the task I wrote *Finis* on the score's last page."

When Wagner heard of Schumann's plan for this oratorio he wrote to him: "The very knowledge that you were composing this text made me happy. Not only do I know this wonderful story but I had thought of treating it myself. But I could not find the right musical form for it. Let me therefore congratulate you for having found it."

Wagner may have been specially attracted by the concept of love-death as the highest form of human devotion. In No. 16 of the score Peri gives her own life for her dying beloved. Schumann explains his use of the key of F♯ minor, which he hardly uses elsewhere, by saying that "the tritone, the exact center of the octave, i.e., F♯, seems to be the highest point."

Schumann saw fit to make changes in the text. He reshaped Moore's tale and corrected Flechsig's translation. Before he even began to write any of the music he completely rewrote the texts for Nos. 11, 18, 22, the choral finale of No. 26, and the solo sections of 20 and 25. It took him two years to get the text in shape; while the music took all of four months, which he completed on June 16, 1843. Clara had watched his creative frenzy with amazement and some concern: "I consider it his very best work. He tackles it with utter devotion and fervor, so intently that I sometimes fear for his health. Still, it makes me happy, too." Schumann reported to his friend Verhulst: "Last Friday I completed my *Paradies und Peri;* it is

my greatest and, I hope, best effort so far. . . . The story simply calls for music. The subject itself is very poetic and sincere; it truly kindled my enthusiasm. Its length is about right for an evening concert, and I pray that I may be able to perform it in one of my own concerts next winter, perhaps conducting it myself."

The composer avoided the division into completely separate numbers as had been customary in the oratorio form since the time of Handel. The work is "through-composed"; the third and sixth "numbers" have no distinct ending. Nor are other endings indicated: rather, the composer simply supplies transitions. A new, declamatory style, with origins as in the *Lied,* distinguishes the recitatives, taking the place of the traditional patterns. At the Berlin premiere, the critic Rellstab expressed his disapproval of these formal innovations. Schumann, contrary to his usual practice, replied in a letter: "You object to two aspects: the lack of recitatives and the connection, without breaks, of the musical sections. To me these are among the work's advantages, representing formal innovations. It would have been good to have this discussed in your review."

While Robert conducted the rehearsals for *Peri* (his first activity as a conductor), Clara was in Dresden. He had asked her to come back, feeling that he needed help in this new kind of task. "I just don't like to rehearse without you; you are my guiding spirit." The first performance of *Peri* took place on December 4, 1843, also marking Schumann's debut as a conductor, and was acclaimed a success. Livia Frege sang the title role; she must have made remarkable progress since the days when Schumann had first heard her. Dörffel, in his *History of the Gewandhaus Concerts,* raved about her performance. "No one, at least in Leipzig, could come near her as an interpreter of that role." Schmidt, the tenor, developed a cold and was about to lose his voice during the performance, so Vesque von Püttlingen, the singer and writer of Lieder, who was in the audience, came forward to sing the role at sight. Schumann was most grateful and later presented him with the autograph of the scene involving the youth afflicted with the plague, the scene he had risen to salvage.

Peri was quickly performed in a number of cities. On January 1, 1848, Hiller could report that it was "soon to be given in New

York." Schumann wrote Ignaz Moscheles, one of the few early proponents of his music, about a performance in London. A recommendation by Mendelssohn, highly regarded in England, helped. Mendelssohn had become acquainted with *Peri* during the first rehearsals of the solo quartets in October, 1843, during which Robert conducted the soloists, a small chorus, and a string quintet while Clara played the wind parts on the piano. Mendelssohn often turned pages for Clara and would at times sing the entrances of the solo parts in his small, pleasant tenor voice, so the following lines were not penned out of mere politeness. They were written in response to Clara's invitation to Mendelssohn to attend the Leipzig first performance, but the letter did not reach him in time, and Mendelssohn was unable to get away from Berlin. "I need not tell you and your dear husband how sorry I am. Not only do I like to come to Leipzig and to hear good music—but I would have specially liked to hear *this* music, Schumann's new composition. Now I must wait until another one will be completed: what a shame! . . . Please tell him that I rejoice with him. Do enjoy tomorrow night's performance, and when you and your friends celebrate the event please remember how happy I would have been to join you."

Soon after this, Mendelssohn wrote a recommendation to Buxton, the London publisher, who had taken an interest in Mendelssohn's own music. "I can tell you that studying and hearing this new work by Dr. Schumann has given me the greatest pleasure.

I had no doubts about its undisputed success which it . . . indeed achieved. I consider it a highly important, noble composition, full of great beauty, profundity, and poetic feeling. The choruses are most effective; the solo parts are melodious and attractive."

Schumann himself wrote to Moscheles about *Peri:* "We are anxious to come to England next year, and we ask for your kind counsel and assistance. My wife will do herself proud, I am sure. Since I would not like to stand by idly I thought of performing some excerpts from *Peri.* After all, it grew in English soil and represents England's poetic flowering at its best. To make this possible it would be good to have the vocal score available there before my arrival. . . . Breitkopf & Härtel are going to publish the score here around Christmas. I mention this because it may indicate to an English publisher some confidence in the work, for the Germans usually aren't quick to publish full scores. On two different evenings *Peri* was received most cordially here; an unforgettable experience for me. One would have to re-translate the text into English, but this should not be too difficult as in many places the original text would fit."

Unfortunately the trip to England did not materialize. It would have greatly helped to establish Schumann's reputation abroad. Not until after his death was Clara able to travel to England, where her concert performances were very successful.

Chapter 16

Schumann's work benefited immensely from the very humdrum life led during the year 1843. But noticeable changes in his personality and behavior became manifest. He devoted more time to writing or advising young artists or helping them along with their careers. Thus when Robert Franz sent manuscripts of his songs, Schumann immediately showed keen interest. As a result of his recommendations, several collections were published by Whistling, Breitkopf, and Kistner. But during this time Schumann increasingly refused to speak, seemingly preferring silence. This turn in his behavior sometimes took grotesque forms. For example important family matters were "discussed" in written form, via the joint family diary. He increasingly and noticeably shied away from large social gatherings. Even in small gatherings of close friends he spoke little. Henriette Voigt, a good friend from childhood days, tells that on warm summer nights they would go on excursion boat rides together, but often sat together in complete silence. Once upon parting Schumann pressed her hand and murmured: "tonight we really understood each other." Franz Brendel recalls another incident. Schumann had discovered an especially good "Markobrunner" [wine] in Gahlis. "He asked me to go there with him. In stifling heat we journeyed through the Rosenthal without speaking a single word. When we arrived the Markobrunner was indeed his main concern. I couldn't get a word out of him. It was the same on the way back. But he made one remark which afforded me a glimpse into what went on inside him. He spoke of the particular beauty of such a summer day when no voices are heard, when nature is completely silent. This mood of nature affected him much.

He observed that the ancient Greeks had an apt description for it: 'Pan is asleep.' In moments like these Schumann only took notice of what was going on around him if it happened to relate in some way to his reveries. Sociability interested him only if he needed relief from solitude."

Schumann was greatly concerned about the family's financial straits. "We spend more than we take in," he confessed in the diary. He was able to sell new works to music publishers, but the one-time fees they were then paying were more than modest. He was paid 55 Thaler for *Myrten* and 140 Thaler for the three Opus 41 quartets. *Peri* brought a greater return—550 Thaler. A fee of this size not only resulted in greater prestige but also accounts in part for turning to writing in the larger forms.

Soon after their marriage Clara extracted a promise from Robert to undertake an extended Russian tour with her. Her motivation stemmed not only from a desire for artistic recognition but also out of concern for the family finances. At the time of the extended rehearsals of *Peri,* the Russian project began to take shape. At the same time Breitkopf & Härtel offered Schumann the editorship of the *Allgemeine Musikalische Zeitung.* Such a position for so prestigious a journal would have assured Schumann a steady income. After much hesitation, however, he declined, advising that he planned to devote himself entirely to composing.

As a result of these various commitments and opportunities it was impossible for Schumann to find that solitude which had become so important. To go on the Russian tour at this time really required that he "give his all." So Clara enlisted Mendelssohn's

The Kremlin, Moscow. Drawing by Robert Schumann, 1844

support in planning and guiding the undertaking. Liszt was also called on to persuade him. Clara wrote: "Robert greatly fears this journey. Might you be able to present it to him in a more attractive light?" Robert, after several postponements, at last agreed to schedule the journey for the first months of 1844. What Robert sacrificed, for Clara's career and the family income, was that which he loved best: to compose in peace. He imagined, however, that he might continue his work while they were traveling.

It may also be that Clara wished to prove herself in the eyes of her father who, after *Peri*'s success, had written a letter seeking a reconciliation. For Clara's sake Robert reluctantly agreed to following up this overture, though he certainly could not forget the past. The tour also offered a temporary respite from the editorial tasks in connection with the *Zeitschrift*. But in the end the loss of six months worth of composing time turned out to be very painful,

even more so than being away from their children.

When passing through Berlin, Robert and Clara at last made the personal acquaintance of "their" poet, Professor Friedrich Rückert. Clara, in a letter to Wieck on February 20, however, refers to the event with the single word: "interesting."

Clara's concerts were enthusiastically received everywhere: in Mitau, Riga, St. Petersburg, and Moscow. Robert, too, won new friends for his music, among them two brothers, the Counts Wielhorsky. In their St. Petersburg palace Schumann conducted his "Spring" Symphony and assisted in presenting performances of his string quartets.

The coaches in which Robert and Clara traveled were cold and drafty; hotel rooms were primitive; travel by sleigh was positively painful. In Dorpat Robert was forced to spend several days in bed. Depressions and dizzy spells made the stay in Moscow an ordeal.

Being the husband of a famous wife, Schumann was beginning to realize, was painful, yet the pain had to remain concealed. He worked hard at concealing his feelings, when Clara was entertaining guests or meeting with tour sponsors, only occasionally offering an ironic comment, but largely he absented himself, living in a world of his own. There were no disagreements with Clara and indeed, in free hours he sought out piano pieces by other composers that might be suitable for her programs, but he hated all men who were composers, considering them to be at the root of his troubles.

"No time or peace for composing" was Robert's summary of the tour. He adverts to "hidden music," referring to poems he wrote in Moscow. Other diary entries deal with trivia, with rheumatism, phobias, melancholy. Such was the life of "Clara Wieck's husband" in Russia. Then there was the matter of too much alcohol for which frequent solitary walks provided no improvement. With great effort he wrote sketches for a portion of the final scene of Goethe's *Faust, Part II* which was at first described as a libretto among his opera projects. While ill in Dorpat he reviewed Goethe's drama for those scenes which seemed suitable to be set. The sketches were written out after his return home and in 1844 became Nos. 1, 2, 3, and 7 of the third section of *Scenes from Faust* to which we shall return later.

Following the Russian tour, it took Robert some time to adjust again to "dull Leipzig." But a return to familiar surroundings and home soon led to ambitious plans. In addition to Byron's *Corsair* he worked on the *Scenes from Faust*. In order to refrain from returning Goethe's text he prepared oratorio-like excerpts. He soon recognized that it would take time to complete a project of this magnitude, but probably never imagined that it would take a decade. He was slow getting started, concentrating first on the last scene which he called *Verklärung* (Transfiguration), which occupied him until the winter of 1844. His zest for creative work, so strong while composing *Peri,* was dealt a fatal blow by the Russian tour. To complete even a handful of compositions was a struggle and hence a disappointment. This, in turn, led to heavy drinking, further undermining his health. Hoping to regain health and peace of mind he gave up his position as editor of the *Neue Zeitschrift für Musik.* Franz

Brendel took his place and under his direction it became the organ of the so-called "New German School." With the publication of Wagner's polemic essay *On the Jews in Music,* the *Zeitschrift* became an aggressive, militant journal. Only upon Brendel's appointment as professor of music at Leipzig University did the journal resume a moderate stance.

The Schumanns' great expectations of Hans Christian Andersen's Leipzig visit turned out to be a grave disappointment. Livia Frege's performance of Schumann songs seemed of no interest to the visitor. He preferred telling his fairy tales to young and old.

In August, Schumann's health took a turn for the worse: he suffered a "complete nervous collapse." Clearly a number of factors contributed to this downturn, including, as Clara put it, his "public humiliation." When Mendelssohn took a year's leave from the Gewandhaus podium in order to conduct his works in Frankfurt and Berlin, the management immediately appointed Niels W. Gade as principal conductor without so much as considering Schumann. Schumann had struggled and suffered much in trying to prove his talent, and the circumstances surrounding Gade's appointment proved overwhelming. He had found in Mendelssohn's Leipzig conservatory an environment producing a minimum of conflicts: the combination of teaching and composing which might have protected him from the political and commercial aspects of the musical world. But his penchant for alcohol condemned him. He failed to take advantage of this opportunity, though it would in all probability have provided financial independence and enough time to successfully pursue his passion for composing.

Nor was life at home conducive to serenity. The Schumanns' living quarters were very crowded and not well suited to creative work. His frustrations can be measured by the number of works of which he conceived but which failed to satisfy him when completed. For days on end he could not work at all and put sketches away or destroyed them. He would often make notes in his sketch book while walking and when he returned he locked himself in his room. Unhappily, if he opened the sketch book at all he commonly burned what little he had noted.

A vacation in the Harz Mountains did not improve matters. Late in October, the couple went to Dresden, hoping that a few weeks there would improve his spirits. He could not sleep for nights on end and was plagued by terrible fears. In the morning Clara would find him dissolved in tears, "giving up all hope for himself." Wieck tried to "pull Robert out of it [his depression], forcibly."

Their elder daughter's recurring illness led them to remain in Dresden, first in a boarding house, and, beginning in December, 1844, in an apartment. With Mendelssohn's departure, Leipzig had lost its chief attraction for Schumann. And after all, hadn't Mendelssohn, at Clara's urging, led them to undertake the disastrous journey to Russia? To be sure, the friendship had never been really intimate due to Robert's introspective, silent nature, his easily aroused suspicions and hurt feelings but Mendelssohn had remained Schumann's staunchest supporter.

Despite his poor health Schumann participated in several concerts that were arranged on the occasion of their leaving Leipzig. On November 29, 1844, some of the city's leading musical personalities, including Mendelssohn, gathered at Raimund Härtel's home. Frau Frege sang Schumann songs; the 13-year-old violinist Joseph Joachim also performed. Clara, "Leipzig's sweetheart," had appeared on November 5, playing (for the first time, after some hesitation) Beethoven's E^b major piano concerto. The Schumanns, in turn, gave a farewell matinee for their friends on December 8. The correspondent for the *Signale für die musikalische Welt* expressed the hope that Schumann would return soon, "with new songs."

Chapter 17

In 1846 the Schumanns moved to Grosse Reitbahn Strasse in Dresden. Their family had seen the addition of four children which added to their problems. Five years in Dresden aggravated Schumann's pathological sense of being hemmed in. Musically speaking the city seems to have been a desert. The view of the arts at court was old-fashioned and lethargic, supporting a superficial style in painting and opera. Twenty years earlier even Carl Maria von Weber had been unable to obtain public support for German opera or any other serious music in the city. No good chamber music ensemble existed. Beethoven was seldom performed since he was not "good box office," and when his works were played "the performers added embellishments *ad libitum*." Small wonder that Schumann complained to Mendelssohn about the reactionary taste of Dresden audiences: "Here they are less open to innovation than any place else."

One redeeming feature was provided by the group of men who held weekly get-togethers: Bendemann, Rietschel, Hübner, Richard Wagner, Ferdinand Hiller, and Robert Reinick were the outstanding members. "There never is a lack of topics for conversation or of pieces to be read aloud: it is a lively crowd." When Schumann met the actor Eduard Devrient, the latter was struck by the composer's absent-minded, apathetic behavior. But Schumann did like to talk with Weber's widow who showed a keen interest in his work. Clara on the other hand developed a close friendship with the singers Wilhelmine Schröder-Devrient ("a true artist") and Jenny Lind who passed through several times. Clara worshipped her; Robert marvelled at her Lieder singing.

Above all others, Schumann developed a close relationship with the painter Bendemann, whose knowledge of and views about art impressed him. He also thought highly of Bendemann's wife, a daughter of Schadow. Bendemann reinforced Schumann in his opinion that Geibel was little more than a ladies' poet. On the other hand, Bendemann deserves credit for Schumann's growing admiration for Hebbel's work.

Schumann's depressed state of mind lasted longer than any previous episode, until early in 1845. The list of compositions for 1844 therefore is short: only a chorus and an aria for the opera *The Corsair,* for which a libretto may have been completed. Any other fragments of music which may have been done in this year have disappeared.

Further disappointments with music publishers occurred. Kistner rejected *Dichterliebe,* as well as an Allegro affettuoso for piano and orchestra, and the D minor symphony. Peters did accept the song cycle *Twenty Lieder by Heine, Opus 47.* Schumann removed four songs and supplied the title *Dichterliebe.*

Among the people Schumann encountered in Dresden, Wagner was to be the most significant. The meeting took place in the "Hiller Circle" where Wagner gave a reading of the text for *Lohengrin,* a subject Schumann had considered after completing *Peri.* He was unable to understand how Wagner could set such a text except as separate musical numbers.

Schumann's condition improved gradually. In the spring of 1845 he cautiously returned to composing by writing contrapuntal studies, as though he wished to involve his intellect rather than his

Richard Wagner

overly stimulated imagination. This "passion for fugues" lasted until that fall but resulted in several masterworks: *Studien und Skizzen für den Pedalflügel* (Opus 56,58), *Vier Fugen für das Pianoforte* (Opus 72), and *Sechs Orgelfugen über den Namen Bach* (Opus 60). They testify to his daily involvement with Bach's works and also were an antidote to the trivial compositions with which he came into contact daily and which "practically turned me into a misanthrope." After these works in the strict style Schumann turned to freer forms of music.

Two more movements were written for the piano concerto in A minor, thus completing that famous composition, and work on the C major symphony was begun. To the conductor Ott he confessed that he still was quite ill when he wrote it. "I'm afraid it shows. Only while composing the last movement did I begin to feel like myself again."

A trip to the Rhine, planned for August, 1845, got no farther than Weimar because the prescriptions Schumann took made him feel "continually ill." Were these medications intended to control his alcoholism?

At about this time Schumann again turned to writing songs, using texts from collections of poetry by Hoffmann von Fallersleben (Leipzig, 1834; Breslau, 1837) and from his *Kinderlieder* (Children's Songs, Leipzig, 1843). Schumann's setting of the little *Soldatenlied* (Soldier's Song) first appeared in a collection entitled *Fünfzig neue Lieder für Kinder* (Fifty New Songs for Children) which also included contributions by Spohr and Mendelssohn. This song attests to the connection between poet and composer several years before they met in Düsseldorf.

Schumann achieved his "first triumph" with the "best of all concertos"—the name that has been bestowed on the Piano Concerto in A Minor. On January 1, 1846, a few weeks before the birth of their son Emil, Clara helped to establish the concerto's reputation in a performance at the Leipzig Gewandhaus, with Mendelssohn conducting and in the composer's presence. This recognition immediately so bolstered his creative energy that in January he began orchestrating the C Major Symphony which had caused him so much difficulty. In addition he wrote *Five Songs For Mixed Chorus,* Opus 55, for Mendelssohn who had just founded the Leipzig *Liederkranz.*

AUGUST HEINRICH
HOFFMANN
(1798-1874)

The poet and linguist used the name of his place of birth, Fallersleben. Although he enrolled at Göttingen University to study theology, his interests turned to collecting and paraphrasing folk and patriotic songs. He also studied Dutch literature, became a librarian, and eventually became Professor of German Literature at the University of Breslau where his research repeatedly took him to Austria, Denmark, Holland, Belgium, and Switzerland. He resigned his position in 1842, just before his dismissal from the university resulting from objections to the political views articulated in his *Unpolitische Lieder* (Hamburg, 1840–41). Exiled successively by several German states, he led an unsettled life. During a sojourn on the island of Helgoland he penned his *Deutschland, Deutschland Über Alles.* The State of Mecklenburg finally granted him residence in 1845 where he formed a friendship with the writer Fritz Reuter. Prussia granted him amnesty and a pension in 1848, enabling him to settle in Weimar where, together with Oskar Schade, he edited the *Weimarisches Jahrbuch für deutsche Sprache, Literatur und Kunst. Geschichte der deutsch-lateinischen Mischpoesie* (History of Mixed German and Latin Poetry) was also completed there, after the publication of which the Duke of Ratibor appointed him librarian of Corvey Abbey. Fallersleben made a significant contribution to the publication of early Prussian literature; his simple, tuneful songs established his popularity. His epigrammatic poems, though not profound, and often tendentious presentations of topical issues, reveal a superb technical facility in capturing the views of his contemporaries. Simple and sincere, he was able to capture the spirit of folk song better than most of his contemporaries. Although he had received no formal musical training he composed attractive and widely sung melodies to accompany some of his verses.

Schumann did not have to move any great distance from the writing of songs for several voices and piano to writing choral works. Indeed, his odyssey characterizes the development of Romantic choral music. His a cappella choruses were written for a small group of kindred souls, mostly amateurs, whom he had assembled in Dresden and would later gather together in Düsseldorf. Opus 55 is based upon texts by Burns, so in *Hochlandbursch* (Highland Lad) four solo voices alternate with the chorus; an effect he used to good advantage in later songs as well. *Zahnweh,* a couplet in which Burns wishes a year of toothaches on everyone who maligns Scotland, is but passingly humorous.

Four Songs for Mixed Voices, Opus 59, make greater demands on the singers but are musically unconvincing. The opening poem of the group was written by Karl Lappe, who also supplied the text for Schubert's *Im Abendroth. Nord oder Süd* includes incidental solos which, while having an effective conclusion, cannot compensate for the excessive word repetitions. *Gute Nacht* (Good Night, Rückert) and *Jägerlied* (Hunting Song, Mörike; used for a magnificent composition by Hugo Wolf) are rather weak, while *Am Bodensee,* poem by Platen, is unworthy of Schumann thanks to its excessive sentimentality. Another chorus, *Hirtenknabengesang* (Song of the Shepherd Boy), set to the last verses of the poem *Hirtenfeuer* by Annette von Droste-Hüllshof and written in January 1846, remains virtually unknown. It was finally published in 1929–30 in the *Yearbook* of Breitkopf & Härtel. The unusual scoring—two sopranos and two tenors—inspired Schumann to write a double canon.

In spite of interruptions the C Major Symphony was completed in 1846. Though admired at the time, it has not retained its former place in the symphonic literature. Save during periods of illness Schumann labored hard, and indeed overtaxed his strength.

The Leipzig Gewandhaus, ca. 1845

In spite of his output he continued to be known (except in Leipzig and Dresden) chiefly as Clara's husband, much as he resented this. When an old friend remarked that Clara must have done much to smooth his way as a composer, Robert abruptly rose and left the room.

His condition necessitated periods of rest during which he devoted himself to his children. He took the oldest, the 4½-year-old Marie, for walks, taught her how to count and to memorize and recite short verses. Three-year-old Lieschen was also taught a few rhymes. Both girls "liked to sing a great deal, with light, clear voices." The memory book in which these observations are recorded also includes a list of books that Robert recommended for their later reading. At the top of the list is the Bible, followed by the poets Ruckert, Schiller, Platen, Grün, and Immermann, and "for later: Jean Paul, Goethe, Shakespeare, Byron, Homer, and Sophocles."

In February, 1846, Wieck, who had been visiting in Weimar, came to see Clara, greatly excited. "There is no one who sings like [Jenny] Lind. Everyone should take her as a model: Minna (one of Wieck's students) must sing like her, and Maier must play like her . . ." Clara, after describing how Wieck was beside himself, added that she "would dearly love to hear Lind—but I intensely

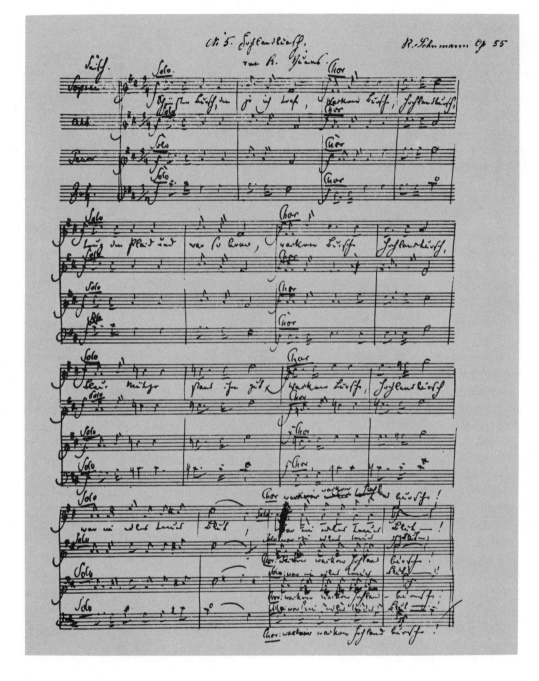

Schumann,
Highland Lad,
Autograph

ANNETTE,
BARONESS VON DROSTE-HÜLSHOFF

Droste-Hülshoff was the most significant female German poet of the 19th Century. A member of an old Westphalian noble family, she received a thorough education. After 1841 she lived in Meersburg Castle on Lake Constance where she wrote most of her nature poetry. It reflected impressions of her Westphalian homeland and also revealed her profoundly religious outlook. Her ballads and tales deal with supernatural and mythical forces in nature. She was one of the first poets inspired by the heath and moor landscapes of that region.

dislike listening to someone talk endlessly about a person whom I have never heard or seen." The opportunity to hear Lind came on April 12. Clara's family insisted that she go to Leipzig. "Lind is a genius—such a voice is heard only once in a great while. She makes a very favorable first impression. Her face is not beautiful, but her beautiful eyes make it seem so. Her singing is ever so sincere. There is no showmanship, no great display of emotion, yet she touches your heart. A certain melancholy quality inevitably affects the listener. At first Jenny Lind may appear to be cold, but this is not the case; the impression may be caused by the simplicity of her singing. No weeping, sobbing, or quavering sounds, no bad habits of any kind."

Such a singer was in Clara's mind the ideal interpreter for Robert's music. Lind's voice was not big, but even one of her very attractive soft notes was easily heard in any hall regardless of size. After the concert Dr. Frege hosted a large reception in her honor, at which Clara "became even fonder of Jenny Lind due to her modest, even reticent deportment." The feelings were mutual, and Robert, who met Lind a few months later in Hamburg also warmed to her at once, just as Clara had hoped. He was full of admiration even though he heard her in a role that probably was beyond her: Donna Anna in *Don Giovanni.* He had to admit that Schröder-Devrient was a better interpreter of that role.

Neither Clara's eagerness to perform nor Robert's desire to organize musical evenings at home could find adequate opportunities in Dresden. So following a stay at Norderney for reasons of health they decided to spend the 1846–47 season in Vienna, perhaps hoping that Clara might find more performance opportunities and he might at last establish himself as a composer in the musical center of Europe. Marie and Elise accompanied their parents. But save for their comfortable living quarters the stay in Vienna was not happy. Clara had not appeared in recital in the Austrian capital for nine years. Now the concert-going public let her down, in part perhaps because her programs contained many of Robert's works. The Viennese understood his music no more than they did Bach, let alone Chopin. Due to Robert's influence those composers also figured prominently in her programs. Robert conducted some of his own compositions at their third concert but Hanslick, then Vienna's most influential critic, noted that the applause was "polite and obviously intended only for Clara." The fourth concert, better attended, produced some profit, thanks largely to Jenny Lind's participation. She sang only two songs: Mendelssohn's *Auf Flügeln des Gesanges* (On Wings of Song) and Schumann's *Der Nussbaum* (The Nut Tree). The day before Lind had given a recital of her own; now she was returning Clara's favor, who had on an earlier occasion replaced her when Lind had to cancel a Gewandhaus appearance. Clara knew that Jenny Lind always would draw an audience. Soon after their arrival in Vienna she had called on Lind and obtained her cooperation. The concert was sold out, "which paid all expenses of our trip and an additional 300 Thaler which we were able to take back to Dresden. Still, the event is one of my saddest memories . . . I couldn't help thinking how one song sung by Lind succeeded in a way that I was unable to match with all my playing . . . Nevertheless her performance of the songs . . . enchanted me . . . Her singing of Robert's *Nussbaum* was a little less successful. She failed to establish the right tempo."

Before the concert Robert had rehearsed some of his songs with her and was impressed. "I shall never forget this rehearsal: even at a first reading she showed such clear understanding of text and music! I have never met anyone who has such easy, unaffected yet profound feeling for these words. And she was sight reading at that!"

Having complained about the dearth of music-making in their Dresden home, Schumann now made up for it in their Vienna apartment. On January 15, 1847, there also was a pleasant meeting with the poets Grillparzer, Stifter, and Eichendorff. Robert and Clara already knew Grillparzer but greatly enjoyed his slighting remarks about Vienna. Stifter made less of an impression, probably due to his heavy dialect and his obesity. Unfortunately, the meeting with Eichendorff was all too brief; several earlier plans to get together had failed to materialize. At a matinee von Marchion sang Schumann's Eichendorff songs. The poet and his children were in the audience and he seemed pleased, declaring that Schumann imbued life into his songs—a remark that reveals Eichendorff's "musical" concept of his poetry.

At a social gathering of *Concordia,* an association of writers and other artists, an unfortunate meeting took place between the Schumanns and Meyerbeer. Things got off on the wrong foot since Schumann was a friend of Mendelssohn, whom Meyerbeer strongly disliked. Furthermore, Meyerbeer had composed texts by Heine, thus making him Schumann's rival. Meyerbeer's Heine songs of 1837 are based on poems that Schumann had set far more convincingly three years later. Schumann's distaste for Meyerbeer's music increased as the years went by. In 1841, Wagner wrote to Schumann (with greater candor than he was to show later): "Don't let them malign Meyerbeer so much: I owe everything to him including the great fame I am sure to achieve soon." But Schumann's opinion never changed. Clara entrusted to her diary her impressions of a Dresden performance (February 1850) of *Le Prophète:* "Robert

Jenny Lind

hissed loudly in many places. Indeed this is godless (or, as Robert rightly said, immoral) music. It must disgust anyone with good sense and an unspoiled disposition." Hanslick, who was present at their meeting in Vienna, noted that they were fortunately seated at some distance from each other but that "neither one of them seemed to be at ease."

With half-empty houses and a noticeable lack of interest in Schumann's music the stay in Vienna had to be considered a failure. The journey home turned into a small concert tour. Schumann's Eichendorff songs and the piano quintet were enthusiastically received in Prague, which improved the Schumanns' morale. Good publicity was available in Bohemia thanks to an article written by a journalist using the *Davidsbündler* name "Flamin" who was a Schumann devotee.

A brief stop-over in Dresden cast a pall over their further journey: they found their little Emil in critical condition, suffering from "hardened glands" which led to the child's death in June. With heavy heart Clara and Robert continued their tour to Berlin. A performance of *Das Paradies und die Peri,* in the King's presence, was well received even though the *Singakademie* had been poorly rehearsed and Robert's inadequate conducting skills created confusion in the orchestra and among the amateur soloists. Everyone tried to give him advice. He spent sleepless nights and stayed in bed except for the full rehearsals, leaving Clara in charge of rehearsing with the soloists, thereby averting the worst. Plans for a repeat performance, with Clara's friend Pauline Viardot-Garcia as Peri, failed to materialize when the singer cancelled the engagement. No doubt she viewed an appearance in this role as an inadequate opportunity for captivating the public with bravura singing. A few days later, however, she sang some Mendelssohn songs with Clara.

The Schumanns enjoyed Berlin: the cultural life was superior to that of Vienna, and quite certainly that of Dresden. Clara was glad to spend time with Fanny Hensel, Mendelssohn's sister, and she was feted in the home of Henriette Sonntag, now Countess Rossi. A move to Berlin seemed an enticing thought. Who could have known that Fanny was to die in June! Any plans for a move came to nothing.

After Berlin, Dresden seemed even more of a desert than before. Schumann's health, however, improved markedly. While Clara was working on the piano reduction of the C Major Symphony, Robert composed the *Phantasiestücke,* the D Minor Trio for Violin, Cello and Piano, and some songs. The latter, the first songs from the Dresden years, were inspired by Mörike poems. A visit by Robert Franz may have been a factor, for this eccentric composer from Halle had written some memorable Mörike songs himself.

In *Die Soldatenbraut* (The Soldier's Bride, Opus 64, No. 1) a gentle, ingratiating mood prevails, despite the pronounced rhythm. It is a stylized military march, expressing a girl's feelings about her soldier sweetheart. The last repeat is effective: the march now is heard faintly, from afar. March and wedding music provide a charming contrast. The song's engaging melody gained it a place on many concert programs and led Schumann to make an arrangement for women's voices. (Opus 69, No. 4). A small, lyric work, it seems to have served as a preparation for works on a larger scale. A certain objective quality in these songs is probably due to Schumann's immediately previous involvement with symphony and chamber music. This objective quality is revealed in *Die Soldatenbraut*'s folk-like flavor.

Das verlassene Mägdelein (The Forsaken Maid, Opus 64, No. 2) is a clear testament to Schumann's feeling for the style of Bach, yet in two passages it employs a kind of chromaticism that was unthinkable in the 1840 songs. The voice part lacks any sense of intense emotion, but is rather a monologue over a floating accompaniment suggesting string writing. This may not be the greatest setting of a poem that inspired other composers, among them Pfitzner; nevertheless it was Schumann's setting that inspired one by Hugo Wolf. Not only did Wolf model his music on Schumann's setting but he made the same minor changes in the text.

The same poem reappears in Schumann's *Romanzen* for women's voices, Opus 69. It is a strophic setting with a folk song flavor. These *Romanzen,* as well as those of Opus 91, call for "optional piano accompaniment." The twelve songs display a great variety of emotions and all present clear evidence of the great love and care Schumann bestowed on their composition.

In July Schumann visited his home town Zwickau, which feted

EDUARD
MÖRIKE

In the 17th Century Mörike's family left their homeland Brandenburg and settled in Württemberg. The poet was born on September 8, 1804, the son of the town physician of Ludwigsburg. After his father's early death he developed a close attachment to his mother. Having attended the *Gymnasium* in Stuttgart and the seminary in Urach, he enrolled, a budding theologian, at the seminary in Tübingen where he developed close friendships with Waiblingen and Hölderlin. A tumultuous love affair with a young waitress inspired some of his great songs. He also began work on his novel, *Maler Nolten* while at Tübingen.

After passing his exams he entered the ministry and became engaged to Luise Rau, a pastor's daughter, but shied away from marriage. While serving as a vicar in several villages he completed *Maler Nolten.* In 1834, he became pastor of the church in Clevesulzbach, an appointment he held for nine years. Klärchen, his sister, kept house for him and their mother until her death in 1841. During the years in Clevesulzbach he completed his most significant work: the collection of poems published in 1838.

In 1843 poor health forced him to take early retirement. With his sister and his wife, Margarethe Speeth whom he had married in 1851, he lived in Schwäbisch Hall and Bad Mergentheim. A teaching position at the *Katharina-Stift* in Stuttgart was created specially for him. Ultimately he was able to teach literature for only one hour a week. During the 24 years of "retirement" he became a father, developed friendships with Theodor Storm and Moritz von Schwind, and made the acquaintances of Turgeniev and Hebbel. His last years brought ill health, reduced circumstances, loneliness and resignation. At Mörike's funeral in Stuttgart in 1875 Frederick Theodor Vischen gave a funeral oration which was itself a significant literary piece and was widely read.

its favorite son with a torchlight parade and serenades. A small music festival had also been planned, but the death of little Emil required that it be postponed from June to July 10. For the occasion Schumann wrote *Beim Abschied zu singen* (A Farewell Song), as a gift to the city. It is a choral piece with soprano solo: *Es ist bestimmt in Gottes Rat* (God Has Ordained, Opus 84, text by Ernst von Feuchtersleben) which calls for ten wind instruments or piano as accompaniment. Schumann conducted the performance himself. The work was not presented again until 1862 at the Leipzig Gewandhaus. Unfortunately it is as sentimental as Mendelssohn's setting of the same text.

A few months after Fanny Mendelssohn's death her brother Felix died unexpectedly on November 4, 1847. Both deaths were diagnosed as "nerve apoplexy"—a stroke, just as Mendelssohn once had predicted to Schumann. Robert attended the services in Leipzig by himself since Clara was again expecting. On his return there was more bad news, though not quite as painful: Ferdinand Hiller, a close Dresden friend, had accepted a position as music director in Düsseldorf. At a farewell banquet at the Brühl Terrace Eduard Devrient proposed a toast to both Hiller and Schumann whom, he saluted as the "master of song of the *Liedertafel*," a designation that caused Schumann to frown although it was accurate, for Hiller had just passed on to him the directorship of the recently founded *Liedertafel.*

To mark his appointment, Schumann wrote *Three Songs for Male Chorus A Cappella,* Opus 62. The patriotic texts by Rückert, Eichendorff, and Klopstock presage coming political developments. *Der Eidgenossen Nachtwache* (Night Watch of the Swiss Confederates) is particularly well written, but *Freiheitslied* (Song of Freedom) and *Schlachtgesang* (Battle Song) have little appeal today.

BARON ERNST
VON FEUCHTERSLEBEN

Feuchtersleben (1806–1849) was a physician and psychiatrist in Vienna. His book *Diätetik der Seele* advocated mental health through will power. His friends included Grillparzer, Schubert, Bauernfeld, Moritz von Schwind, and Stifter. In his popular scientific essays and in his poetry he is a good representative of the Austrian Biedermeier epoch.

The *Ritornels for Four-Part Male Voices,* Opus 65, also written for the *Liedertafel* in the form of canons, are masterfully done, providing a variety of timbre using alternating solo and choral passages.

Schumann was no friend of the "eternal 6/4 chords of male chorus style," and he soon tired of the medium. His real interest lay in the training of a mixed chorus, suitable for oratorio performances and offering greater challenges to him as a composer. His "Invitation for the Formation of a Choral Society" was successful: rehearsals began on January 5, 1848. This was Schumann's opportunity to perfect himself as a conductor and "to make an effective contribution."

To one collection of *Romances and Ballads for Mixed Voices,* composed in 1840, Schumann quickly added two further works (Opus 75 and 91) in the form. In a letter to Hiller dated April 10, 1849 Schumann reports that "several volumes of ballads for chorus are being published; they sound very good." Not much else can be said in favor of them. Strangely, Schumann gives the princess's question "Was siehst du mich an so wunniglich?" (Why do you gaze at me with such desire?) in *Schön Rohtraut* (Beautiful Beloved, Opus 67, No. 2; text by Mörike) to male voices only. *Meerfey* (Mermaid, Opus 69, No. 5, text by Eichendorff) is scored for five-part women's voices and optional piano accompaniment. The title is Schumann's; Eichendorff's title is *Verloren* (Lost). In addition Schumann wrote the text for a second stanza, apparently missing from Eichendorff's original. The piece gives the impression of student exercises in the strict style. An undulating pattern recurs relentlessly save for the last five measures. A quiet ending does mitigate the impression made by what precedes it: a laborious, awkward study. More imagination is displayed in the setting of Kerner's *Wassermann* (The Merman, Opus 91, No. 3); as well as a more meaningful grouping of voices.

The tenor solo in Goethe's *König von Thule* (The King of Thule, Opus 67) was added later; perhaps intended to represent the king. Verses one to three are given to the soprano, verse four is shared by soprano and tenor. The tenor is silent in the first half of verses five and six but takes the leading position in the second half of each. It is difficult to make any sense of this arrangement.

The badly worn manuscript presents some problems to musicologists. According to Hans Schneider the second half of Goethe's *Haidenröslein* had been covered up, the third part of Uhland's *Schifflein* having been pasted over it. For some time it was therefore assumed that the latter existed only as a fragment. Similarly, the hastily written *Romanze vom Gänsebuben* (Song of the Gooseherd), based on a Spanish poem, appears scattered over several pages of the manuscript, leading to a similar assumption. The two parts of Robert Burns's *Johannis* (Cock up your Beaver), entitled *Der Rekrut* in Schumann's published version, are almost identical. Schumann wrote down only those portions of the second part that contain differences.

Vom verwundeten Knaben (The Wounded Boy, an Old German poem) later served as the model for a much more successful song by Brahms. Sometime later Schumann added a superfluous alto solo to the choral setting. In the choral version of Schiller's *Der Handschuh* (The Glove) 23 measures are unfortunately missing. They probably were written down on a leaf that was lost. The Opus 87 version might have been more effective, as a choral work, than the solo song of 1840 noted above.

Chapter 18

During 1847 Schumann composed the piano trios Opus 63 and 80, both highly original works. He also wrote the overture and first act of his Romantic opera *Genoveva,* Opus 81. This was not Schumann's first attempt at musical drama, for in 1838 he had begun work on a libretto by Becker, *Doge und Dogaressa,* based on E. T. A. Hoffmann's novella by the same title. Nothing, however, came of it. The composer found no "profound German qualities" in the subject. From the time he first encountered the vocal scores of several Mozart operas, Schumann had dreamt of writing an opera himself. Some of his thoughts on such a project were distinctly odd: "An opera without text—wouldn't that be dramatic?" Unfortunately we shall never know what he had in mind; nothing was ever committed to paper.

He considered a wide variety of dramatic materials including Calderon's *Bridge at Mantible.* He also considered *The Veiled Prophet of Khorosan,* the legend of a Nabi who, during a period of Assyrian rule, struggled to maintain the faith of the Jews in their fathers' creed; as well as *Till Eulenspiegel.* In 1844 Schumann became interested in Byron's *Corsair.* Andersen's *Glücksblume* (Flower of Fortune) has already been mentioned. The composer corresponded with Zuccalmaglio about a legend, *Mokanna,* and an historical subject, "The Moorish Invasion of Spain." Plans for a Faust opera were even announced. Clara was enlisted to write Annette von Droste-Hülsdorff about a suitable operatic subject, but writing librettos was viewed as hack work by the poet. *Mazeppa* by the Polish writer Slowacki was also taken under consideration.

Soon after *Genoveva* Schumann's thoughts returned to possible new opera subjects. "In the future I intend to concentrate on writing operas." To C. Wettig, a young composer whom Schumann had encouraged in the *Zeitschrift,* Robert gave this advice: "There's no use theorizing and writing about it. You must roll up your sleeves and get to work! Take any subject from history or literature. Take Shakespeare, Calderon, perhaps also Boccaccio. Arrange the material in a way that is right for the stage and for music. Then look for a poet who can versify your material. You mustn't wait until some poet happens to come your way with a suitable libretto." In the same spirit Schumann looked over the *Odyssey, Bajazet* by Racine, *Sakuntala* by Kalidasa and even Cicero's letters for himself.

Having gained expertise in writing for voice, and spurred on by the success of scores of operas, particularly those first presented in Paris, Schumann impatiently searched for a subject. Aside from the enormous number noted above, his "book of projects" included several later undertaken by Wagner: the Nibelungen, the song contest on the Wartburg (i.e. Tannhäuser); Lohengrin, and Master Martin and His Apprentices.

Inquiries addressed to Griepenkerl and Marbach seeking suitable texts brought no replies, but Schumann finally found his man: the painter and poet Robert Reinick who had already written a libretto for Hiller. Schumann suggested that Reinick fashion an opera text from the Genoveva legend as told by Ludwig Tieck and Friedrich Hebbel. The choice of such a folkloristic, German subject showed good judgment. As in the case of Weber's *Freischütz,* the legend of the outcast countess had many of the qualities of

Romanticism including a forest setting. It served as the background for a tragic story, elaborated and dramatically treated by Friedrich Müller (not a source for Schumann), Tieck, and Hebbel. Though the text seemed a good choice it presented problems, for Reinick's arrangement did not fulfill Schumann's expectations.

Müller had submitted two outlines. One of them combined Genoveva's ban with an added, secondary plot which Schumann discarded, holding to his own plan which has Genoveva's expulsion and salvation occur in close succession in Act IV. Reinick tried to comply with the composer's every wish, but Schumann was put off by the tearful text.

Might the great Hebbel be of help? Schumann wrote to him: "I have received two acts; the remaining two ought to arrive any day. But in spite of the arranger's best intentions I cannot warm up to his style. Above all, it lacks *strength,* and I intensely dislike the typical language of librettos. I simply cannot set such tirades to music; they mean nothing to me. In my despairing state of mind it came to me that the direct way might be best—that I should turn to the true poet and ask him for help . . . I would not expect you to rewrite for an opera that which you already have completed in such a profound, masterly way. All I would ask is that you take a look at the text as a whole, give me your opinion, and lend your able assistance here and there. This is my earnest hope."

In a friendly but firm letter Hebbel declined to participate at this late stage, leaving Schumann no choice but to write his own libretto. The refusal grieved him all the more because Hebbel had made a profound impression on him when they met. His very intense approach to artistic creation seemed to be in harmony with Schumann's own. He called Hebbel "probably the greatest genius of our time," at the same time worrying that "if he doesn't overtax his strength he will arrive at the top," a warning Schumann might well have saved for himself.

Hebbel not only failed to find the meeting productive but rather annoying. He still recalled it in 1862: "After a brief greeting during which little was said I sat down next to him for a quarter of an hour. He stared at me, saying nothing, so I too remained silent, to see how long he would keep this up. When he didn't open his mouth once, I jumped up in desperation. Schumann also rose, took his hat, and walked next to me, silently. By now I had become annoyed and likewise kept silent. When we arrived at the hotel I quickly took leave without inviting him to come to my room."

Work on the *Genoveva* text was completed while Reinick was away from Dresden for several weeks. But upon his return he found that Schumann had made so many changes that he did not wish to have his name used as the author. As a result, the subtitle now reads "After Tieck and Hebbel."

Synopsis. After a solemn service Bishop Hidulfus of Trier calls for war against the Moorish prince Abdorrhaman whose armies are threatening the realm of the Franks. Siegfried is appointed commander of the troops; during his absence his young wife Genoveva is to be protected by Golo. But Golo is in love with Genoveva and would much prefer to go off to battle with the others. Siegfried leaves and Genoveva, fainting, falls into Golo's arms. He kisses her. Margaretha who was Golo's former nurse, but was banned from the castle because she practiced magic, observed this scene. She encourages Golo's passion and promises that she will help him to win Genoveva's love.

Genoveva, lonely, longs for Siegfried. She is frightened by noisy servants. Golo reports that news of a Frankish victory has caused the servants' high spirits. Without giving it much thought Genoveva asks her friend to sing a song with her. When Golo suddenly becomes overly familiar the troubled Genoveva can think of no way out but to call him (mindful of his obscure origin) a "dishonorable bastard." Deeply offended, Golo curses her and lays plans to kill her.

Soon after this the steward Drago tells Golo of a rumor that Genoveva is involved in an adulterous affair with her chaplain. Golo maliciously confirms the rumor and urges Drago to force his way into the young woman's bedchamber. Drago is discovered there and the people, taking him to be the supposed lover, kill him. Genoveva is thrown into the tower where she is to await Siegfried's judgment.

Meanwhile Siegfried lies wounded in a hospice in Strassburg. Margaretha leaves to find him, pretending to be a nurse. She undertakes the delay of his recovery by poisoning his water to gain time

Scene from Genoveva

for Golo, all the while telling of a magic mirror in which she can reveal past distant events. But Siegfried's only thought is to return home. Golo arrives with a letter intended to reveal Genoveva's infidelity but Siegfried so trusts Genoveva's fidelity that Golo is tempted to confess his guilt. But doubt arises in Siefried's mind, so turning to Margaretha's magic mirror he seeks to learn if the accusations against Genoveva are true. In a great rage he shatters the mirror and runs off. Drago's ghost arises from the shattered pieces and entreats Margaretha to reveal the truth lest she suffer death by fire.

Through a wild, rocky landscape Kaspar and Balthasar escort Genoveva, supposedly condemned to death by Siegfried, to the place of execution. Her prayer for strength is answered by consoling voices. Golo arrives, carrying Siegfried's ring and sword as symbols of his authority, to proclaim the death sentence. Once more he tries to win Genoveva for himself by promising to help her escape. When she refuses he orders her execution and rushes away. Genoveva in vain proclaims her innocence. At that moment distant horn calls and voices are heard: those of Siegfried and his followers whom Margaretha has led to the place. Once more united, the couple is led to the castle in a triumphal procession. There Hidulfus, among shouts of joy by the people, once more blesses their union.

Much of the character drawing in all this is left unclear and

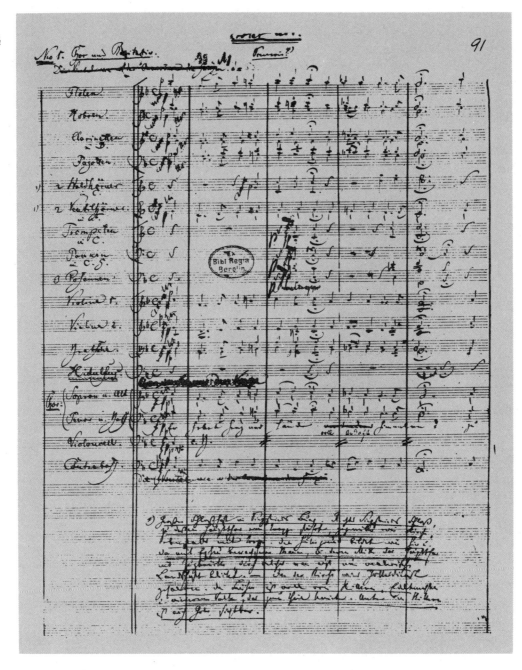

seems arbitrary. Schumann's own rather wooden additions to the text do not improve matters, possibly because he felt constricted by existing rhyme schemes. Nor did Wagner's criticisms, advanced with some arrogance, improve his self-confidence, even though some of them might well have been heeded. Schumann hid behind the excuse that Wagner was trying to spoil his effects, and even his closest friends lacked the courage to dissuade him from using such a hodgepodge of a text.

The score was completed late in the fall of 1848. Schumann asked Julius Rietz for his opinion as Rietz was to conduct the third and following performances. "Wherever an excess of music endangers the dramatic effect it must be sacrificed. I'd be thankful for any suggestions . . . Wagner is a poetic and clever person, but his evaluation does not go into purely musical matters. And Reissiger [the first Kapellmeister in Dresden] understands only his own music and that of the Philistines."

Schumann was satisfied with the text and did not seem to have sensed any dramatic flaws. He wrote to Heinrich Dorn: "*Genoveva!* You mustn't think of the old, sentimental one. To me it represents real life, the way any drama should. The text is based chiefly on Hebbel's tragedy."

Some of Schumann's notes from the days when work on *Genoveva* was in progress survive, laying out his ideas about the treatment of chorus, soloists, recitatives, and orchestra. (They were published by Boetticher.) He indicates that "the choral writing must be kept as light as possible. Unison writing for tenor and bass with octave doubling by soprano and alto produce a strong effect. Real four-part writing, spreading out the voices, only rarely is appropriate. Choruses must always be vigorous; high registers are to be avoided for all voices."

Considering Schumann's inexperience with the form, we must admire his careful consideration of his musical resources, and not only in connection with the choruses. He avoided the style of currently popular Italian composers, which is not surprising in view of his opinions aired in the *Zeitschrift*. Weber's *Euryanthe* served as a model. Like Wagner, Schumann considered traditional recitative outmoded; instead he provided musical declamation but avoided startling effects. Such practice was later to influence his Lieder style, but in the case of *Genoveva* merely resulted in the absence of contrast that was detrimental to the work's stage effectiveness.

"It represents real life:" Schumann's claim is not validated in the poorly drawn character of Golo, nor is it supported by the character of Margaretha. Demonic qualities are conveyed only in her music, and are there only suggested. The central character seems lifeless: she suffers her martyrdom in innocence. The sentimental passages at the beginning of Acts II and IV do not express the dramatic action which, following Hebbel, focuses on Golo and fails to provide for any character development of the title role. Nor did Schumann provide her with distinctive music. Her aria in Act IV opens with a distinctive horn theme (Example 61) which Schumann soon abandons without apparent reason and without exploiting its further potential.

The second finale in particular is unconvincing and lacks cohesion; indeed it seems to contain all the undesirable characteristics of French grand opera à la Meyerbeer. Though some of the transparent chromaticism which distinguishes Schumann's late works appears, and though some passages anticipate Wagner's *Tristan* sounds, with complex inner voices, these occasional areas of

Example 61

144

brilliant writing fail to offset the oratorio-like heaviness and a laggardly pace which becomes tiresome. Some musical symbolism that corresponds to the unraveling of the inner action occurs from time to time, it is delicate but never clearly delineated. Schumann did not share Wagner's path of associating themes with recollections; he shied away from anything that specific. Only in the overture, and perhaps in the incantation scene before the magic mirror, do we find distinctively profiled thematic material. A text of greater poetic substance might have compensated for the undramatic, song-like treatment of the high points. Had Schumann composed other operas he might have overcome the weaknesses of his first effort, but they remain unwritten.

The music for *Genoveva,* then, is epic in character; it does not express in any direct way the experiences of the protagonists. Rather the events seem to be related by a narrator. Rhythmic monotony gets in the way of dramatic action. His lack of dramatic experience led Schumann to transplant techniques used in the oratorio *Peri* to his opera, thus sealing its fate.

Otto Jahn, the Mozart biographer, pinpointed the opera's faults in terms that remain valid today: "There is hardly a single section that is self-contained, ending in a traditional manner. Instead, an uninterrupted stream of music reflects the continuous action. This seems strange to, and difficult for the listener. Though the composer's reasons are not difficult to understand, the listener is required to make a great effort . . . Furthermore, all situations are treated as though they were of equal importance. That Schumann should devote so much care and love to each and all is laudable, but again, it interferes with easy comprehension."

There is something ironic, but typical of Schumann's destiny, in his hope that *Genoveva* would exert a seminal, rejuvenating influence on German opera, for any such impact must surely be credited to his earlier oratorio. However, if we look for purely musical beauties in the opera we will find them in abundance. Siegfried's aria—when, after his recovery, he longs to return home—is full of pulsating energy. Golo's confession of love moves on forcefully with increasing tension, but suddenly dies away when Genoveva calls him back to reality; a skillfully handled scene. Similar high points are unfortunately absent in the concluding double chorus which is drawn out and void of inspiration. All that remains of the opera today is the overture which combines its principal themes and develops them symphonically.

Two years were to elapse before *Genoveva* was performed. The Leipzig theater wanted first to derive maximum benefit from the international success of Meyerbeer's *Le Prophète.* Schumann briefly referred in the *Zeitschrift* to Meyerbeer's work in the form of a death announcement! But his enthusiasm for his own opera was irrepressible. We shall come back to the reasons for its failure, but he refused to seek them in himself and his limited dramatic talent. Rather he blamed the operatic establishment of the day. Writing to C. F. Peters who published the opera he exclaimed: "If my work doesn't provide you a quick profit, the fault lies with the miserable condition of the theatrical world, especially the unspeakable bad taste of the public." (Letter of August 22, 1851).

Schumann completed the instrumentation of *Genoveva,* "to my great joy," on April 4. The next day's diary entry mentions "*Manfred*—great enthusiasm—sketches." By November 22 he already had completed the music for that play.

Chapter 19

In *Manfred,* Schumann perceived an image of himself: a life remaining incomplete and unfulfilled, the result of his progressive illness. There is little doubt as well that Manfred *is* Byron. John Galt, who was with Byron on the ship *Malta Pocket* in August of 1809, recalled:

> Everyone was under the spell of the mysterious aura that surrounded Lord Byron. It is true: occasionally he would descend from the clouds and be like any human being. But his element was the mysterious; he was at home in the onslaught of the storm and in the hidden recesses of guilt. . . . When he described Manfred he described himself.

It is evident in the opening scene of this "dramatic poem" that, though subjective and free, it is indebted to Goethe's *Faust.* Byron did not deny that he was well aware of Goethe's drama: "1816 in Coligny, Mathew Monk Lewis translated it for me, mostly by reciting it. Needless to say it made a deep impression on me." Even stronger was the impact of the Swiss Alps upon the poet and surely Byron's separation from his wife and emigration from England furnished additional reason to commit *Manfred* to paper. It cannot really be called a drama in the conventional sense; rather it is an epic work that has been dissolved into poetry—into dialogues and monologues. By using this form the writer made it impossible to stage the work which in turn kept it from realizing any lasting success.

The story, briefly recounted, tells of Manfred the magician, who, driven by guilt related to actions in his earlier years, takes solitary refuge in his mountain castle. There he converses with ghosts who are in his service. They cannot help him find peace, but they conjure up the apparition of a seductive young woman. As he is about to embrace her the apparition dissolves into nothing, but her voice curses him: "Thou shalt be thine own hell!" On the summit of the mountain *Jungfrau* Manfred contrasts the radiant world of the Alps with his own dark soul. No earthly beauty can move him. About to throw himself over the precipice, he is held back by a hunter who leads the magician to his mountain hut. In a monologue Manfred reveals the sources of his guilt: his incestuous love for his sister that led to her death. Shunned by society and alienated from the world, he now is approached by the Fairy of the Alps who offers him her help. Manfred rejects her offer as she is not one of the spirits in his service. Ariman, prince of the spirits, gives permission to Nemesis to conjure up the ghost of his sister, Astarte, who lies at the root of Manfred's suffering. She tells him of his imminent death, but when he begs for her forgiveness she departs. As Manfred lies dying a venerable abbott tries in vain to hear Manfred's confession and to bring him back into the folds of the church. To him, and to the demons who are about to take possession of his soul, Manfred shouts: "Away! I shall die as I have lived—alone."

This fictional tragedy reflected for Schumann the reality of his own. According to Clara, Byron's poem inspired him "extraordinarily." He read the work to a few friends; when he reached the moment of Astarte's apparition he was overcome with emotion and sobbing and was forced to stop. His strong emotional

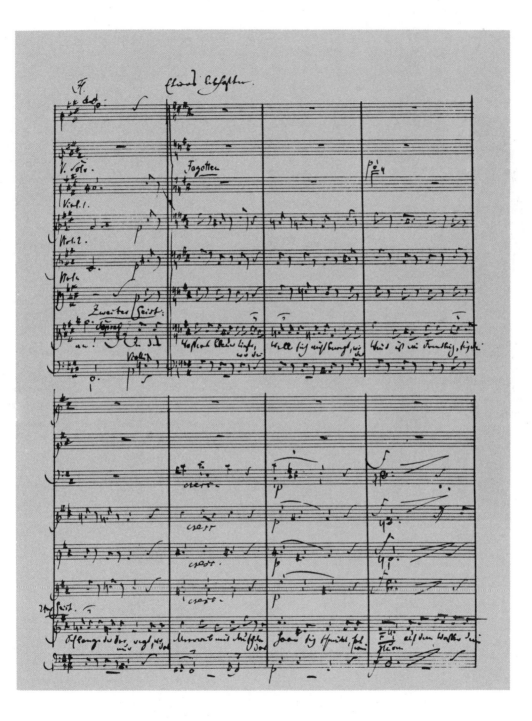

Franz Liszt as Conductor

reaction to this scene was to be decisive in his musical setting of it.

Having finished the composition of the overture, Schumann decided to celebrate this "birthday" with a bottle of champagne.

Schumann did not alter any of Byron's text, even though Suckow's translation is rather bombastic. He did not want to interfere with the flow of the language, particularly in those places where the text establishes moods independently of the music. He made good use of expressive devices that were part of his new style, including melodrama: spoken text accompanied by the orchestra. Its use is particularly convincing here. *Manfred* is based on the Romantic leitmotiv of "Salvation," so frequently found in early German Romanticism. Had Wagner not taken this leitmotif to further heights, *Manfred* might well have become the prime example of 19th Century musical innovation. Those portions that are sung or are purely orchestral are more convincing than the sections using melodrama, a medium that later turned out to be equally unsuccessful in works with piano accompaniment.

The following scenes were composed by Schumann:

PART I
Song of the Spirits—*Dein Gebot zieht mich heraus* (Alto and Soprano)
Apparition of a magic image—*O Gott, ist's so* (Melodrama, Manfred)
Curse of the Spirits—*Wenn der Mond auf stiller Welt* (Four bass voices)
Kuhreigen [*Ranz des vaches*, alpine dance]—*Horch, der Ton* (Melodrama, Alfred; hunter, accompanied by English horn)

PART II
Entr'acte
Incantation of the Fairy of the Alps—*Du schöner Geist* (Melodrama, Alfred)
Hymn of Ariman's spirits—*Heil unserm Meister* (Chorus)
Chorus of Spirits 1) *Wirf in den Staub*
2) *Zermalmt den Wurm* (Chorus)

Astarte's incantation—*Schatten! Geist!* (Melodrama, Nemesis)
Manfred's address to Astarte—*O höre mich, Astarte!* (Melodrama, Manfred)

PART III
Ein Friede kam auf mich (Melodrama, Manfred)
Farewell to the Sun—*Glorreiche Sonne* (Melodrama, Manfred)
Blick' nur hierher (Melodrama, Abbot, Manfred)
Finale: *Requiem aeternam* (Manfred, Abbott, Chorus)

For the apparition of the Fairy of the Alps, Schumann's instrumentation is suitably light. Great urgency characterizes the invocation of Astarte (Example 62).

In the overture, the most impressive part of the score, Schumann succeeds well in representing the protagonist's split personality. Precisely because there is no "program," the music tells us a good deal about Schumann as a person and about his compositional skill. He urged Franz Liszt, the conductor of the work's first performance, to take special care. "I consider it one of my healthiest creations." Though it avoids brilliant orchestration it represents a high point in Schumann's symphonic oeuvre. Even if the listener is unfamiliar with the drama, the music conveys a clear statement, just as the music of Beethoven's comparable overtures does. From the first angry, syncopated chords (Example 63) to the final collapse, with its dying-away conclusion in E♭ minor, there is a prevailing air of pessimism and resignation. As Wilhelm Furtwängler once said to this writer, "the message of the poet and the message of the composer agree."

Having completed the score, Schumann, quite typically, abandoned the plan for a stage performance. But the desire to have it performed on stage was rekindled in 1851 when he conducted the overture in Düsseldorf. It inspired him to write Liszt: "My hope [for a staged performance] is reawakened by you: did you again give it some thought? I have no doubt that it is feasible. A few problematic places will have to be discussed with the stage director, e.g. whether the spirits in Part I should be visible, as I think they should . . . It would be something new, really unprecedented."

Schumann suggested that Liszt not call the work "opera, *Singspiel,* or melodrama;" instead the printed program was to designate it "Dramatic Poem With Music." The music's sole function was to serve the poem, an "eloquent testimony to the poet's power and skill." Schumann opined that "interpreting the role of Manfred was of paramount importance." The music was merely the "outer wrapping," a view that will find little support today, given the impossible translation. An attempt to reconcile one of the recent

Example 63

Example 62

Hof-Theater.

Weimar, Sonntag den 13. Juni 1852.

Zum Erstenmale:

Manfred.

Dramatisches Gedicht in vier Abtheilungen, von Lord Byron,
nach den Uebersetzungen von A. Böttcher und Posgaru.
Musik von R. Schumann.

Manfred,..............................	Hr. Pätsch.
Gemsenjäger,..........................	Hr. Winterberger.
Abt von St. Maurice,...................	Hr. Jaffé.
Manuel, ⎫ Diener Manfreds,	Hr. Streit.
Hermann, ⎬	Hr. Grambach.
Königin der Alpen,....................	Fr. Don-Lebrun.
Ahriman,.............................	Hr. Genast.
Nemesis,.............................	Fr. Stör.
Erste ⎫	Fr. Genast.
Zweite ⎬ Schicksalsschwester,.........	Fr. Pätsch.
Dritte ⎭	Frl. Moltke.
Geist Astarta's,.....................	Fr. Hettstedt.
Böser Geist,.........................	Hr. Franke.
Geister.	

Die Scene ist in den höheren Alpen, theils in Manfreds Schloß, theils im Gebirge.

Die neue Dekoration ist vom Hof-Theatermaler Hrn. Händel.

Die Gesänge sind an der Kasse für 1 Sgr. zu haben.

Zweite Vorstellung im Eilften Abonnement.

Preise der Plätze:

	Thlr.	Sgr.	Pf.		Thlr.	Sgr.	Pf.
Fremden-Loge	1	—	—	Parterre-Loge	—	15	—
Balkon	—	20	—	Parterre	—	10	—
Sperrsitze	—	20	—	Gallerie-Loge	—	7	6
Parket	—	15	—	Gallerie	—	5	—

Anfang halb 7 Uhr.   Ende gegen 9 Uhr.

Die Billets gelten nur am Tage der Vorstellung, wo sie gelöst worden.

Der Zutritt auf die Bühne, bei den Proben wie bei den Vorstellungen, ist nicht gestattet.

Das Theater wird um 5 Uhr geöffnet.

Krank: Fr. Knopp. — Frl. Trandorff.

Announcement of first performance of Manfred

---

translations with Schumann's music might well be worthwhile. An arrangement by Richard Pohl for *one* narrator was used successfully by Ludwig Wüllner, the singer-actor, as described by Fritz Busch in the memoirs of his childhood.

As a stage work *Manfred* did not succeed. Not long ago it was attempted by the Rome Opera but soon taken out of the repertory. Byron himself tried to prevent its presentation on the stage of Drury Lane Theater, realizing that it was a drama to be read. Schumann also had to overcome serious reservations before Liszt, the indefatigable, brought the project to fruition. "The enormity of the undertaking made me shudder; but I also realize that once you lend a helping hand we eventually shall succeed, even if a first attempt should run into some obstacles."

Ill health prevented Schumann from attending the first performances on June 13 and 17, 1852, in Weimar. He expressed his gratitude to Liszt by making him a present of the autograph score. Schumann never was to hear a complete performance of his *Manfred*.

Chapter 20

Whenever there was an opportune time for intensive work, Schumann would seize it. He once wrote to Louis Ehlert that his "desk drawer contained many compositions from this happy period." Bötticher and Eismann mention three unpublished songs. There are drafts for *Ammenuhr* (text from *The Youth's Magic Horn), Der Weisse Hirsch* (Uhland), and *Das Schwert* (Uhland); they carry an instruction to the copyist to "make a clean copy," indicating that they surely were intended for publication.

In December 1848 Schumann returned to the piano, and to Rückert. Since the 1830s Schumann's writing for the piano had been chiefly devoted to etudes and chamber music, with the exception of concert pieces with orchestra for Clara's use. But now Rückert's poetry served as the inspiration for the six impromptus for four-hand piano entitled *Bilder aus dem Osten (Pictures from the Orient).* Bötticher has shown that in his copy of the Rückert texts Schumann had marked the *Makaman* (Arabic: verses interspersed with prose) Nos. 2, 6, 7, 13, 16 and 24. Later, in the preface, he pointed out that the sixth *Makaman* Impromptu was based on "The penitent Abu Seid in old age."

His *Album for the Young,* Opus 68, points to his and Clara's growing family. "When I wrote these pieces my musical mood was better than ever," he reported to Carl Reinecke. "Musical ideas came to me freely. I've become specially fond of the pieces; they are happy reflections of our family life. You will notice in them some of my humor from the good old days."

Other works followed these pieces for young people. *Advent Lied,* Opus 71, for soprano solo, choir and orchestra, also is based on a Rückert text. In it Schumann for the first time deals with sacred subject matter. He rejected the term "cantata" as "over-used" and instead chose "Geistliches Gedicht" for the subtitle. The work consists of seven separate sections. Christ's entry into Jerusalem has a pastoral flavor; His reception there is cast in the form of a festive chorus and constitutes the second section, ending in a fugato. The Prince of Peace is addressed (No. 3) by the soloists and a chorus of women's voices. A prayer for the Lord's return is set as a chorale. "Mankind's indignation" brings greater emotional intensity, after which the work concludes with another prayer for victory by the forces of light.

Adventlied is conceived on a larger scale. Here again Schumann shies away from obvious effects—from the manner of storytelling that so often imparts an operatic quality to an oratorio. Settings that call for "program music" tended to inhibit Schumann's inspiration; here he seems most at ease in the prelude and interlude. Following Handel, Haydn and Beethoven he is searching for a new, classic style—but it seems tentative, experimental: a body as yet without a soul.

At this time the revolutionary upheavals of 1848 had not yet reached Dresden. In arguments with skeptics Schumann showed great sympathy with the cause of freedom, yet he was opposed to any kind of violence. Financial and other concerns caused him to concentrate on work on the opera. Because of a difficult pregnancy Clara was unable to concertize and thus could not contribute to the family coffers. Schumann turned to his brother Carl for help with their rent. When Clara was again able to perform she contributed her fees to various charitable causes as the revolutionary struggles brought hardships to many. Some of the Schumanns' own financial problems were relieved by the publication of the *Ballads for Chorus,* which soon enjoyed good sales. As usual, Schumann carefully supervised the layout of the title page: "The words 'Ballads for Chorus' on the title page should stand out more than the word 'Romanzen.'" From this one should not conclude, however, that he considered the dramatic effects of these choruses to be more important than their lyrical qualities. Rather he wanted to stress what he considered their innovative aspects.

Schumann's preference for homophonic choral texture does not represent a diminishing of his compositional abilities. The same preference is found in *Ungewitter* (The Storm, Opus 67), written in 1840, but had already been used in his works from the "Year of Songs." To the contrary, the later choruses show, if anything, greater profundity and self-assurance.

In a collection of songs for women's voices, Opus 69, we find a setting of Uhland's well-known poem *Die Kappelle* (The Chapel). It shows Schumann intent on writing music that was folk-like and easy to sing. For the accompaniment a fashionable instrument of the time was used: the *Physharmonika,* invented in 1818 by Häckl and featuring a keyboard activating strings as well as pipes. The wind supply was generated by pedals in the manner of a harmonium. Use of this instrument was intended to appeal to a large audience, even though the composition itself is in the strict Baroque form of a double canon. Hans Pfitzner provided orchestral accompaniments for some of these songs.

Four Songs for Double Chorus, Opus 141, represent Schumann's most mature choral writing. They were intended for large choral societies and represent the sum of his experience in writing for chorus. Goethe's *Talismane* suggests the character of a motet. *Zuversicht,* text by Zedlitz, is the most impressive piece in this set, going far beyond routine homophonic writing.

Schnitter Tod (Death, the Reaper), the first chorus in Opus 75, is a setting of the well-known medieval poem. The first four verses are in minor keys; the fifth verse, dealing with defiance and confidence, changes to major and is the most moving. Eichendorff's *Im Walde* might represent a wish to make amends: it had been included in the *Liederkreis* without the second verse, which is included here. But the choral version lacks the inspiration of the solo song. In spite of this it came to enjoy the favor of many choral groups. In *Der traurige Jäger* (The Mourning Hunter, Opus 75, No. 3; text by Eichendorff) we are moved by the ostinato passage, representing the sad hunter playing his horn calls "while his heart is breaking."

Occasionally Schumann's contemporaries must have been troubled by his daring harmonies, always employed for special, expressive effects. He remonstrated with Franz Brendel who had succeeded him as editor of the *Neue Zeitschrift für Musik:* "I was pleased with the frank reviews of my choral ballads—but I am not aware of any harmonic harshness except where it would be justified by the text. And I must solemnly protest against the accusation of 'striving for effect.' That notion is most distasteful to me."

From time to time Robert and Clara would ask Lüttichau, the director of the court theater in Dresden, for free tickets to performances. He seems to have been rather "stingy" with these—but when the couple did have a chance to observe the artistry of Mme. Schröder-Devrient they were no less impressed than Wagner had been. It may be that this great singer-actress was the principal reason for Schumann's renewed interest in song writing. At this point in his career he invented the medium of the song cycle for several solo voices.

Next to *Spanische Liebeslieder,* Opus 138, and their German counterpart, *Minnespiel* (Love Songs, Opus 101, texts by Rückert), *Spanisches Liederspiel* (Opus 74, texts by Geibel, based on Spanish poets) is the most important of these cycles. They portray individuals recounting for each other their feelings. Schumann imbued these songs with a richness of color and a fiery temperament that express well their southern European flavor. Their folk-like qualities also help to make this cycle one of Schumann's most gracious works. He wrote to Reinecke: "I think that *Liederspiele* is quite novel as to its form, and sounds very cheerful . . . These, I predict, will be among my most successful songs. This I credit to the charming, cheerful poems." They later were sensitively transcribed by Geibel, a very popular poet, from works of earlier Spanish writers.

But Schumann was proven wrong: the period during which he wrote these nine pieces (plus an added one for baryton) came to be

JOSEPH CHRISTIAN
BARON VON ZEDLITZ
(1790–1862)

Zedlitz attended the *Gymnasium* in Breslau with
Eichendorff. After serving as an officer he settled in
Vienna where he remained except for some trips to
Southern Germany and Italy. His poetry was popular and
patriotic; his short stories and plays followed Spanish
models.

regarded as one of artistic decline. There were few performances.
In the two solo songs, five duets, and two quartets we experience
the story of a love, from the first bashful encounter to assured
happiness.

In *Erste Begegnung* (First Encounter, Opus 74, No. 1) we immediately hear Spanish rhythms, most attractive in these concise
phrases. Here as in most of the Spanish songs the title was provided
by Schumann. A few lines of text ("Und am Rosenbusch, o Mutter /
Einen Jüngling seh ich") do not occur in Geibel's poem and
presumably were added by the composer. *Intermezzo,* Opus 74, No.
2, is a serenade telling of a nocturnal abduction. It charms with
harmonies moving in the same "blissful thirds and sixths" that we
will encounter in Brahms's *Liebeslieder* Waltzes. Next is a passionate
duet for women's voices, *Liebesgram* (Love's Sorrow, Opus 74, No.
3). The text, an imaginary dialogue, had already been set as a solo
song. The present version produces a more dramatic effect, partly
through the nostalgic ending, in the major mode, of each verse.

The piano establishes the melancholic, nocturnal mood of *In der
Nacht* (At Night, Opus 74, No. 4). Its meandering lines correspond
to the intervals then heard in the solo voices. The song is characterized by these and by harmonic instability. It is a jewel among
Schumann's duets, regrettably not well known. Its most moving
moment occurs when (at the reference to "hopeless grief") there is
a momentary turn to the major mode.

More cheerful moods prevail in the quartet *Es ist verraten* (It
Cannot Be Concealed, Opus 74, No. 5). Spanish color is called for
by the indication "In the tempo of a Bolero." The four singers tease
the girl who cannot hide her feelings of unrequited love. Her
sorrow is contrasted (in the manner of a Baroque opera buffa) with
the mirth of the others. In *Melancholie,* Opus 74, No. 6, love's tor-
ment is first painted with bold strokes in the piano part and then
transferred to the voice. Here, too, there is an unrestrained quality
evocative of Southern temperament. But pain soon gives way to
other emotion: in the following song, *Geständnis* (Confession, Opus
74, No. 7), the tenor avows his ardent love, boldly, à la Florestan.
Botschaft (Message, No. 8), continually changes from serious to
roguish moods, in a way that is typical of the cycle as a whole.
Bolero rhythms dominate and the basic mood remains cheerful.
Finally, in *Ich bin geliebt* (I Know I Am Loved, No. 9), the "evil
tongues" and their gossiping are accentuated by "slurs" in the piano
part.

There are only two numbers in *Liederspiel* that call for a bass
voice. Most likely Schumann wanted to make up for this imbalance
by writing one additional song: *Der Contrabandiste* (The Smuggler,
Opus 74, App.)—one of the rare examples of a buffoonish
Schumann song. Sixteenth-notes, difficult to execute, suggest the
prancing of the "dear horse." There is little concern with the
meaning of individual words here, but the prevailing virtuoso
quality led Carl Tausig and later Serge Rachmaninoff to arrange the
piece for solo piano.

Schumann suggested to the publisher Kistner that the design of
an artistic title page should be entrusted to the painter Ludwig
Richter, Schumann's friend, to replace the "cheap" graphics of
Schuberth, but Kistner did not comply. (Richter's son had been
Schumann's composition student.)

During April and May of 1849 Schumann worked steadily in spite of the unexpected death of brother Carl. The Dresden uprising in May also interfered with creative work. Just before, on April 29, Clara had arranged a morning recital. The program featured the Piano Trio in F Major and the completed protions of *Liederspiel.*

On May 3d, there were uprisings in Baden-Baden, the Palatinate, and Dresden, against which Prussian troops were enlisted. The Schumann family packed their belongings and left, at first for Maxen, then for Kreischa, in order to avoid the possibility that Robert might be forced to join the insurgents. An article in the *Augsburger Allgemeine Zeitung* shortly thereafter informed the family that the revolution had been put down. They also read that a warrant for the arrest of Kapellmeister Richard Wagner had been issued: he had sided with the insurgents, hoping thereby to advance his musical career.

Robert Reinick had supplied verses to accompany a series of woodcuts by his friend Alfred Rethel, entitled *Auch ein Totentanz* (Another Dance of Death). Here Death becomes a "hero of the revolution." When, after all the suffering, "order" had been restored, Rethel described the catastrophe to his mother: "A great, magnificent effort that would have been to Germany's honor was brutally put down by cold-blooded military action. At first I had regarded this movement with suspicion, expecting a "red" republic, communism and all that goes with it. But it turned out to be supported by the truly noble enthusiasm of the people . . . a mission, divinely inspired, rather than something brought about by radical talk in bad newspapers or by demagogues."

Schumann, like Rethel, supported some aspects of the popular uprising including the amalgamation of the many small independent German states. But he objected to the abuse of this yearning for freedom by a few who endeavored to superimpose other political objectives upon it. Rethel's series of "Dance of Death" woodcuts found allegorical reflection in Schumann's *Spielmann.*

Was the composer losing touch with his own time? While Wagner manned the barricades, Schumann retreated to his creative work, and though he worked at a hectic pace, his compositions became increasingly subdued. One gains the impression that those

qualities that account for his greatness by that time belonged to the past. On the surface it seems that the retreat was voluntary, but it really seems to have taken place out of an inner necessity. True enough: men of genius often are not part of the age in which they were living, and revolutionary upheavals often have an adverse effect on their intellectual vitality. In this case, however, appearances are deceiving: Schumann carried the banner for artistic change up to his last years, when despair related to his illness overwhelmed him. Only rarely, now, did work of his youth have a bearing on his writing: he did not wish to coast on his former accomplishments. If occasionally he reverted to a style or technique of the past this was the exception to the rule. The past never appeared to him as some luminous aura, so he kept a distance between himself and his youth works, losing no opportunity to belittle them. To live as a prince of music, affecting his fellow men and giving them happiness—this was a dream that accompanied him to the grave. Illness, depression and alcohol were to blame. Great events that affected the course of history impinged upon him but only spurred him to greater efforts in his own work.

A look at the *Four Duets for Soprano and Tenor,* Opus 78, is in order. They rank above the first series of duets in freshness of inspiration. Ambitious musical goals are revealed in the choice of Goethe's *Ich denke dein* (I think of Thee), written by the poet for a melody by Zelter. Moreover, it was eventually set by over 80 other composers. *Wiegenlied am Lager eines kranken Kindes* (Cradle Song For An Ailing Child, text by Hebbel) concludes this group—a sincere reflection of a father's feelings. In the music, suspensions and certain chord sequences remind us of *Kind im Einschlummern* (Child Falling Asleep) from the *Scenes from Childhood* (Examples 64 and 65).

Liederalbum für die Jugend and *Minnespiel* are groups of songs that had been put aside in April which Schumann now hastened to complete. A small piano collection, the *Album für die Jugend,* intended for use in the home, had been written between *Genoveva* and *Manfred*— one might say for recreation, but also as an 1848 birthday offering for their daughter Marie. "It comes straight from our family; I felt as though I had gone back to my beginnings as a composer." A plan to include pieces by other composers eventually was dropped.

Example 6 4

Example 6 5

Musikalische Haus- und Lebensregeln (Musical Rules for the House and for Life), originally also to be included, were published separately later. Though some pieces were given new titles they remained musically unchanged. Ludwig Richter, painter and friend, was asked to design the decorative title page. He came to see the Schumanns to learn what Robert had in mind. While Clara played the pieces the composer sat next to her, "his head lowered and his eyes half closed." Before each piece he whispered some explanatory remarks.

The collection was a success, at a time when Schumann again had turned to song writing. He therefore thought of writing something in a similar vein. The result was a new species of children's songs, such as Taubert and Reinecke were to develop further. Again Schumann was more interested in character drawing than in the expression of personal feelings. To his publisher Emanuel Klitzsch he made suggestions about the songs and their order: "They them-selves will explain best what I had in mind. I composed poems suitable for young people, chosen from only the best writers, proceeding from the easy to the more difficult. Mignon provides the conclusion, providing insights into a more complex soul."

Schumann succeeded admirably; he found the tone of what then was popular, thus ensuring the songs' appeal to young singers. None of the pieces became a true folk-song—but Schumann's intention was to lead subtly to a higher level of artistry. Because the range of subjects is wider, that intention is carried out even more convincingly here than in the album of piano pieces. The songs reflect Schumann's, the teacher's, interpretation of what attracted young people to music. Wallowing in emotion would have had the opposite effect, as would the pseudo-innocent and the purely playful. The composer tried to understand the emotions of growing up, to express the feelings and concepts to which young people can relate. In this sense these miniature pieces, though easy to play, can be considered small works of art.

The moderately-paced pieces in this collection of songs some-times suffer in performance from dragging tempos, so that their meaning is distorted. Schumann never wanted his music to be burdened with pathos: the metronome markings in the complete edition (which Clara helped edit) testify to this. Perhaps there is some truth to Joseph Joachim's claim that Schumann's metronome did not work properly, resulting in tempo markings that are too fast. The high metronome numbers given to instrumental works of moderate speed (not all songs have metronome markings) should, at any rate, avoid overly emotional interpretations and help per-formers to think of Schumann's own tempos as "intelligent" and lean. Later in life Clara was inclined to perform lively movements in an expansive, sentimental manner, but that is a different matter. They had always disagreed about tempos, as shown by their diary communications: "dearest little Clara, I cannot agree with you. Only the composer knows the proper interpretation of his works." Her pedal markings, dynamic indications, also those metronome markings that are hers, were of course the result of her own growth as a pianist which continued to the time, much later, when she participated in editing of Robert's complete works. During her long career Clara's style of performance underwent many changes. Nietzsche heard her play in her old age and offered his sarcastic verdict: "Gentle lyricism and uncontrolled, intoxicated emotion." In such remarks he took issue with her interpretive style rather than with Robert's music which he esteemed highly.

In *Der Abendstern* (The Evening Star, Opus 79, No. 1) the device of descending fifths is borrowed from the song *Mein schöner Stern*. It serves to express poetically the child's longing for a star. Schumann substituted the title *Schmetterling* (Butterfly, Opus 79, No. 2) for Fallersleben's original *Wie gut bin ich dir* (How Fond I Am of You) in order to avoid any sentimentality. One might chuckle when in *Frühlingsbotschaft* (Message of Spring, Opus 79, No. 3) we hear the cuckoo's call sounding more like a military fanfare—perhaps not surprising, since the text was written by the author of *Deutschland über Alles* [the German national anthem]. Schumann here, in his search for a distinctive, musically expressive style, was intent on avoiding realistic tone painting—more intent than other contemporary composers, such as Hugo Wolf. While earlier composers, e.g. Schubert, inevitably resorted to the musical equivalents of bird calls, Schumann avoided them, even in situations such as this, where the text practically demands them.

The musical material of this song is further elaborated in *Frühlingsgruss* (Spring Greetings, Opus 79, No. 4; text by Fallersleben). In the piano part we hear horn-like passages with no obvious intention in the text. Four of Fallersleben's poems deal with spring; it is the basic theme of the entire collection. Schumann avoids folk-song flavor, but the song is childlike and lively, following the prosody of the text throughout. It achieved great popularity.

Politically, Fallersleben was counted among the radicals; his poem *Vom Schlaraffenland* (From the Land of Plenty, Opus 79, No. 5) may have implied some social criticism. Schumann, however, interprets it purely from a child's perspective. He did not set the fifth verse. *Sonntag* (Sunday, Opus 79, No. 6), innocent and quiet, must have appealed to Brahms; there are echoes of it in his *Komm bald* (Come Soon) (Example 66).

Example 66

Zigeunerliedchen I (Little Gypsy Song, Opus 79, No. 7) is based on Geibel's translation of an anonymous poem. It resembles *Talismane* in that several (three in this instance) four-line verses are combined to make up a single composition. Though the music is essentially light and airy, with a slightly Hungarian flavor, one also catches glimpses of the persecuted gypsy's feelings of bitterness and aggression. *Zigeunerliedchen II* shows particularly well how feelings of melancholy and despair can be expressed with great economy of means. *Des Knaben Berglied* (Mountain Song of the Shepherd Boy, Opus 79, No. 8) adds Ludwig Uhland to the list of those who supplied *Lieder* texts for Schumann, though he is more frequently represented in the choral songs.

The revolutionary undertones, so characteristic of Uhland, barely come through in the fanfares of *Des Knaben Berglied,* in part because Schumann did not compose the second verse.

It is no mere accident that Schumann's *Liederalbum für die Jugend* includes some songs for several voices. This is either implied by the text or can be justified on formal grounds. Mendelssohn, in his duets, does not draw individual characters; he is interested in purely musical matters. But Schumann always explores "the inner life of a poem." Thus the two or three protagonists of a poem became

LUDWIG
UHLAND

Ludwig Uhland (1787–1862), poet and literary scholar, attended the *Gymnasium* and university in Tübingen. From 1802 to 1808 he studied law as well as medieval literature, especially, French and German poetry. His first poems were published, some under the pen name Volker. A stay in Paris followed in 1810; he studied Napoleonic law and avidly read manuscripts in old French and middle high German. On his return to Germany he reluctantly accepted a position as an attorney in Stuttgart. The Wars of Liberation aroused his patriotism. Since he resided in Württemberg, a member of the Confederation of the Rhine, he could only participate to the extent of expressing his hopes and good wishes. Soon after, in 1815, he published the volume of poems which (in its 10th, enlarged edition) provided Schumann with texts. These poems show Uhland as an accomplished representative of early Romanticism. He was fond of

dealing with medieval life and was chiefly attracted to folk subjects. This may account for his success and far-reaching influence. He was able to write simply and concisely, equalled only by Goethe and Heine. What he lacked in passion he made up in his unassuming and clear style. He was not above some sentimentality, especially in his early writing. Ballads and romances were his forte. They display the simple, down-to-earth language that Schumann preferred. Uhland also wrote plays. *Ernst, Duke of Suabia* and *Ludwig of Bavaria* both lack energy and momentum and were only moderately successful.

After 1816 Uhland turned to politics and science. He took part in the disputes surrounding the Württemberg constitution and later became a deputy for the liberal party. An essay on Walter von der Vogelweide led to a professorship in German literature and brought him to Tübingen in 1829. He soon resigned from this position when, in 1832, the government refused to grant him a leave to become a deputy. His marriage to Emilie Vischer relieved him of material worries so he was able to divide his time between political activity and scholarly work. He had withdrawn from politics for several years when the unrest of 1848 once more caused him to become active. He was a member of the left in the first German national assembly when he spoke out vigorously against hereditary monarchy, and he accompanied the Rump Parliament to Frankfurt and Stuttgart. In 1850 he retired and settled in Tübingen, occupying himself with the completion of literary studies. Uhland's old age was happy: his simple, modest and uncompromising character moved him to decline any official honors, which led to the high regard in which he was held by members of all political parties.

musical personalities also, unless the concept of a simple folk song mandated otherwise.

The text of *Mailied* had been called "Fliegendes Blatt," i.e., "fly sheet" or "broadside," but actually goes back to the Rococo poet Christian Adolf Overbeck. His poem became well known through Mozart's setting. Its original title had been "Fritzchen an den Mai." The three songs *Das Glück* (Good Luck; Hebbel), *Frühlingslied,* and

Die Schwalben (The Swallows, from the *Wunderhorn* collection) offer great challenges to the singer, both in the fast-paced dialogue and the spirited scherzo.

Marienwürmchen (Lady Bug, Opus 79, No. 14; *Wunderhorn*) and *Hinaus ins Freie* (Into the Open, Opus 79, No. 12; text by Fallersleben) contrast in both key and mood. In the second song, rising triadic figures at the beginning of each verse express feelings of joy and vitality occasioned by the coming of spring. *Der Sandmann*, Opus 79, No. 13, is taken from a collection of poems by Hermann Kletke (1813–86). It is a charming song: humorous, playful and imaginative, supported by a fleet-footed accompaniment in which the "fine little boots" fairly dance. To come up with a second verse of equal stature Schumann repeats some passages of the text. *Marienwürmchen* became popular as a children's song; in its great simplicity it indeed sounds as though it were one, old and traditional. *Die Waise* (The Orphan Girl, Opus 79, No. 15; Fallersleben) is surpassed by the piano piece *Armes Waisenkind* found in the album of the previous year. Schumann had planned to omit the fourth stanza, a mournful conclusion, but Clara considered it essential.

Whenever Schumann composed a work for a specific, festive occasion he tended to fall into conventional patterns. *Weihnachtslied* (Christmas Song, Opus 79, No. 17; No. 16 in the complete edition) is a case in point. It uses an anonymous translation of an Anderson poem. Careful listening will reveal the mystic quality that distinguishes Schumann's later works. The cantus firmus G-F#-E-A, without any evident meaning, extends over two measures and recurs in the second stanza. "Alleluia," the choral refrain, seems somewhat overdone in this context. Quite convincing, on the other hand, is the dry, pedantic beginning of *Die wandelnde Glocke* (The Walking Church Bell, Opus 79, No. 18; Goethe) which then leads into the absorbing tale, coupled with a strong sense of the grotesque. The intentional rhythmic monotony is interrupted by accents and jarring chords when the bell comes, hobbling along. Even though the great Goethe is involved Schumann deviates from the text three times, for the sake of his melodic line. The song is just right for a child's comprehension; it is in no way inferior to Loewe's famous setting.

Frühlingsankunft (Spring's Arrival, Opus 79, No. 19; Fallersleben) demonstrates Schumann's new regard for declamation of the text. In order to point up the intended meaning of the poem, the words "zerrissene Wolken" are emphasized at the expense of "tragen," the word that supplies the rhyme. A reflective mood is indicated by the piano accompaniment with its 16th-notes, subtle counterpoint, and interludes. Contrary to his usual practice

Schumann omits the poet's repetition of a word ("Herz" in measure 26) because his musical concept allows no room for it. In *Des Sennen Abschied* (The Herdsman's Farewell, Opus 79, No. 23; text from Schiller's *Wilhelm Tell*) a flowing Swiss melody is played on the shawm rather than on the *Alphorn* as is indicated. At the point where the tune sung by the herdsman reaches a daring modulation it suddenly ends, as though he did not know how to go on (Example 67). This is the play's opening scene. Its music here recalls the Swiss herdsman's tune, the *ranz des vaches*. Meyerbeer once used the melody, note for note, in a song, though he did not go to the trouble of using Schumann's imaginative changes of keys. At the thought of the coming of another May the melody strays to E major—but the awareness that it really is fall, and spring far away, leads to the return to C major. Schumann repeats the words "im lieblichen" and the last six measures.

Example 67

Er ist's (Come, Spring!, Opus 79, No. 24; Mörike) is a superb poem. Schumann does not altogether do it justice for he changed the text in several places for no apparent reason. The words "von fern ein leiser" are omitted, so that all that remains of that line of text is "horch, ein Harfenton!" Elsewhere Schumann introduces word repetitions; they influenced Hugo Wolf in his setting of the poem which is far more convincing. A comparison with Robert Frantz's version also is worthwhile. Towards the conclusion Schumann's music does capture the feeling of great elation, though for once he requires more volume and power than a young, untrained voice might be able to muster.

William Tell was a very appropriate play for Schumann to read at this time. On the manuscript of *Des Buben Schützenlied* (The boy's

Ludwig Richter: title page for
Lieder für die Jugend, *Op. 79*

hunting song, Opus 79, No. 26) Schumann noted: "May 3d, (revolution in Dresden)." The boy's song, however, does not suggest that Schumann was unusually inspired, for the musical lines do not bring anything new. The melodic declamation is in stubborn conflict with the text's basic rhythm.

Schumann's style in *Schneeglöckchen,* (Snow drops, Opus 79, No. 27, Rückert), on the other hand, sounds easy and natural as though it came from his most successful period of song writing. He omitted four verses of the poem. In *Lied Linceus des Türmers* (Song of Lynceus the Watchman, Opus 79, No. 28, from Goethe's *Faust, Part II*), the "young" of the collection's title have reached manhood. At the volume's conclusion we find Mignon's *Kennst du das Land* (Opus 79, No. 29, from Goethe's *Wilhelm Meister*) which, as we shall see, also furnishes the opening for the group of Goethe songs, Opus 98a.

All of Schumann's experience as a song writer is reflected in these *Lieder für die Jugend,* with the exception of ballad-like qualities. The latter was saved for repertory that addressed itself to adults. After Schumann's contributions—modest, unpretentious and therefore convincing—no one else undertook to stimulate interest among young people in the *Lied* by providing works specifically written with them in mind.

Again great care was given to the design of the printed volume. For the title page Schumann desired something "simpler, with fewer figures," and Ludwig Richter seemed to be the ideal person to supply it. After an initial conversation Richter accepted for a moderate fee.

Work provided the antidote to the upheavals of the revolution and to other problems. *Album für die Jugend, Minnespiel,* and the *Jagdlieder für Männerchor* (Hunting songs for Male Chorus, Opus 137) were composed in Kreischa near Dresden, the Schumann family's refuge during these turbulent times. Other works written there include the *Four Marches for the Year 1849* for piano, Opus 76, and the motet for double chorus of male voices, *Verzweifle nicht im Schmerzenstal* (Opus 93; Rückert). The latter most likely was written out of sympathy with those who had taken part in the May insurrection. The conciseness for which Schumann was increasingly striving is replaced in this work by a certain long-windedness. For a performance in Düsseldorf in 1852, the organ part was replaced by orchestral accompaniment, but this did not make the work more colorful or harmonically more interesting. The *Jagdlieder für Männerchor* also date from the Kreischa sojourn. Heinrich Laube's *Jagdbrevier* supplied the texts; the score calls for four horns ad libitum. Clara published these works posthumously. Laube, otherwise a witty travel writer, contributed poetry that was disappointing, heavily German in a sentimental way. *Frühe* (Daybreak), the fourth chorus, is the only one that is fresh and lively.

Clara's diary faithfully records the events of the time, including political discussions at home. One reflected on the need for a free press as well as the hoped-for abdication of the hated princely government. In November Robert summed up: "The period was most stimulating for me. I never accomplished more, and I never was happier as an artist." But his art increasingly was to be an escape. "I am affected by everything that goes on: politics, literature, people. I reflect on everything in my own way; my thinking finds release in music." It seems that the changes he went through at this time of political change were affected by it; but also were due to his artistic development and not to problems related to his illness. As he approached the end of his career Schumann was looking for new ways to come to terms with reality. The revolution, a time of great upheaval, now was a thing of the past, and he searched for new meaning for his life. What this meaning was is hard for us to determine, even knowing his music. When he was young, men with similar middle-class backgrounds sought to express themselves through tears, embraces, and confessions—but this now was out of fashion. While others turned either to the bombastic or the overly refined, Schumann was about to set out on a road to a new simplicity.

Clara found it strange that all the frightening events in the outside world "affected his poetic sensibilities in the opposite manner." She had played through the just completed *Liederalbum* on an instrument belonging to the organist-choirmaster in Kreischa. "All these songs exude an air of greatest peace—everything seems like spring, laughing, blossoms." Robert's response to the political movements of the time is hard to define. Remarks in letters and the diary merely contain generalities. Did daily life come to a

HEINRICH LAUBE
(1806–1884)

Laube was born in Silesia, the son of a mason. After studying theology, church history, and literature he became a private tutor. In Leipzig he became an editor for the *Zeitung für die elegante Welt,* the leading journal of the "Young Germany" movement. Because of his liberal writings he was expatriated in 1834 and was imprisoned in Berlin for nine months pending trial. Another 18 months were spent in a kind of exile, restricted to the castle of his friend, Prince Pückler-Muskau. Later he was active as a journalist in Vienna, a delegate to the Frankfurt National Assembly, and became director of the Vienna Burgtheater. In 1871 he founded the Stadttheater there.

At first Laube wrote extensively for "Young Germans"; later his interest in the theater led to play writing and the translation into German of French plays. His memoirs and reviews represent an interesting contribution to theater history of his time.

standstill? One took it more seriously. Were there more inhibiting contradictions than before? That would hardly have been possible. One came to the defense of weak men and disregarded the strong ones. Blockheads, without any talent, enjoyed playing the part of a "loner" or "oddball." People continued to read their family magazines and to visit the theater, unconcerned with the birth pangs of a new age—pains that Schumann viewed as decadent and pathological exaggerations. Politicians cared not a whit about the thoughts of artists, and public institutions remained isolated from whatever was new.

On the day after Robert's birthday the Schumanns returned to Dresden, much to Clara's regret. The city seemed to have been turned into a fortress by the Prussian occupation, but nothing seemed to interfere with Robert's obsession with work. For the time being he had risen above depression and alcoholism and found in his art a release from the discords in the world around him. His work—hectic, proceeding at breakneck speed—was not without traces of carelessness.

Once more he turned to writing songs, but his frame of mind now differed from what it was in 1840. He composed under great pressure of time, as though he knew that the years ahead, including his conducting duties in Düsseldorf and the deterioration of his health, would make creative work impossible. His mania for work suggests that he wanted to assure himself of a bountiful compositional harvest while he still could. In this he differed from Schubert who was simply swept along by the torrent of musical inspiration. Schumann seems to have been clearly aware of the end of his composing life and his mounting physical afflictions. We must be careful, however, in making these judgments, as we might arrive at wrong conclusions and the characterization of his late compositions as otherworldly.

Wörner rightly indicates that Schumann's orchestral experience now "is evident in every measure we hear." Through his performances of works for chorus and orchestra he became increasingly familiar with their possibilities. It is reflected in his treatment of vocal cantilena and in his occasional turn to a kind of Sprechgesang—a vocal style closely observing the melody and rhythm of speech. Schumann again experimented with new subjects, especially with the dramatic ballad. In doing so he rose above the constraints of his depressions. The degree to which he applied himself to his work varied, but when Moser remarked that there were "hardly more than a dozen songs" after 1849 as significant he merely repeated an often-stated, biased point of view. Young singers should not be discouraged by the difficulties of Schumann's late songs for they will be rewarded by their beauty. This is not to deny that some of the orchestrally conceived material in the accompaniment, prior to this time normally transformed into genuinely pianistic writing, now often appears to be a mere keyboard reduction.

Having returned to Dresden, Schumann, after reading Wilhelm Meister for the third time, tackled the composition of the poems that Goethe had sprinkled throughout the text: the songs of Mignon and the harper. It was a new world for Clara; for Robert it was a rediscovery. His was a special fondness for literature, which led him to explore it with a diligence and receptivity to its beauty that went beyond what one might expect from a song writer or a composer preoccupied with operatic projects. While still in Kreischa Schumann had begun to compose the Mignon songs. Out of these grew the Requiem For Mignon which, according to his own account, was "sketched on July 2–3, 1849 in Dresden." Clara, whose son Ferdinand was about to be born, first heard the Wilhelm Meister songs when Robert played them for her on July 3d; she was "profoundly moved."

We already have met Mignon; her Kennst du das Land formed the conclusion of the Jugendalbum. It inspired Schumann to set other poems from the novel. It should be noted here that virtually all composers of Lieder have also been inspired by these poems. According to his diary Schumann had planned to collect all his Goethe songs in a single volume. Thus the Ballade des Harfners (The Harper's Ballad, entitled Der Sänger by Schubert and Wolf) became No. 2 of Opus 98a, so that Kennst du das Land, Opus 98a, No. 1, served as the introduction. The famous poem is treated here in a manner suitable for an "Album for the Young" so it should not be compared with Beethoven's and Schubert's settings. In all his Goethe songs Schumann, characteristically, was not so much fascinated by the exuberance of youthful poetry but by the expressions of grief found in the Wilhelm Meister excerpts and in the thoughtful qualities of the West-östlicher Divan (Divan of East and West). Schumann's reaction to great poetry, always intense, is here stimulated by characters who are veiled in mystery—not in the quasi-mythological manner of Schubert but psychologically fascinating for the composer. By probing their mysteries Schumann did not rob these characters of their stature, but found a place for them in the language of Romantic music. This happened at the expense of clarity of musical form, as will be seen when we compare Schubert's *Wilhelm Meister* settings with those by Schumann: the latter are characterized by imbalance and unrest.

The increasing sense of resignation in *Kennst du das Land* seems arbitrary; it proceeds from the forceful first "Dahin" to the rather passive repetition of the figure at the end in the piano. Between these we hear constant repetitions of the intervals d-g and g-c. These skips of a fourth are gradually obscured by their harmonic treatment. Finally there are no more modulations; G minor emerges as the established tonality. The meaning of this aphorism about Mignon's longing is not made clear until the last measures. Schumann here strives for continuous musical flow, as shown by the ritornello-like use, between the song's stanzas, of the opening measures (Example 68). It is a difficult objective to achieve, for there are many passages that do not blend—that remain distinct as they observe the meaning of the text.

Example 68

Mignon's enigmatic personality is characterized in the piano part by many leaps, mournful chromaticism and dissonant appoggiaturas. Unlike Beethoven, Schumann refrains from describing the landscape in any pictorial sense. There is an occasional nod towards tone painting, such as the triplet motion when the text refers to "gentle wind." Zelter and Beethoven did the same. Both the lofty and the idyllic are treated distinctively by Schumann, just as both might exist in Mignon's mind. Livia Frege indicated how pleased she was to have the song included in the Goethe collection. Schumann must have been doubly pleased: the song had been written "with excitement, but also to the accompani-

ment of much noise by our children in Kreischa."

In the *Ballade des Harfners* Goethe presents his allegorical view of the place of the artist in society—for composers, including Schubert and Wolf, not the most fertile source of inspiration. Compared with these two, Schumann did not fare well. He tried to compensate for the poem's length with an abundance of thematic material, developing six themes just to represent the harp. The piano slavishly follows the singer, responding to the subtlest nuances of the text. So many isolated beauties, however, did not result in a song that is of one piece. The scene begins "with free declamation," which prescription is maintained literally, the only connecting link being the stylized representation of the harp at beginning and end. It is not clear whether discrepancies in the text are due to Schumann's use of an early edition or whether he decided on the changes himself. Thus he writes "in reinem Galse" rather than "in purem Golde."

In *Wer nie sein Brot mit Tränen ass* (Who Never Ate His Bread in Tears, Opus 98a, No. 4) the harper emerges as a great seer, articulating not only his own judgment but also speaking for all. Intensity grows as we reach the harp-like broken chords; finally the venerable man reflects that "on this earth every failing must be avenged," and the song ends on a note of resignation. Earlier, as he voices his accusation, the fervor grows, "at first slowly, then with greater force," while the voice part remains tied to the muffled bass notes of the piano, relentlessly expressing the heavy burden of fate. The accompaniment displays a magical, almost impressionistic quality. To accomplish the transition to the less tense mood of the ending, Schumann repeats the last line of Goethe's text—not a convincing effect.

Heiss mich nicht reden (Ask Me No Questions, Opus 98a, No. 5) seems quite dramatic when compared with settings by other composers. Schumann is the only one to give expression to Mignon's wish to confide rather than remain silent. His fondness for repeating words, however, does not improve the song. Mignon as portrayed here can express pain and resignation more convincingly than the old, blind man. Her feelings, mature beyond her years, give this song the quality of an operatic "scene" in which the opening stanza takes the place of an *accompagnato* recitative. Her protestations, "heiss mich nicht reden" are heard in the dark, insistent C minor accents of the accompaniment. After the "recitative"-like first part of the song the C major section leads into the "aria." Wagner's influence can easily be heard. In fact, Schumann goes beyond what he knew from *Tannhäuser,* appropriating a thematic technique pointing to the as yet unwritten Wagnerian music dramas (Example 6 9): "Nur ein Gott vermag sie aufzuschliessen" ("only a god can unlock them [my lips]"). It seems as though Mignon were thinking of ancient Wotan! At the song's end, apathy reigns, not the release of having unburdened herself which had been so eloquently expressed by the music.

The harper's *Wer sich der Einsamkeit ergibt* (He Who is Lonely and Succumbs, Opus 9 7a, No. 7) does not include Goethe's second verse, probably because it is not compatible with the prevailing mood of the music. An echo of Beethoven's *An die ferne Geliebte* is this time probably unintentional.

An die Türen will ich schleichen (As from Door to Door I Wander, Opus 9 8a, No. 8) inspired Schumann's greatest Wilhelm Meister song, as it did in the cases of Schubert and Hugo Wolf. Here Schumann wrote a song that was unified and convincing. The hesitating gait of the syncopations, the imploring sixteenth-note figure, the quick, harp-like sounds, strong melodic invention and effortless modulations—all these combine to achieve a moving masterpiece. Though the repetition of "eine Träne" may have

faulty accentuation (Example 7 0), the effect is specially touching. In the brief piano postlude the various themes once more are intertwined. This song shows well how skillfully the composer knew how to integrate voice and piano parts, one imitating the other.

Mignon sings *So lasst mich scheinen* (Let Me Appear Now, Opus 9 8a, No. 9) to the accompaniment of a zither, before she exchanges the angel costume she had worn at a children's charade for her everyday clothes. Comparing the song to Schubert's version, Georgiades criticizes Schumann: "[he] did not succeed in establishing a basic mood for the entire song." But one wonders whether this had been the composer's intent, since he transformed Goethe's regular stanzas into an irregular arrangement of groups of two and three measures. A feeling of fluctuation results, probably intended to picture someone whose behavior is guided by spontaneous thoughts and emotions. In the postlude, intervals of a second

Example 7 0

Example 6 9

163

Example 71

increasingly dominate the melody (Example 71); their "sinking" quality clearly expresses Mignon's debility and lack of strength.

Schumann's late songs are full of subtle interrelations—of correspondences and deviations. They may be expressions of the composer's fondness for the enigmatic but may also characterize persons or situations. The definitive, unequivocal is avoided. All this need not be evidence of an inability to control larger relationships, to unify a work, as has been said about these pieces; more likely it represents the intentional avoiding of too much repetition and precise identification. A slightly hysterical quality dominates the melodic structure of *So lasst mich scheinen,* introducing only occasional flashes of E^b major into the underlying G major.

Requiem For Mignon, Opus 98b, for solo voices, chorus and orchestra, is one of the major works of 1849; it was completed on July 3. Schumann called this his "most productive" year, which we can interpret as "year of most intensive work." The Requiem can be seen as a continuation of the Goethe songs. On that July day Robert played excerpts for Clara. She noted that "this moved me more than anything else has in a long time. Words and music seem to spring from *one* soul. Words cannot describe the feelings of bliss that overcame me on hearing this magnificent music. Whenever Robert writes something that entirely delights me, tears of joy ensue." She no doubt was happy to help with corrections. Many of those found in the vocal parts are hers, especially in the final chorus, *Kinder, eilet ins Leben hinein.* Robert first wrote down the vocal parts in short score form, beginning with the choral sections. Instrumental parts were not added until work on the full score began. Richness of imagination is shown in the alternating choral and solo portions, displaying profound lyric-mystical emotion. Such qualities identify the work as a Requiem, not in the traditional meaning of music for

mourning but as a "memorial service in the poetic sense intended by Goethe" (Wasielewski). Counterpoint is avoided in favor of simple, eloquent melody. The choral sound has variety and many subtle nuances. We can understand why Brahms chose this work for his debut as conductor of the Singakademie in Vienna. Goethe's own words characterize the Requiem: "Sad but not without grace; moderate grief, mournful but not without beauty." These qualities unfortunately also contribute to the impression of a somewhat long-winded presentation. But life is imparted by the choir's antiphonal singing, with questions and answers, and by the active ending, representing a new-found will to live. A private performance by Schumann's choral society was given on May 8, 1850; he conducted the first public performance on November 2 in Düsseldorf.

Goethe continued to be much in the picture: Liszt conducted the preliminary version of the *Scenes from Faust* in Weimar, to observe the poet's 100th birthday. The final chorus also was given in Leipzig and Dresden. While Liszt was successful, using conventional music for the conclusion, the Leipzig audience did not warm up to the preliminary version, used there because the vocal and instrumental parts of the later version had not yet been copied. In Leipzig the reason may have been the startling ending, dying away to a *pianissimo.* The *Scenes From Faust,* as a complete work, will occupy our attention later on.

Schumann was working furiously. He wrote music based on earlier plans, e.g. the pieces for four-hand piano, the Concert-Allegro, and the Romances for oboe. Throughout this period he had no official title or position. He was made painfully aware of this when he laid the plans for a commemorative service for Chopin, who had died on October 17, to be held in the Frauenkirche. Permission for this performance was refused by the authorities. Nor was there much chance of his being offered Wagner's position of court Kapellmeister, a position that had become vacant when Wagner fled to Switzerland. To be sure, this position would hardly have been the right assignment for Schumann. Predictably, Clara's hopes that with the discreet help of friends Robert might obtain the post, were not fulfilled.

But one had to make ends meet. Schumann, through Dr. Härtel, tried to learn whether Julius Rietz, principal conductor of

164

*Goethe in his study, dictating
to his secretary, John, 1831*

the Leipzig Opera and the Gewandhaus, was indeed slated to succeed Otto Nicolai in Berlin. As it turned out, Heinrich Dorn was given that post. Rietz remained in Leipzig which removed the need for Schumann to prove himself in that taxing position.

Schumann's changing attitude toward treating texts goes back to a time prior to the Goethe songs. Individual words are melodically highlighted and different parts of a song express different moods. Above all, voice lines tend to incorporate elements of recitative, due to Schumann's desire for intelligibility that sometimes goes beyond purely musical considerations. To reconcile different elements never was an easy task for him, leading later generations to the facile and oft-repeated opinion that his creative talent had already deteriorated. Actually we witness the emergence of a mature style which, for lack of time, he was never able to perfect. It may be true that Schumann's late lyric work resembles a landscape full of ruins—but within that landscape some admirable structures remain.

Rückert's *Adventlied* ("*Dein König kommt in niedern Hüllen,*" Your King Arrives in Lowly Garb, Opus 71, for soprano solo, choir and orchestra) is an early example. According to Müller-Reuter it was not written down until November 25-30, 1849. Schumann originally had conceived it for male double choir with full orchestra and optional organ. There is a great gap here between a truly sacred style with Bach, Handel and Palestrina serving as models, and another style, metaphysical rather than religious in orientation, which suggests a devotional mood rather than a strong faith. At first Schumann objected to the work's title, desired by the publisher; eventually he yielded and gave up his preferred designation, "Geistliches Lied." Instead of romantic, sensuous sound Schumann looked for a meditative mood. Before a performance of the work at the Paulinen Church in Leipzig he confessed to Strackerjahn: "To devote his efforts to sacred music must be the artist's highest aim . . . As we get older we set higher goals for ourselves. I hope this time will soon come for me." Schumann was seeking for a dispassionate attitude in an abstract, neoclassical sense. W. Dahms claimed that Rückert's verbosity led to the same quality in some of Schumann's vocal music, even before this time, but this assumption ignores many songs, including early ones, in which Schumann

Clara Schumann, ca. 1850

demonstrates his ability for concise expression. When Dahms, however, criticizes the *Adventlied* for its "deplorable tender-heartedness" he is putting his finger on the one quality that is characteristic of the composer's resignation in his late years—a quality far more noticeable than his command of form, easy counterpoint, clear fugal writing and thematic fluency.

A theme heard in the first measures played by the orchestra provides the link between the interwoven parts. With the solo soprano leading only sporadically, the choir bears the essential role. Soon after the score was completed, the first performance took place on December 10, 1849, at a concert given by the Gewand-haus Orchestra "for the benefit of the poor."

Liederspiel, with its ensemble of several voices, had been so successful that Schumann wanted to duplicate its effect in his *Minnespiel aus Rückerts Liebesfrühling,* Opus 101. While Schumann looked at the summer of 1849 as felicitous and most rewarding, these songs, written in November, speak of darkness and depression, especially the last of the solo songs. There is none of the vigor

of the Spanish songs; instead the music sounds soulful and contemplative.

Schumann enlarges *Meine Töne still und heiter* (Sweet and Gay My Songs Float Upward, Opus 101, No. 1) by adding another Rückert poem, taken from the almanac *Moosrosen* (beginning with the words "die Liebste"), dating from 1826. One might think that this additional poem furnished the impulse for Schumann's return to Rückert's *Liebesfrühling,* but there may be a more plausible explanation: thinking ahead to their 10th wedding anniversary in the following year, a renewed interest in the source of the earlier love poems would seem natural. But the resulting new songs were tinged with melancholy. On June 8 Schumann records in his diary: "My 39th birthday. Dear Clara—and my melancholy."

An unusual device distinguishes *Liebster, deine Worte stehlen* (Dearest, When You Speak, You Capture, Opus 101, No. 2) from the songs, duets and quartets of *Minnespiel:* while the text of Rückert's refrain remains the same, Schumann supplies different melodies and rhythms for each. Its short concluding arpeggio provides the transition to the duet *Ich bin dein Baum* (I Am Your Tree, Opus 101, No. 3) and again furnishes the initial motion (Examples 72 and 73). The mellifluous dialogue between alto and baritone imparts life to this duet.

Example 72

Example 73

Mein schöner Stern (My Beauteous Star, Opus 101, No. 4) was meant to express Robert's gratitude for Clara's companionship during his recurrent periods of hypochondria and depression. Whenever he completely understood and expressed the meanings of "his" poet an extraordinary song resulted, as it did here. That he refrained from making any changes in the text confirms this. A down-beat followed by the interval of a descending second becomes an up-beat in the voice part, as though it wanted to continue the idea stated in the accompaniment (Example 74). Often the voice anticipates harmonic change by a quarter-note, creating friction that keeps the song from becoming too hymn-like and smooth. The quartet that follows, Opus 101, No. 5, provides a more pretentious but not more substantial scherzo version of the duet from Opus 37.

Example 74

O Freund, mein Schirm, mein Schutz (My Love, My Hope, My Guide, Opus 101, No. 6) is vaguely related to Biblical texts. Schumann easily finds the proper style, based on his Bach studies, in this case especially the Bach cantatas. Still, the "modern" composer speaks to us in this work. Schumann creates his own concept of Baroque sound by interpreting the words in a way new for him, writing an ostinato bass that is related to the meaning of the text.

In the duet *Die tausend Grüsse* (A Thousand Greetings, Opus 101, No. 7) the tempo, already lively at the beginning, increases furiously towards the end. There is something operatic and extroverted in the music, but it does not seem forced or superimposed. We are not far from the hectic scene in the second act of *Tristan* where the lovers are reunited—a scene which Clara later found "indecent" dwelling as it did on graphically explicit rhythm.

The concluding quartet returns to the poem *So wahr die Sonne scheinet* (As Certain as the Sun is Shining, Opus 101, No. 8) but does not reflect the text any more precisely than the duet had done.

In 1849, Louis Ehlert published an essay containing just about all the clichés about Schumann that posterity was to eagerly adopt. "He found the artistic solution to all the conflicts with which we struggle in our lives . . . In all his striving a gentle, conciliatory spirit prevails." Such an idyllic interpretation made it easy for later generations to interpret Schumann's last years as representing "a decline of his once so flourishing imagination, of his artistic inventiveness and his self-criticism." What we actually see is the artist's attempt to purify the passionate emotions of his youth by turning to an economy and simplicity of means. His ability to work and his artistic imagination may have been hampered by his illness, but they continued to be there.

Nachtlied (Night Song, Opus 108), a chorus in which Schumann comes to terms with the poet Hebbel without going through an "intermediary," communicates an intense, atmospheric mood. The text, in three sections, first speaks of "Schwellende Nacht voll von Lichtern und Sternen" ("engulfing night, full of lights and stars"). Calmness reigns, barely aware of the "steigendes, neigendes Leben" ("pulsing life"), and sleep provides a "protective circle." The melodic line given to the violas at first is brooding and jagged. When we reach the words "du nahst dich leise" ("softly you are

167

approaching") it has shed all decorative detail and expresses complete calm. A masterpiece, unjustly forgotten.

The *Spanische Liebeslieder,* Opus 138, were completed in November, 1849, incorporating some material written in April of the same year. This time Schumann thought of accompaniment for four-hand piano. "As we found out during several performances in a circle of friends, this [kind of accompaniment] is much more effective." The statement, addressed to the publisher Kistner, is evidence of such performances of the songs, as a group, by four amateur singers with some musical training. Only in such an intimate setting are the songs likely to come across, though a few individual songs made their way to the concert stage. The quality of voices Schumann had available in the musical circles of Leipzig, Dresden, or Düsseldorf helped these songs on their road to success, but such voices are rare today. Moreover, recordings and television have had the sad result of making such spontaneous, joyful music-making in the home rare.

The *Spanische Liebeslieder* (with four-hand accompaniment, translations by Geibel, published posthumously) again contain some national flavor. In the opening number for piano (Opus 138, No. 1) we hear a Bolero, while the Intermezzo that separates the two groups of songs has the flavor of a "national dance." During the solo numbers the second pianist rests. Following the not very substantial overture we hear the first song, *Tief im Herzen trag' ich Pein* (Buried Deep Beyond Relief..., Opus 138, No. 2). Schumann's setting does not bear up well when compared with what Hugo Wolf accomplished with the same text in his *Spanisches Liederbuch.* A succession of musical ideas, loosely connected, conveys the impression of great, unfettered mental anguish. A guitar-like accompaniment furnishes unobtrusive support.

Spirited and witty, *O wie lieblich ist das Mädchen* (Oh, How Lovely is the Maiden, Opus 138, No. 3, text by Gil Vicente) is bound to captivate the listener. The piano interludes contribute to the effect: effervescent, tossed-off phrases that take over where the voice line, inconclusive, leaves off. They represent not only the laughter of the song's lovely maiden but also the affection of her admirer. It is up to the interpreter to give variety to each stanza, in the manner of a Schubert song.

In *Bedeckt mich mit Blumen* (Cover Me with Flowers, Opus 138, No. 4) the two women's voices express identical sentiments in interwoven melodies in the minor mode, surging and passionate. *Flutenreicher Ebro* (Ebro, Bordered with Blossoms, Opus 138, No. 5), entitled *Romanze,* stands out above the other songs in the group with its abundance of melody. Stephen Heller's *Improvisata* for piano, Opus 98, is entitled *Über die Romanze Flutenreicher Ebro;* in it (it was written during Schumann's lifetime) he quotes the melody. No. 6 is an intermezzo for the two pianists, recalling a Spanish "national dance''; No. 7, *Weh, wie zornig is das Mädchen* (Oh, How Angry is the Maiden), with its pretense of fear, reminds us that Schumann's humor could emerge even under tears. He must have had a good laugh hiding the voice part's main theme, "Weh, wie zornig," in the measure preceding the last stanza, challenging the pianist's ability to bring it out clearly (Example 75).

Example 75

In *Hoch, hoch sind die Berge* (High Are the Mountains, Opus 138, No. 8; text after Pedro di Padilla) Schumann emerges as someone steeped in German folk song rather than as a proud Spaniard. Later Brahms learned how to handle this genre more convincingly, though clearly influenced by Schumann. *Blaue Augen hat das Mädchen* (The Maiden Has Blue Eyes, Opus 138, No. 9) follows, a playful duet with a hint of opera buffa quality. Finally the quartet *Dunkler Lichtglanz, blinder Blick* (Light That's Dark, Sightless Glances, Opus 138, No. 10) sings the praises of love, thoughtfully at first in minor, then, with ecstacy, in major.

Soon after the summer composition of Goethe songs with their unstable emotional qualities in 1849, Schumann was troubled by rumors of a cholera epidemic. It caused him once more to seek solace in drinking, the cause of his "sudden illness." As a result the Byron songs, written in December, are of lesser stature, showing little more than promise. A harp accompaniment had originally been planned; perhaps Schumann found the experiment unsatisfactory, the instrument providing insufficient variety. One feels that he had set his sights high, but apparently he did not feel comfortable writing these songs. He therefore resorted to high-flown, empty emotional gesturing whenever the text permitted. Nor was he well served by Körner's translation, one of many, of the Byron poems. *An den Mond* (To the Moon, Opus 95, No. 2) is the title Schumann gave to "Leuchte der Schlaflosen" (in other translations "Sonne der Schlummerlosen"); this version also was set by Mendelssohn. Schumann's song fails to impress. It might be worthwhile to try substituting a harp for the thick piano accompaniment, thus perhaps saving Schumann's only encounter with legendary bard-songs. A notation on the music refers to harp *and* piano.

No more rewarding was Schumann's turn at this time to melodrama. By combining spoken words with the sound of the piano he adds a special timbre, that of indefinite pitch, to the total musical effect. The function of language is thereby changed, representing almost pure sound instead of expressing specific thoughts. He derived the idea for these three "Declamations" from the poems and felt "obligated" to the authors for having inspired him "to try new paths of artistic expression." Actually, Schumann was not "composing works in a style as yet unexplored," as he called his melodramas. There are 18th Century precedents in imitation of ancient Greek models which were then further developed by Rousseau, Benda, Reichardt and Abbé Vogler. With Zumsteeg's *Frühlingsfeier,* after Klopstock, the declaimed, i.e. spoken ballad with musical accompaniment had found its way into concert performance. This was the likely model for Schubert who, much interested in composing ballads, wrote only one melodrama, *Abschied von der Erde.* Melodramatic passages abound in opera before Schumann, almost amounting to a fad: *Fidelio, Der Freischütz, Der Vampyr* [Marschner], *Preziosa* [Weber]. Composers after Schumann also availed themselves of the fascinating effect that the spoken word can have (more so than sung recitative) in moments of greatest

dramatic tension. Other examples, at one time highly acclaimed, are Liszt's *Lenore,* text by Bürger (already set as a melodrama by Kunze in 1788) and Richard Strauss's *Enoch Arden,* words by Tennyson. Objections to melodrama were voiced long before motion pictures began using spoken dialogue and music on the same sound track. Such objections bear directly on Schumann's three works which combine declamation and piano accompaniment. Schoenberg, on the other hand, clearly understood why he used the speaking voice at indicated pitch levels in combination with instrumental music.

Schumann's attempts in his melodramas to give both the spoken words and music independence were unsuccessful—no unified musical impression was achieved. *Schön Hedwig,* Opus 106, text by Hebbel, begins with a festive overture in D major, given to the piano. It describes the setting and anticipates the conclusion and its meaning. After this what little music there is relates to Hedwig and her predicament as she is importuned by questions; it forgoes any realistic treatment of the narrative. To intensify and not detract from the poet's verbal message seems to have been the intent. The attempt was only partly successful.

Two other "declamations" of May, 1852 should be considered. *Die Flüchtlinge* (The Fugitives, Opus 122, No. 2) uses a translation of a work by Percy Bysshe Shelley, the early English Romantic of whom Schumann was very fond. It is more convincing than Schumann's melodramatic first-born, even though the translation is so frighteningly naive that the performer might well wish to supply his own.

Of the three melodramas, *Die Ballade vom Haideknaben* (Ballad of the Boy From the Heath, Opus 122, No. 1, text by Hebbel) is the most significant. Its music reminds us of dramatic passages in Weber or Wagner, partly due to the extensive chromaticism. Here the boy becomes the victim of the gory crime of which he had dreamt. Spoken words and musical action never coalesce: they only exist in proximity of each other. It is as though Schumann looked to melodrama to escape from his difficulties in writing opera. But the tension between words and music, always an essential challenge for Schumann, gives way to the supremacy of the spoken text, and the result is failure.

PERCY BYSSHE
SHELLEY

Shelley (1792–1822) came from a well-to-do, well regarded English family. After his education at Eton he attended Oxford. He was expelled for having published a pamphlet on atheism, after which he went to London, and abducted the 16-year-old daughter of the proprietress of a cafe. Later he lived with Mary, the daughter of the social revolutionary Godwin, a follower of Rousseau. Shelley was the philosopher among English romantic poets; in his writings he showed himself to be a passionate champion of freedom. He lived with Mary in Italy and Switzerland. Longing for union with nature he wrote long odes on wind, water and the heavens, about color and tones. Shelley drowned when his ship *Ariel* capsized in the Gulf of La Spezia.

For a number of reasons Schumann considered his position in Dresden to be untenable. Despite his ardent wish the first performance of *Genoveva* was not to take place there. After five years of concentrated artistic work he still was not part of the city's official musical life. Lüttichau, the general director of the opera, a busy man given to intrigues, avoided Schumann. He expressed his lack of esteem in a variety of ways, making it clear to Schumann that he was not welcome at the opera.

Several accounts note that both Robert and Clara were nervous and irritable during this period in 1852. The year during which he worked harder than ever had consumed his remaining strength. At the end of the year he unveiled the *Neujahrslied,* Opus 144, to a Rückert text. It calls for orchestral accompaniment and was written in a few days. Completing the orchestration became his first task in Düsseldorf. He conducted it soon after, in January of the following year, but due to insufficient rehearsal it was not a success, much to his regret. The text lacks substance; the music does not reveal real engagement. The old year and the new are represented by solo voices and are addressed in solemn choruses. All join in the final chorale, *Nun danket alle Gott.* It hardly conveys any of Schumann's thoughtful, original style but seems rather upright, honorable—and stiff.

Chapter 21

In November, 1852 Schumann received a confidential inquiry from his friend Hiller in Düsseldorf: would he be interested in the position of municipal music director there? Hiller was intending to go to Cologne to direct the Gürzenich Concerts. While Clara regarded this possibility as a decided advancement it upset and bewildered Robert. He was becoming increasingly nervous because he believed that his musical future depended on the success of his opera *Genoveva* which had been seriously delayed. His *Peri* had just been well received in Düsseldorf—a good omen. But had Mendelssohn not been greatly annoyed at the state of music there? Twenty years before he had found it to be "in disarray." Furthermore, the move would be costly. And wasn't it true that Clara was just becoming established as a pianist, having given highly successful soirées with the Dresden concertmaster Schubert at the Dresden Opera?

Robert did some looking into Düsseldorf and was annoyed by what he found. "I looked up Düsseldorf in an old geography book; it listed among the city's attractions three convents and an insane asylum. I was willing to accept the former but was bothered by the latter." His thoughts turned back to 1845 when he cut short a stay in Maxen because from his window he looked out on the insane asylum "Sonnenstein." In answering Schumann, Hiller pointedly omitted replying to his question about the asylum. On the other hand, Immermann, the beloved writer of *Merlin* and *Tristan and Isolde,* had lived in Düsseldorf. During one of Clara's brief concert tours the Schumanns had met Immermann's widow in Bremen who gave them much information about Düsseldorf.

Schumann's lack of success in Leipzig facilitated the decision.

In February Clara performed the *Introduction and Allegro Appassionato* for piano and orchestra at the Gewandhaus: it was not well received. Rehearsals for the opera *Genoveva* were difficult; the Schumanns were annoyed by "a peculiar, unpleasant attitude among the music experts"; the performance of *Minnespiel* on the occasion of a private birthday party for Schumann resulted in a cool reception—"Nothing but Mendelssohn's music pleases them," as Clara put it. Still, the concert tour through North Germany was a success, both for Schumann as a composer and financially. Robert finally signed the Düsseldorf contract, largely at Clara's urging and for financial reasons. As soon as his acceptance had been received he was paid his first salary, though his duties did not begin until fall. The decision having been made in March, Robert now found a new peace of mind, so that composing once more became possible, even while traveling.

Liebeslied (Love Song, Opus 51, No. 5; text from Goethe's *West-östlicher Divan*), if not a profound work, is charming, with a warmth reminiscent of Mendelssohn, though it does have a certain brittle quality characteristic of Schumann. Goethe's lines do not strongly invite a musical setting but they appealed to Schumann's fondness for the enigmatic, the hidden. The text, from the beginning of the *Divan,* supplies the clue to earlier mystifications. The exact date of composition is not known but is believed to be April, 1850. It is based on a sketch from the time of Robert's and Clara's engagement, a time when they exchanged clandestine, coded messages. Other settings of the *Divan* poems come from the same period.

Aufträge (Messages, Opus 77, No. 5; text by Christian L'Egru)

Düsseldorf, ca. 1840

clearly demonstrates that Schumann could still at times make great demands on the technical skills of the pianist. An attractive song, it displays virtuosic elan, yet its simple form of three repeated sections keeps it from sounding hectic and exaggerated. This is another love song in a lighter vein, with precise declamation and a playful piano part. Such an effective song deserves to be better known.

Resignation, Opus 83, No. 1, is a distillation of the qualities of Schumann's late songs. The text was contributed by Julius Buddeus, a friend of the Schumanns and a descendant of the widely respected Jena theologian. This song (as is true of many Hugo Wolf songs) would be more effective with the transparency of a string quartet accompaniment rather than the piano. Indeed, many of Schumann's late works no longer bear the marks of thinking in pianistic terms. The song reverts to a style used in the last songs of the *Jugendalbum.* It concentrates on the declamation of the text, slighting purely melodic elements. This compositional approach leads to a richer harmonic language, subtly reflecting every nuance. Being a free fantasy, the song offers special challenges to the interpreter. There is no longer any trace of the traditional strophic song. In this miniature Schumann created what Wagner had envisioned for the musical theater: a mixture of speech-like song and of melody derived from words. For this reason an understanding of *Resignation* cannot be derived by examining its particulars, for its musical shape, formally very free, reveals itself only in a broader perspective. The opening measures make for a recitative-like introduction (Example 7 6): The beginning of the piano part, dissonant and on the off-beat, is unusual. A chromatically rising motif, hidden in an inner voice, expresses longing, the dominant emotion pervading the entire song. Such freely-flowing "melody" runs counter to the conventions of the time, leading one to wonder what Schumann, had he lived, might have created to take a place next to Wagner's "Art Work of the Future" of the second half of the century. In this context the opening motif is not a leitmotif, as has been assumed; it is a continuing thread rather than a broken one that had to be re-tied. There is no real recitative, no elaborate arioso, no "cantata song" in Schubert's manner: rather we meet an entirely new medium of a vocal fantasy.

Is there anything autobiographical in *Resignation?* One must be careful with such programmatic interpretations. There *is* a change of mood, but "autumn" here does not seem to allude to Schumann's mental state. A new, striking language, void of metaphors:

Schumann's longing for it is as strong as the love described by his friend Buddeus.

Die Blume der Ergebung (The Flower of Resignation, Opus 8 3, No. 2; text by Rückert) combines Schumann's mature chromaticism with a melodic style harking back to earlier years. Sketches from those years undoubtedly were used in this new way. During a period when he had set sail into unknown waters Schumann, in this song (and in the following *Einsiedler,* also of April, 1 8 5 0) seems to have sought shelter in the safe harbor of cantabile melody. This metaphor may explain the subdued sound, never blossoming forth: gentle, "objective," intellectual.

Schumann's intention of becoming ever simpler, calmer is not entirely realized in *Der Einsiedler* (The Hermit, Opus 8 3, No. 3; text by Eichendorff). Historians may be right when they speak of the composer's "resting from his labors," of last successes before the onset of darkness, though such interpretations are too easily made. A slow tempo and static, chorale-like harmonies do not capture the

Example 7 6

delicate, floating mood of the poem, one of the most effective Romantic creations. Perhaps the composer did not wish to "touch" or "disturb" Eichendorff's poem. Taken by itself the solemn melody seems right; characteristically Schumann provides unexpected harmonies by way of remote keys, including some hints of the Phrygian mode. The calmness of the night, the "consoler of the world" is invoked, not in the ecstatic tones of verses by Novalis or music by Mendelssohn, but with simple, understated gestures.

Opinions differ greatly about *Der Handschuh* (The Glove, Opus 87; text by Schiller). This diversity of opinion may in part be due to uncertainty about the date of composition. The 1851 publication date gives no clue as to the time of writing; it is not indicated in the *Componierbuch*. Wasielewski mentions 1850. Given choice of text and style of composition (Schumann had been fond of the poem since 1834), 1840 seems more likely—a year when several "long ballads" were written. Such a placement surely applies to at least the first two-thirds of *Der Handschuh*. It has been called "unsuitable for music," "too full of operatic pathos," "musically rather feeble," "bordering on parody," and "the best setting of a Schiller ballad in the entire song repertory." Indeed there is little here that approaches the intensity of Schumann's best ballads save for the descriptions of the "frightful cats" which compare favorably with the corresponding section of the *Löwenbraut*. If Schumann here reworked a subject he had tackled earlier he was not successful. The pianist is faced with what amounts to a keyboard reduction of a vocal score. There is declamation and tone painting, quite lively, but an excess of thematic material spoils the effect. At first the singer recites in a free, realistic manner, which borders on the comical. Irony is established supposedly in the middle section in 6/8 time, but it does not overcome the underlying heavy feeling. Nor does the ending, with its incisive chords, establish the intended dramatic mood.

An early date of composition seems likely when we consider Schumann's discussions of Vesque von Püttlingen's songs. He lists text characteristics which seem to demand a musical setting. Subjects which he considers particularly "musical" include "an arrogant ruler," "a suppressed people," "a great king," "the sorrow of a mother." Only music, he observed, can express the contrasts

WILFRIED VON DER NEUN

Wilfred von der Neun (real name Friedrich Wilhelm Traugott Schöpf) was born in Dresden in 1826. After serving as a minister he settled in Niederlössnitz near Dresden. Using a pen name alluding to the ninth Muse, he published in 1852 a volume of poems, *Herz und Welt*. Only in its third edition does his real name appear.

and tensions inherent in such settings. Schumann did indeed prefer such contradictory elements in his ballads, noting that "no one knew better than Loewe how to paint a convincing picture" in this manner. But unhappily Schumann's efforts to realize the same qualities often misfired despite the fact that he considered himself a "realist" who had long since rejected subject matter that seemed "staged" in the manner of Romantic painting. So it is hardly surprising that the tale of the valiant knight who retrieves his lady's glove from the wild animals' cage did not turn out to be a masterpiece. Only parts of a choral version have been preserved.

In matters of literary taste Schumann's judgment was not always reliable, especially during periods when intensive work resulted in stress. The *Sechs Gesänge* (Six Songs, Opus 89) is but another demonstration of his faulted judgment. And yet the settings of poems by Wilfried von der Neun are distinctive, not merely reversions to an earlier styles.

On May 14, 1850, Schumann invited the poet Schöpf to meet him in Leipzig. The meeting took place on May 28 and was continued on June 4. Poet and composer discussed music to be written for the setting of the poems—an unusual procedure. Schöpf later recalled: "While we walked in the garden [Schumann] occasionally would hold a blade of grass between his lips. Thus his voice would be even softer, and the silences more frequent . . . A person of substance, quite amiable: thus I remember him."

For *Es stürmt am Abendhimmel* (Storms in the Evening, Opus 89, No. 1) the timbres of an orchestra are needed to do justice to the accompaniment. Typical of this period, Schumann gives only bits of melodic material to the singer. In this kind of "speech song" we detect the first influences of Wagner. Dramatic expression here takes precedence over any intrinsic musical values or thematic work. In spite of some evident banality and intense dramatic expression Schumann manages to refrain from posturing. The broad, sweeping lines of the dark ending are convincing, as they are in *Herbstlied*. Brahms did not hesitate to use such effects in his Platen songs.

In *Heimliches Verschwinden* (Secret Disappearance, Opus 8 9, No. 2) Schumann uses again the resumption of an interrupted thread in a way that was to be perfected by Hugo Wolf. Again and again the basic mood is interrupted and then recaptured. An accompaniment consisting of arpeggiated triplets reminds of Schumann's earlier practice.

Herbstlied (Autumn Song, Opus 8 9, No. 3) concentrates on a single musical thought. The brief initial theme in the bass (Example 7 7) suffices to evoke images of autumn, of the end of life, of magic moods, joys of times past, and hope inspired by the beauties of nature. Such concentration on one musical motif, which really serves only to balance the melody, is quite typical. Brittle harmonies beautifully capture the twilight mood of the forest; then "the glorious color of the treetops speaks of distant bliss," concluding the song with rustling arpeggios, leading once more into that initial, pliable bass motif. Hans Pfitzner owed much to this technique.

Example 7 7

Schumann, while writing this song, probably did not recall a letter he had written to Emil Flechsig in 1 8 2 7, at the time of saying goodbye to his high school sweetheart, Liddy. There he characterized a similar mood:

The sun had barely set—the mountain top aglow—the forest seemed on fire. All God's creation dissolved into a purple sea. As I was regarding it, thinking about God's greatness, a black cloud appeared in the east, quick as lightning, rising and growing.

Schumann's melody is carefully declaimed. Tremolos in the piano grow and fade, leading into a *pianissimo* conclusion, with vibrating ninth-chords in a low bass register—a dark, twilight effect.

Abschied vom Walde (Farewell to the Forest, Opus 8 9, No. 4), a rather vague mood picture, is followed by the fresh and lively *Ins Freie* (Into the Open, Opus 8 9, No. 5). If the intended bounding effect is not fully realized in performance, it is partially due to the heavy piano part and to the representation of "songs resounding" which is less than convincing. In *Röselein, Röselein* (Little Rose, Opus 8 9, No. 6) we hear the graceful sounds of earlier times. A dash of irony is added, suggested by the rather forced humor of the text. A phrase in the piano, rather mechanically alternating with the song melody, suggests a similar phrase in *O wie lieblich ist das Mädchen*. Another poem by von der Neun, *Gesungen!* (Let Us Sing, Opus 9 6, No. 4), perhaps an afterthought, features a technique found in several of the Goethe songs: several minor keys appear at the same time. The song shows a level of inspiration that is rare in these last songs.

According to the *Componierbuch* the Opus 8 9 songs were written May 1 1–18, 1 8 5 0, and were dedicated to the singer Jenny Lind. This dedication was occasioned by her visit half a year earlier, when Clara had appeared at a concert in Hamburg with Robert conducting. He had written to Lind, asking whether Clara and he might meet her in Berlin on their way back to Dresden. Instead, Lind promptly journeyed to Hamburg to take part, on the spur of the moment, in one of Clara's concerts in northern Germany. Clara notes that "on the morning of Thursday the 2 1st, Lind visited us for a brief rehearsal. It turned out to be a long one as she sang many of

Robert's songs. And how she did sing them! Such sincerity, depth of feeling, and yet such simplicity! She sang *Marienwürmchen, Frühlingsankunft,* [Clara erroneously writes *Frühlingsglaube*] from the collection which she did not know—sang them *at sight.* What an unforgettable experience; what a wonderful person on whom God has bestowed such talent! She is a true artist: everything she says is right to the point, not wasting any words . . . I shall always remember how she sang these songs, and am tempted to say that I should never want to hear anyone else interpret them. Needless to say, Robert is just as enthusiastic. To hear songs performed in such a way, from the soul, is a delight for the composer . . . The evening concert in Altona was magnificent—everything was right: a full house, an enthusiastic audience, magnificent singing . . . I had been afraid that there might be a slight in all this for me and was relieved that this was not the case. But now to her and her singing. Robert's *Sonnenschein:* incredible. Robert said to her: 'one fairly feels the sun on one's back,' it was sung with such freshness and childlike innocence. Her singing brought out all the spiritual and intellectual meaning of *Der Himmel hat eine Träne geweint* . . . If we only could persuade her to sing nothing but good music and to get rid of all that rubbish by . . . Meyerbeer, Bellini, Donizetti, etc.; she is too good for that."

Clara and Jenny continued in a happy relationship and of the same mind for several years, but their friendship cooled considerably in 1855 when Clara gave concerts in Hannover. Sharp disagreements arose because Lind had no use for the *Schumann Variations* of Brahms, the Schumanns' new friend, insisting that his music represented "a wrong approach." Could it be that Lind had noticed Brahms's infatuation with Clara and harbored resentments for that reason?

Rehearsals for *Genoveva* finally started in Leipzig in mid-May which contributed to the delayed move to Düsseldorf. "Nervous irritation" and another bout with alcoholism added an element of uncertainty even to the short trip from Dresden to Leipzig. As opening night approached, the resentment of the chorus, busy with many other engagements, increased. Rietz, the resident conductor, had led the early rehearsals conscientiously, but the dress rehearsal was turned over to Schumann who arrived late and in ill health.

Clara and Robert Schumann's handwriting

The first performance generated much excitement, with many notable musicians in the audience. Liszt, who two years later produced the opera in Weimar with no success, was among them. Louis Spohr, himself a distinguished and unjustly forgotten composer of operas, did no better with it in Kassel. Others attending included Meyerbeer, Hiller, Moscheles, Gade, and Moritz Hauptmann.

Save for the popular Günther-Bachmann, who sang the role of Margaretha, the cast was good but not first-rate. Siegfried was sung by Brassin, the father of a well-regarded pianist. Caroline Mayer, a thoroughly trained musician, was Genoveva. It was said that her voice, without vibrato, sounded like a clarinet. The tenor Widemann sang Golo.

The performance did not live up to the high expectations held by all for it. The shortened overture and the Golo-Genoveva duet *Wenn ich ein Vöglein wär* (text from Herder's collection of folk songs, 1778) received most applause; indeed they remain the best parts of the work. Schumann had taken the duet, slightly modifying the ending, from his Opus 43.

The reviews of *Genoveva* were largely polemic and nonsubstantive. Departing from his earlier views, Schumann now resented unfavorable reviews and indeed ended a long-standing friendship with Krüger, the lead music critic for the *Leipziger Allgemeine Zeitung,* who published a scathing review. Schumann hoped that in time his efforts "in the field of dramatic music, too, would be properly appreciated." He blamed *Genoveva*'s failure on the shallow taste of the public and the strangle hold of foreign operas on fashionable opinion.

With the failure of the opera, the material advantages that Schumann had hoped to derive by establishing himself in a new artistic medium were now in doubt. Negotiations with theaters in addition to those already mentioned were protracted and finally collapsed. Only Hermann Levi, the director in Karlsruhe, was successful with *Genoveva* where the opera remained in the repertoire into the 1860s.

During the interval before the move to Düsseldorf Schumann wrote a number of songs in which he intended to express with utmost clarity those things that were "beyond words:" emotions, atmosphere. He had first stated this position in broad terms in his article *Über Ausdruck in der Musik* (On Expression in Music): "to have thoughts, emotions, passions clearly emerge through music." Indeed, Schumann's music seems to hold its own even when it must compete with a text. To give expression to a variety of inner states seems to be easier in a song, where poet and composer speak at the same time, than in purely instrumental works. Yet such coordination of feeling and reason was surely no easier for Schumann than for other composers. Goethe's *Nachtlied* (Night Song, Opus 9 6, No. 1) is a case in point. When Schumann turned to poems such as this famous Goethe text (properly entitled *Wanderers Nachtlied*) he concentrated on a middle-of-the-road manner of expression. In the song's first part, "classic" calm and resting at ease represent control, but the floodgates are then opened: words are heard as sounds, but pauses between them obscure their meaning. A melancholic mood pervades the poem, derived from its gently flowing basic rhythm. With the concluding bass progression (F to G) the song as a whole is intensely illuminated. The greatest musical intensity is reached in the four measures of "Die Vögelein schweigen." A few years earlier Liszt set the same text on a larger scale; though the music seems out of step with the shape of the poem, the song displays a more distinctive artistic concept on the composer's part.

Stadt-Theater zu Leipzig.

Dienstag, den 25. Juni 1850.

Mit aufgehobenem Abonnement.

(Zum ersten Male:)

Unter Leitung des Componisten,

Genoveva.

Oper in 4 Akten, nach Tieck und F. Hebbel.

Musik von Dr. Schumann.

Personen:

Hitulfus, Bischof von Trier.	Herr Wilcke.
Siegfried, Pfalzgraf.	Herr Brassin.
Genoveva.	Fräul. Mayer.
Golo.	Herr Widemann.
Margaretha.	Frau Günther-Bachmann.
Drago, Haushofmeister.	Herr Salomon.
Balthasar, } Dienerschaft im Schlosse.	Herr Stürmer.
Caspar, }	Herr Meißner.
Angelo, }	Fräul. Zeimer II.
Conrad, Siegfried's Edelknecht.	Herr Steps.
Ritter, Geistliche, Knappen, Knechte, Landvolk, Erscheinungen.	

Der Text der Gesänge ist an der Casse für 3 Neugroschen zu haben.

Preise der Plätze:

Parterre: 10 Neugroschen.   Parket: 20 Neugroschen.
Parterre-Logen: Ein einzelner Platz 20 Neugroschen.
Amphitheater: Sperrsitz 1 Thaler, ungesperrt 20 Neugroschen.
Logen des ersten Ranges: Ein einzelner Platz 20 Neugroschen.
Logen des zweiten Ranges: Ein einzelner Platz 15 Neugroschen.
Erste Gallerie: 15 Neugroschen.   Ein gesperrter Sitz daselbst 20 Neugroschen.
Zweite Gallerie: 10 Neugroschen.   Ein gesperrter Sitz daselbst 15 Neugroschen.
Dritte Gallerie: Mittelplatz 7½ Neugroschen.   Seitenplatz: 5 Neugroschen.

Anfang halb 7 Uhr.   Einlaß halb 6 Uhr.   Ende nach 9 Uhr.

Nachricht.

Man abonnirt auf den Theaterzettel mit vierteljährlich 12 Ngr. 5 Pf. in der Buchdruckerei von J. F. Fischer Poststraße Nr. 1B. — Bestellungen nehmen die Zetteltäger an.

Playbill, first performance of Genoveva

AUGUST GRAF
VON PLATEN (-HALLERMÜNDE)

August Graf von Platen (-Hallermünde) was born in
Ansbach in 1796. He joined the Bavarian Cadet Corps in
1806, became a page boy at the royal court, and participated in the campaign against Napoleon. Having
obtained an extended leave from military service he
studied law, languages, philosophy and natural sciences in
Würzburg and Erlangen, establishing contacts with some
of the major literary and intellectual figures of the time.
He served as librarian at Erlangen, until he settled in
Italy in 1826. In 1835 he died of a fever in Syracuse. His
poems reflect a passionate search for beauty. A representative of "Post-Classicism" he possessed a supreme
command of the strict forms of ode, sonnet, and *ghasel*.

Schumann, as did Liszt, repeats the last portion of Goethe's text.

Among the poets to whom Schumann turned for both inspiration and text was Count August von Platen, although the composer
selected a rather weak poem.

Schumann's text was taken from Platen's first collection of
poems written in 1833, not long before his death in Syracuse. *Ihre
Stimme* (Her Voice, Opus 96, No. 3), though grouped with many of
Schumann's lively, earlier songs, conveys but a pale reflection of the
poem's emotional impact.

In the catalog of Schumann's works, *Mein Garten* (My Garden,
Opus 77, No. 2; text by Fallersleben) is dated 1850. Scholars
believe, with good reason, that it was based on sketches, or other
material not used elsewhere, and to which Schumann now returned.

FRIEDRICH
HALM

Friedrich Halm was the pen name used by Baron Franz
Josef von Münch-Bellinghausen (1806–1871). After
studying law in Vienna he entered, a mere 20 years old,
the Austrian civil service. His teacher, the esthetician Enk
von der Burg, influenced Halm's literary ambitions,
which he kept secret for a long time. In 1834, using the
pen name he was to keep, he submitted his play *Griseldis*
to the Burgtheater. It was so successful that it soon
appeared on other stages. He had a talent for establishing tense emotional situations and a fine use of language; qualities which are also found in his less successful plays *Der Adept, Camoens,* and *Ein mildes Urteil*—
dramas turning on esoteric subject matter. His romantic
drama, *Der Sohn der Wildnis,* conquered the German
theater; with its warmth and direct appeal it surpassed the
fashionable tendentious plays of the day. Yet the critics of
the time objected to what they perceived as unnatural
subject matter and cheap effects. Meanwhile Halm had
been promoted to the rank of government councillor
(1840) and in 1845, became the custodian of the Imperial
Library with the title *Hofrat*. His radical reform measures
greatly improved the operations of this incomparable
collection. He served as general manager of the two
court theaters. From 1869 to 1871 he served as the
general manager of the two while continuing his literary
work. Schumann encountered a selection of his plays,
bizarre stories, and poems that had been published in
1850. Next to Brahms, Richard Strauss was most successful in setting Halm's lyrics to music, thus reserving a
modest place for him in the annals of poetry.

OSKAR LUDWIG WOLFF
(1799–1851)

He was born in Altona, and studied medicine and philosophy in Berlin and Kiel. A series of political essays, *Improvisationen,* were so successful in Hamburg that he continued to write in this new genre in Berlin. Goethe developed a lively interest in Wolff, helping him to obtain a professorship at Weimar. In 1832 he moved on to Jena, teaching modern languages and literature. As a writer he did not meet early expectations. Though well planned, his plays and novels seem slight; he was best with less structured forms. *Bilder und Lieder* (1840) contained some compelling verses which Schumann set. Wolff possessed a puckish sense of humor which found its outlet in *Naturgeschichte des deutschen Studenten* (Natural History of the German Student) which he published under the pen name "Pliny the Youngest."

Evidence in support of this view is the similarity to Chopin's *Nocturne in G Minor* (a composer after whom Schumann often modelled himself) and a quotation from Beethoven's *An die Ferne Geliebte,* dear to Schumann. This quotation occurs at the words "Ob sie heimisch ist hinieden." Its simple melodic line is supported by a simple accompaniment. In a modulation to F major, dreamy and full of longing, Schumann hints at something not related to the poem: happiness *has* been found.

In Halm's *Geisternähe* (Your Spirit Near, Opus 77, No. 3) Schumann again returns to a subject that occupied him from time to time throughout his life: the beloved one's marriage to another. This song, as with many of his later songs, shows but slight identification of the composer with the texts being set. His nervous, overly sensitive psyche at best supplied an elegiac echo. This detachment seems to reflect the composer's growing withdrawal, eventually leading to silence and escape.

The poet whose work was used for *Stiller Vorwurf* (Silent Reproach, Opus 77, No. 4) was Oskar Ludwig Wolff, the biographer of Banck, and Schumann's former rival for Clara. The memory of this rivalry may be why in many editions the poem is

PAUL HEYSE

The son of a well known philosopher and linguist, Paul Heyse studied in Berlin where Geibel introduced him to the artists' club *Tunnel,* whose membership included Kugler, Eichendorff, Fontaine and Menzel. Heyse, a student of Romance philology, went to Italy in March of 1852. He shortly thereafter was offered an appointment in Munich by the King of Bavaria which enabled him to devote himself entirely to writing. He gave up this annual stipend in 1867 but continued to live in Munich. A late representative of the Classic-Romantic tradition, his activities were far-ranging, including support for more liberal moral standards. His great facility in writing and with languages at times led him to fall into glossy superficiality. His more than 100 novellas in particular, though they established his reputation, lack depth and a sense of the tragic. Though he was a dedicated playwright, he never achieved lasting success in that genre. His novels were largely placed in an idealized artistic milieu. They caused strong protests because they represent an eudaemonic philosophy. Heyse's great linguistic skills naturally led him to translate Italian and Spanish works, which Schumann first encountered individually in journals and which the composer used extensively particularly in his Spanish song cycles. The first collection of Heyse's poems appeared in 1852.

attributed to an "unknown author." *Stiller Vorwurf* may also be a revision of a song written for Clara in 1840. Its very careful declamation and the abrupt changes in harmony point to techniques which would be further developed by Hugo Wolf.

Husarenabzug (The Hussars' Departure, Opus 125, No. 2) is Schumann's only setting of a poem by Karl Candidus (1817–1882). One wonders whether Brahms inherited the volume of poetry used by Schumann, his idol. While Schumann's setting is weak, the younger composer later was to create several magnificent songs based on these rather mediocre poems.

The text for *Frühlingslied* (Spring Song, Opus 125, No. 4) was written by Ferdinand Braun, with whom Schumann corresponded regularly. Eric Sams takes issue with the "anomaly" of separating subjects and verbs by rests. It would seem, however, that, given the fast tempo, Schumann does this intentionally to call the listener's attention to the piano's interjections.

Paul Heyse (1830–1914) was an accomplished poet—not only in the opinion of his friend Theodor Storm, but as evidenced in his lyrics for *Frühlingslust,* Opus 125, No. 5. Two manuscripts for this song exist, the first of which bears the date June 11, 1850 and shows a few slight variants. Schumann did not assign it a number. (In the thematic catalog it is listed as Opus 125, No. 5; in the Complete Edition as No. 2).

Setting von Strachwitz's *Mein altes Ross* (My Old Horse, Opus 127, No. 4) may have been Schumann's way of paying tribute to that writer, who died in 1847 at the age of 25.

COUNT MORITZ
KARL WILHELM VON STRACHWITZ

A native of Silesia, he studied law in Breslau and Berlin. He, too, was a member of the *Tunnel.* His ballads exerted a decisive influence on Fontane. He devoted himself entirely to writing on his Moravian estate although poor health led him to travel in Scandinavia and Italy. He died of cholera in Vienna. A formal perfection distinguishes his spirited, individualistic poetry, though it is overshadowed by that of Platen and Geibel. His *Neue Gedichte,* published in 1848, was the source for Schumann's setting.

Chapter 22

Neither the Dresden public nor the local musicians took much notice of the fact that Robert Schumann was about to leave the city, but two farewell parties were given for the couple by their friends. At their concert the choral society performed *Wenn zwei auseinander gehn,* a choral piece written by Schumann for the occasion. As he always did at gatherings of many people, especially those at which he was the occasion for the gathering, Schumann indulged himself in his worst behavior. At the concert he thought the singing abominable so insisted upon a second performance. At the third try he conducted himself, with even worse results, as Eduard Devrient noted in his diary.

In Bendemann's home the Lenau songs, written shortly before, were presented, closing with the gentle *Altkatholisches Lied: Requiem.* During the intermission Bendemann served his best wine, only to be told by Schumann that it was poor and unfit for the occasion. All present agreed that Schumann's behavior was insufferable. Schumann showed no emotion during the recital of the Lenau songs, despite the fact that these Opus 90 songs are on a consistently high level.

Schumann felt a strong kinship with Lenau's intentions. All the songs in the first group display a dark mood, reflected in the common themes, related keys and programmatic ideas. The opening *Lied eines Schmiedes* (Song of a Smith, Opus 90, No. 1) provides a splendid model, although (or because?) it stems from the ironic setting of Lenau's *Faust.* With its subdued march rhythm over pounding basses it provides the first variation on the subject of melancholy in this group of songs. Despite the rough syncopation

the piece is relatively uncomplicated. Schumann omitted Lenau's third verse. Changes of wording occur in *Meine Rose* (My Rose, Opus 90, No. 2), particularly in the change of meaning resulting from the repetition of the first stanza as a conclusion. This change resulted in a musically inconsistent structure, a failure that is not compensated for by Schumann's use of portions of some 1840 songs,—especially in *Stille Tränen.* The poetry establishes a nocturnal mood. The piano imitates the sustained mournful melodic line. In the third measure voice and piano unite. The central portion raises the typically Romantic question: can devotion and sacrifice give new life to a heart that is breaking under the load of sorrow, as water revives a flower? The poet provides no answer, but Schumann's first stanza, repeated *pianissimo,* replies with a resigned "no." A da capo is used as a means of poetic expression. The outer stanzas, in B♭ major, are effectively set off by the middle section in G♭ major.

Having reveled in beautiful melody, Schumann now reverts to his psychologically conditioned late style. *Kommen und Scheiden* (Meeting and Parting, Opus 90, No. 3) displays this clear abandonment of coherent melody. Fragments of text are treated in an impressionistic manner; memories of the beloved's appearance are loosely strung together. Such an impressionistic treatment has precedents in Schuberts *Der Doppelgänger* and *Die Stadt.* A single arabesque provides the thematic nucleus for Schumann's song. It is as though the words are whispered; one is reminded of the composer's habit of pursuing his lips when deep in thought. In measure 16, Schumann crossed out the words "im Hain", apparently uncon-

A circle of poets at the home of Justinus Kerner in Weinsberg. Left to right: Theobald Kerner, Lenau, Gustav Schwab, Count Alexander of Württemberg, Karl Mayer, Dr. Justinus Kerner, Friederike Kerner, Ludwig Uhland, Varnhagen von Ense.

cerned about eliminating the rhyme in Lenau's poem.

Both text and music of *Die Sennin* (The Alpine Dairy Maid, Opus 90, No. 4) bear similarities to *Des Sennen Abschied* of the previous year. The poem was first published in the *Musenalmanach* of 1836 and was the composer's source. Though the song initially paints a pleasant genre picture, a dark, oppressive mood soon takes hold and prevails to the end. The poem itself loses some of its effect by an insistence on rhyme that results in awkward wording. ("Wenn dich Liebe fort bewogen oder dich der Tod entzogen.") *Einsamkeit* (Solitude, Opus 90, No. 5) demonstrates how Schumann in his middle and late periods had found new musical ways to interpret a poetic text. Gushing waves, the sound of wind, rustling leaves; all were part of Schubert's language which was adopted by Schumann and given his own, distinctive impressions as though seen through the prism of his "beautiful sadness." A calm representation of nature no longer suffices; an elegiac mood prevails from the begin-

**NIKOLAUS NIEMBSCH
VON STREHLENAU
(1802—1850)**

generally known by the last two syllables of his name, was born in Hungary, studied law in Vienna and then turned to medicine, though he did not become a physician. His personality, both fiery and melancholic, found expression in poetry and epic writing. The publication of his poems in 1831 led him to Stuttgart where he developed a close relationship with Justinus Kerner and Gustav Schwab. But in spite of these friendships and his rising literary fame Lenau felt compelled to leave for America: where he hoped to discover in virgin forests what he found lacking even in the solitude of the Alps. In 1832 he purchased land, which he then leased to a travel companion in order to travel horseback through the western United States. The brutality and injustices of the West disillusioned him, so that within a few months he returned to Europe where his distinctive, colorful poetry was much admired. Shorter prose works fascinated readers in their mixture of realism and elegiac moods. They were written, along with many poems, soon after his return. The years 1833–43 found Lenau in Vienna and Swabia. *Faust,* Lenau's first large work, was written at the Weinberg home of Kerner, the neurologist who was devoted to him. An unfortunate attempt at a stage version was made by a certain Gramming—something entirely unsuitable for this succession of sketches that display a good deal of scepticism. Though successful as a poet, Lenau remained dissatisfied, a state of mind reflected in the melancholy of his poems.

Affairs of the heart, serious upsets and disappointments, the restless life of a wanderer, and the constant conflict between his personal inclinations and his intellectual goals—all contributed to Lenau's pathological nervousness and irritability.

Schumann used texts taken from the collection *Recent Poems* as well as the 1831 edition. While only fragments of Lenau's *Savonarola* and *Die Albigenser* were published they too display the genius of the man. He did not live to see the publication of his last poem, *Don Juan.* In the summer of 1844 Lenau surprised his friends with the announcement of his engagement to the daughter of a senator from Frankfurt. A few months later he became insane. He was taken to the asylum in Oberdöbling near Vienna; from which death did not deliver him until six years later.

ning. Gliding up and down in half-step motion the piano's eighth-note figure provides a stylized impression of the murmuring fountain, its suspensions shaping the entire musical line (Example 78). The harmonic motion seems to stem from the dominant, introducing an element of uncertainty and foreboding. Formally we are closer to Ariel's song, accompanied by cello, from Part II of the *Scenes from Faust,* but with opposite expressive content: ecstatic love there, hopeless melancholy here, emphasized by non-functional

Example 78

Robert Schumann, ca. 1850

harmony in an impressionistic vein that shows no concern for traditional modulations nor the representation of specific emotions.

To realize how closely Schumann identified himself with a text one should compare his setting of *Der schwere Abend* (The Heavy Evening, Opus 90, No. 6) with that by Robert Franz. Schumann realizes an intimate dialogue between singer and pianist in the key of E♭ minor—a key that seems to accentuate the oppressive mood. The dotted-rhythm motif in the piano part (Example 79) is closely related to *Dichterliebe,* where we find it in No. 13; here a darker color suggesting wind instruments prevails. Once more the voice part ends in a deceptive cadence while the piano, with sweeping, syncopated chords, dwells to the end on the nearness of death. The rhythm of funeral bells provides the basic pattern; its musical interpretation resulted in one of Schumann's most glorious songs.

Example 79

The *Requiem,* Opus 90, No. 7 belongs here. Adolf Follen (1794–1855) had published his translation (based on an anonymous Latin text) in the 1819 volume of *Altchristliche Lieder.* Of the nine stanzas contained therein, Schumann selected only three. It would seem that the singer, expressing her grief over the death of her beloved, should be joined by a chorus, but this was not to be.

Schumann's setting seems overly effeminate. If we compare his setting with Schubert's *Ave Maria,* similar in mood, we immediately note Schubert's much more straightforward rhythm, not allowing the constant text-related fluctuations found in Schumann's setting. The reference to the unfortunate poet, "Ruh von schmerzensreichen Mühen aus," was not felt by Schumann as

Six Poems by Lenau and Requiem, *Op. 9 0*
Title page of the first edition

meant for him. In composing *Requiem* he once more thought of song in times long past. The running 16th-notes, according to his instructions, were to sound "like a harp."

Schumann had added this song (based on Old Catholic models) to the Lenau group on the erroneous assumption that the poet had died. It proved to be a premonition, for on the very day of the first performance, given at the gathering in Bendemann's home, word was received of Lenau's death. Thus Schumann's departure from Dresden proved to be a memorial service for the poet. "The event, together with the songs, put all of us in a mournful mood, but I was able to banish it at the end with the rendition of Robert's wonderful, sprightly *Jagdlied*," Clara wrote in her diary.

Schumann requested Kistner to publish the songs earlier than had been intended in light of Lenau's death. "One might decorate the title page with emblems of mourning, such as a black drape through which a star is visible. The center leaf, with a cross and the Latin text, ought to be by itself, as it is in the manuscript. I should be pleased if you would lend me a hand in thus creating a modest monument to the great but unfortunate poet. Knowing you ,I am certain that you will find the appropriate design." This was done in accord with Schumann's wishes.

Delighted that Schumann's happy dream of becoming a conductor now would come true (a hope that was not to be fulfilled), the family journeyed to Düsseldorf late in the summer of 1850. It seemed to be the ideal position. Now he would be able to compose and to conduct his own orchestra, in performance of his own works.

The furniture was unloaded on September 8 and put in storage for a time. A few days were spent at the Breidenbacher Hof taking care of the tiresome details related to finding an apartment. On the day they moved in, an evening reception with music was given by the orchestra which, after the strenuous move, the couple barely had enough energy to attend. Julius Tausch, the choral director, conducted Robert's *Genoveva* Overture. He immediately made an unfavorable impression on Schumann, and indeed it was Tausch who later became the cause for Robert's resignation. He was then one of Düsseldorf's outstanding musicians, conducting both the *Liedertafel* and the male choral society. After the overture, members

KARL LEBERECHT
IMMERMANN

Born in Magdeburg, Immermann (1796–1840) briefly studied law but was called to arms when Napoleon returned from Elba in 1815. He participated in the battles of Ligny and Waterloo, entered Paris with Blücher's army and was demobilized as an officer. He proved his strength of character in 1817 when members of a Halle fraternity brutally attacked a poor student who did not wish to join their ranks, whereupon Immermann turned to the King with his pamphlet "Concerning the Student Unrests in Halle." He worked as a law clerk in Aschersleben until 1819 and then as an auditor in Münster. There he met the wife of Lützow of the Free Corps with whom he lived after her divorce. His comedy *Die Prinzen von Syrakus* was first given in Münster; which was followed by a collection of poems. Two tragedies, *Petrarca* and *König Periande und sein Haus* clearly reveal him to be a Romantic. In 1824 he was appointed to a judgeship in his native Magdeburg. While in Magdeburg he translated Scott's *Ivanhoe,* wrote essays on esthetics as well as the tragedy *Cardenia und Celinde* which created a considerable stir. Transferred to Düsseldorf, where artistic life was beginning to flourish, he added a new dimension to his literary undertakings with historical dramas, heroic poems, and some poems in a lighter, parodistic vein, and comedies. Of special significance was *Merlin,* a fantastic and profound *Mysterium.* A "literary tragedy" entitled *Der im Irrgarten der Metrik umhertaumelnde Kavalier* (The Gentleman Tottering Around in the Maze of Meter) was directed against Platen. A new collection of poems dating from ca. 1830 provided Schumann with several texts.

Immermann's life took on a new and invigorating dimension when he was asked to direct the Düsseldorf theater from 1835–38. He gave up his judicial appointment in order to devote himself entirely to his "model stage." Though the company was quite ordinary, his remarkable ingenuity in selecting repertory indeed made the Düsseldorf theater a model throughout Germany. In time the "model theater" failed, due to lack of financial support. No other large theater was in a position to retain the talented Immermann so he turned his creative energy back to writing, creating an idyllic-humorous novel *Münchhausen,* a satirical, scurrilous picture of his time which is now a classic of German literature.

In the fall of 1839 he married a granddaughter of the Halle chancellor Niemeyer. Firm in the belief that he finally had found happiness he wrote a new version of *Tristan and Isolde.* At the same time he worked on his memoirs. With his *Münchhausen* he pointed to a new way in which to describe contemporary life.

of the amateur chorus sang several of Schumann's songs: *Widmung, Die Lotosblume, Wanderlied.* This was followed by a performance of the second part of *Peri.* All that Clara could bring herself to write in her diary about the occasion was the single word: "nice."

Düsseldorf appeared to be fertile soil. There were piano students for Clara, and Robert was "greatly pleased" with the work of his colleagues, save for Tausch, and also with the taste of the citizenry. Schumann's first concert in October, 1850, which included the *Adventlied,* was a great success for the composer-conductor. None could have imagined the composer's impending collapse in that moment. The beneficial effects of the new environment are revealed in the compositions that followed: the Cello Concerto, Opus 129, and the *Rhenish Symphony* with its "musical pictures of life on the banks of the Rhine."

But mixed with these works we find songs that are clear premonitions of the onset of darkness. Remarks in the diary confirm this sense: "Bad moods and changeable moods," or remarks about "people who use the weaknesses of others to gain advantages for themselves." From remarks about moodiness, hypochondria, "lonesome walks" to "distant quarters," about moments of panic, being irritable and having compulsions to flee—from these one could but draw a painful conclusion. Schumann's choice of text for the first song is significant: *Herzeleid* (Heartache, Opus 107, No. 1; text by Titus Ullrich [1813–1891]) contains references to madness and death by drowning. They may have struck a sympathetic note in Schumann's mind at this time, shortly before his collapse and attempt to drown himself in the Rhine.

Though a copy of the song *Auf dem Rhein* (On the Rhine, Opus 51, No. 4) carries the date 1846, it refers only to a note Schumann then made, indicating plans for future composing. The poem itself by Karl Leberecht Immermann is inconsequential.

Immermann had died of "nerve inflammation" in 1840. His poem may have attracted Schumann for two reasons: not only does it border on the mystic, and ritualistic, but deals with suicide. In some ways it points to Schumann's actions in connection with his attempted suicide. In 1854 Schumann threw his wedding ring into the Rhine and then followed it, as confirmed by eyewitnesses. The golden treasure of Immermann's poem is protected by the river "until Judgment Day." Schubert's song *Der Sieg* may well have also been on Schumann's mind (Examples 80 and 81). The song's opening section is solemn and restrained; the continuation, using similar melodic material, is heartfelt and even more muted. (The indication "ritardando" applies to the entire measure, not merely to the high note.)

The music for *Jung Volkers Lied* (Young People's Song, Opus 125, No. 3) is fresh and lively—but the text, from Mörike's *Maler Nolten* was mutilated by Schumann. Clara's prudishness most likely was to blame; her influence now was stronger than at the time of *Dichterliebe*. "Mutterleib" (mother's body) and "in ihrem Schoss empfangen" (conceived in her womb) were expressions that would not do; nor is the mother described as "schön, frech" (beautiful, shameless). Schumann does not indulge in tone painting, as the subject might have suggested. In this song and in *Husarenabzug* (Opus 125, No. 5) we first encounter a technique familar from Hugo

JOHANN GOTTFRIED
KINKEL
(1815–1882)

Kinkel was appointed professor of church history in Bonn in 1837. His acquaintances there included Geibel, Freiligrath, Simrock, and Müller von Königswinter. His liberal views resulted in a transfer to the faculty of philosophy. In 1848 he became a member of the National Assembly in Frankfurt, a republican of the left. He participated in the insurrection in Baden and the Palatinate, was wounded, taken prisoner, and sentenced to life imprisonment. Carl Schurz was able to free him from Spandau, after which he fled to London.

In 1866 Kinkel returned to become professor of archeology and art history in Zürich where he became acquainted with Jacob Burckhardt and C. F. Meyer. His poetry is virtually forgotten today. He wrote political essays, epics in verse form, and tried his hand at playwriting.

Wolf's songs; the expression of cockiness and high spirits by using eighth-note chords, staccato, with rapidly changing harmonies.

Schumann adds an attractive touch to Mörike's poem *Der Gärtner* (The Gardener, Opus 107, No. 3); he intentionally confuses the listener with a series of variations on the basic "rider on horseback" rhythm. Hugo Wolf composed the same text; the influence of Schumann's setting, especially its ending and postlude, is apparent. Wolf even adopted the galloping rhythm of dotted triplets, but in spite of such borrowings Wolf's song is far more effective.

Example 80

Mässig langsam.

O un_bewölktes Le_ben! so rein und tief und klar.

Example 81

Ziemlich langsam.

Auf dei - nem Grun - de ha - ben sie an ver - borg - nem Ort

Schumann took the text for the solemn *Abendlied* (Evening Song, Opus 107, No. 6) from Kinkel's collection of poems published in 1850. In it we hear the "angelic voices," artistically transformed, which became a painful obsession of the composer; he heard them constantly. The mood is established by triads outlined in quarter-note triplets; over these the melody moves calmly in eighths and quarter notes. In order to leave the melodic line intact Schumann did not shy away from writing accents where they do not belong (as he had done before), especially on the first syllables of words such as "Majestät." A careful performer should deemphasize these accents. Schumann also substituted the word "Tiefe" (depth) for "Thale" (valley) in order to justify the low bass notes. If Brahms, who entered Schumann's life in 1852, was fond of writing chains of 4/3 chords, this Schumann song may have been his model. In those places where optional variants are provided, the line that goes with the piano part is to be preferred, as always.

The small cycle *Vier Husarenlieder* (Four Hussars' Songs, Opus 117; text by Lenau), "dedicated to the singer, Herr Heinrich Behr," remained incomplete in the sense that Schumann did not publish the song *Frühlingsgrüsse*. Its cockiness, though kept under control, takes us back to an earlier time, with its lively and arresting rhythm. *Der Husar, Trara* (Opus 117, No. 1) presents a special challenge: when sung at the right tempo the extremely rapid delivery precludes the normally expected pronunciation of "rolled" r's. One wonders why Schumann repeated the first stanza in *Den grünen Zeigern* (The Green Sign Posts, Opus 117, No. 3) at the end for it obscures the change from carefree days of youth to manhood—apparently for the sake of the bass line. The rhythm, in the Hungarian manner, is independent of the bar line—intended, perhaps, as an homage to Lenau's native land. In all, Schumann's effort to write dashing military songs was only mildly successful.

Chapter 23

During the first year in Düsseldorf, Schumann's major undertaking as a composer was *Der Rose Pilgerfahrt,* Opus 112, a fairy tale for solo voices and chorus with piano accompaniment, text by Moritz Horn. Schumann, always ready to make revisions and arrangements, soon turned it into an "oratorio" with orchestra accompaniment. Quite likely the earlier, reduced scoring would have assured the work a more lasting place in the repertory. In a letter to the author of the text, dated September 29, 1851, Schumann confirms this: "I originally had provided an accompaniment for piano only; in view of the delicate subject this seemed entirely adequate and still seems so." In fact, the rather insignificant chorus *Ei Mühle, liebe Mühle* was often performed as a duet with piano accompaniment.

About the time-consuming work on the orchestration Schumann writes: "It's a thankless job—not only hard work but also uninteresting. Once I have finished something it no longer interests me. I always want to move on to other things." The newspaper reviews, however, welcomed the new orchestration. This version was first given at a concert of the *Musikverein* on February 5, 1852, in the "wooden shack," the Geissler Gartensaal. (The Düsseldorf Tonhalle now occupies the site.) It pleased everyone. "Fräulein Hartmann and Fräulein Schloss" sang the soprano and alto parts. A Leipzig performance followed soon after, on March 14. Many notable German musicians attended, headed by Liszt, Joachim, Richard Pohl and Ludwig Meinardus.

In the 19th Century the work was a great favorite of virtually all choral groups. Today we realize that Schumann, guided by the sentimental text, provided an excess of melodic charm. Moritz Horn, an actuary in Chemnitz, had sent his text to Schumann early in 1851. Some reservations about composing such a "middle class epic" seem to have occurred to Schumann when he wrote: "Certainly, it is suitable for music, and I already have thought of many melodies. But many cuts should be made, and more dramatic qualities are needed . . . If you would be willing to make some changes for the sake of the music I should really like to compose it . . . Right now it all is fresh in my mind, and if you will make these changes: the sooner, the better." Horn soon obliged, for at the end of May Clara remarks that "in spite of the intolerable street noise he manages to write much wonderful music."

From the manuscript, located by Hans Schneider, it is clear that the work was essentially committed to paper at this time, though only with piano accompaniment and without the final chorus. Again and again Horn's text resulted in teary, sentimental music. A fairy queen changes the rose into a mortal virgin who experiences human love with so much feeling that any composer willing to tackle the subject would have succumbed to sentimentality. Richard Wagner criticized the weak text severely, and even Kretzschmar, who wrote a detailed review, remarked on this weakness, although he concluded by placing the work in the company of Ludwig Richter and the Düsseldorf painters, the Grimm Brothers and the exponents of German Romanticism.

Though Schumann apparently found the text coherent he did not succeed in transforming it into a musical whole, although it possesses some beautiful details. Compared to the early choral works, placed in distant times and places, *Rose* has an ordinary,

Robert Schumann,
Der Rose Pilgerfahrt:
A page of the autograph

everyday setting. The "paradise" described here is that of lower middle-class life, or of a stylized rustic setting. It does not seem too far removed from the comfortable musical world of today's "light classics". Insecurity as to stylistic standards, so widespread today, may also have troubled the composer.

The "Salvation Theme" almost inevitably enters into Schumann's thinking. He writes to Horn: "The evolution rose-young woman-angel seems poetic; it also represents a concept of upward evolution dear to all of us." That in *Rose* a woman should be longing for love is no accident: in that age love was considered the sole destination of a woman. She was to be wife and mother, to conceive and give birth—closer, therefore, to nature than was the male. The image of the rose was appropriate.

The theme of love and death also appears in *Rose*, but a clear motivation for her longing for death seems to be lacking. Her life on earth is comfortable and contented, so salvation through death seems contrived. As in *Peri*, the three stages of salvation correspond to the Christian concept of the soul's existence: paradise—life on earth—eternal life.

In a similar vein the idea of a rose becoming human can be seen as "overcoming" its earlier, natural state; eternal life then follows as an even higher state. An English interpreter found that the work's sentimentality was admirable and "typically German," but it seems naive to conceive of a foreign culture as nothing more than a collection of relics from long ago. Schumann's music does little to compensate for the banality of the text. Forester, miller and grave digger appear, but remain two-dimensional, like a collection of genre pictures kept in the parlor. Setting this kind of subject to music was to reduce oratorio to a more intimate level, for the libretto made a large-scale work impossible. Perhaps Schumann intended with this work to distance himself from the bombastic productions of his day, to withdraw to a more comfortable milieu. The choral writing shows great restraint, avoiding anything that would "dress up" a scene. Choruses do not represent reality in this work, but the spirit of nature, or "the people", in a rather idealistically conceived manner.

The individual characters lack definition, even more so than in Schumann's opera. They move in a remote, fairy-tale world never

Der Rose Pilgerfahrt
Title page of a later edition

establishing contact with reality. We are hardly moved by the rose's suffering: it remains an ornament and has no influence on the subsequent plot. There is a little more outer action than in *Peri;* as the libretto contains a number of dialogues. Scene 6 shows traces of individual character drawing but never achieves the stature of realistic drama. Martha's words are accompanied by a rising figure in the orchestra (Example 82), with dynamics changing from a hesitant, timid *piano* to a rough *forte.* The melodic line is broken by leaps, but the dialogue continually moves in even quarter-notes, dampening any dramatic effect.

Example 82

hat man im Haus erst eu-er-glei-chen,

The work, in two parts, consists of 24 connected numbers. As in *Peri,* definite endings are reserved for the few choruses. Even after the impressive mourning procession *(Wie Blätter am Baum)* the entrance of the tenor soloist, a cappella, continues with material from the preceding melody. In every case a new piece is prepared and conditioned by what came before: a held note, a continued tone color, an anticipated modulation. The overall effect is that of a consistent stream of music in which only color and intensity vary although it occasionally stops flowing altogether; for instance, when the grave digger, accompanied by almost inaudible string chords, reminisces about his "dear wife" who is resting far away.

Schumann's harmonic language in this work uses keys that stand in relationships of thirds and fifths. There are frequent changes from major to minor as well as sudden shifts to remote keys, as for example, when the tenor describes Rose's maternal bliss and the "veil of tears" through which she offers thanks to God. Schumann, with the interpolation of measures full of bold harmonic changes, manages to dispel an overly placid, idyllic mood. But there are long stretches which tire the listener by constantly falling back on what had proved to be effective in Schumann's earlier songs and choral works. This resort to older techniques appears in the tenor part, for example, in the obtrusive appoggiaturas (interval of a third) on accented words. And, much as Schumann admired his late friend—did he have to imitate Mendelssohn's style whenever a chorus of elves was called for? Such literal quotations had surely been embarrassing enough, in *Genoveva.* In *Rose,* the male chorus "Bist du im Feld gewandert" is a little more ambitious; here the description of nature, with horn accompaniment, introduces harmonies that go beyond Schubert, Marschner or Mendelssohn. Fortunately Schumann does not indulge in the text repetitions so customary in oratorios. Thus we have some quite short ensembles, such as the quartet: rose—miller—miller's wife—grave digger.

There is much that is buoyant and cheerful in *Rose,* closely tied to its Rhenish milieu, but Schumann is at his best in the more serious parts. Especially moving is the rose's death: "Schwarzer Tod, das ist kein bleicher, das ist ein Tod voll Morgenrot." (Death—not pale, but full of the promise of the morning's red sky.) Musical motives frequently are text-inspired, as in the women's chorus No. 20, *Ei Mühle, liebe Mühle,* where we hear the rattling of the mill. No. 22 begins with the appearance of a band; before the dance starts we hear the tuning of instruments.

Schumann emphasized to Moritz Horn that he wanted to write music "in the folk style." In spite of this, *Der Rose Pilgerfahrt,* though intended for amateur performance, reveals in every measure the composer's artistry and great skill. Inner voices in the orchestra reveal his mastery in this lively writing and harmonic shading. The ideal seems to have been the kind of "music for singing and playing" still advocated in school music today.

The first performance took place on July 6, 1851, in the large music room of a new, quieter apartment in Düsseldorf. The small version presented was given with the piano part played by Clara. Schumann was pleased by the favorable reception. The *Singkränzchen,* about 30 singers who took turns meeting every other

192

week in a member's home, participated. Their policy was to try out "works which larger groups would not take on, such as Lieder, excerpts from operas, pieces with accompaniment and the like." In November 1851 Clara complained that rehearsing and socializing were not kept separate. "The Kränzchen met at Hildebrand's. Robert was annoyed because of all the talking, with Hildebrand setting a bad example. That's the way it is here: they have lots of energy for making conversation, but not for singing." Still, the first performance of *Rose* must have gone well, for Schumann reported to Plitzsch: "Last month we had a little performance. The work is a fairy tale . . . somewhat like *Peri* in form and mood, but a little more rustic and German." Two years later the work and its creator were acclaimed in The Hague. With much applause a wreath was placed on Schumann's shoulders. He hardly noticed, "but the rest of us did, and I [Clara] thought to myself: that's the way it ought to be!"

Fairy tales were among Schumann's favored subjects during the early days in Düsseldorf—witness the *Märchenbilder* for viola and piano and the *Märchenerzählungen* for clarinet and piano.

There were also plans for an oratorio, *Luther,* about which he corresponded with Ferdinand Pohl. He conceived of a poetic but folk-like treatment, outlining his concept in a letter to the librettist: "The oratorio definitely should be on a popular level, comprehensible to farmer and burgher alike . . . My aim is to write the music in that vein, i.e., certainly not artful, complicated and contrapuntal, but simple and strong, with effective rhythms and melodies." Luther was in Schumann's eyes "a great man of the people;" in this choral work Schumann endeavored to present his

A printed invitation to a musical matinee

hero in that light. The approach reminds one of his writing his Third Symphony, for which he journeyed along the Rhine, collecting songs sung by the people. There is a memo with the advice to "always listen to folk songs; they are a treasure trove of the most beautiful melodies and provide an insight into the characteristics of different nations."

The work was planned to lead to a great climax, which in turn would lead into the concluding chorale, *A Mighty Fortress. Luther* remained a project, but Schumann may have begun composing it: on two pages of the piano version of *Rose* there are fragments of a clarinet part for *Luther.* What might have been a major contribution to the intended new style remained unwritten.

Chapter 24

Schumann's new position pleased him initially, but he lacked the qualities necessary to be truly successful: physical coordination, presence of mind, and especially the ability to communicate verbally. His players waited in vain for interpretive suggestions. He would have them play through a piece once; if it didn't go well he would, without offering any suggestions, merely repeat it. Occasionally he might remark that he had different ideas about this or that, but he would not explain what he had in mind. His lack of conducting skills was not immediately noticeable as the orchestra had been well trained by Hiller, Rietz, and Mendelssohn. Only with time would his insufficiencies become evident.

Due to his difficult personality, Schumann found himself isolated from the musicians who looked to him for inspiration and strong leadership—qualities which he knew he did not possess. According to Clara Faltin, Schumann in rehearsals "tended to let things slide, but his wife, sitting in the front row, would try to pull things together, occasionally giving a warning signal that brought her husband back to reality." Such measures were not likely to increase Robert's self-confidence on the podium; to the contrary, they must have added to his feelings of insufficiency. By the autumn of 1851 it was already clear that he no longer was able to lead even a small ensemble such as the *Singekränzchen*. Lack of interest on the part of its members led it to go out of existence, while the *Quartettkränzchen* disbanded because its participants were inadequately prepared. Only a small number of musicians were included in the Schumanns' circle of friends, although chamber music continued to be cultivated in their home thanks to Clara's initiative.

ELISABETH
KULMANN
(1808–1825)

The German-Russian Elisabeth Kulmann was the daughter of an Alsatian family who had emigrated to Russia. Her very first publication had attracted attention; even Goethe and Jean Paul found favorable things to say about her and her poems. She spoke Russian, German, and Italian fluently, translated Anacreon and Alfieri's *Saul* into Russian, prepared Russian versions of non-European fairy tales, and translated Oserow's tragedies into German. Her works were published in 1833 by the Russian Academy of Sciences. Schumann owned the complete edition of her fiction, the eighth printing of which appeared in 1857.

Robert was happy within the family circle. To his friend Bennett he spoke of the "creative urge which continually inspires me." And so in May, 1851, before the Schumanns embarked on a summer journey, some new products of this inspiration were to issue from Robert's study—a long, narrow room full of bookcases and music racks. These were the songs based on texts by Elisabeth Kulmann.

Schumann's choice of these saccharine poems has led to the assumption that mental decline was clouding his judgment. But there are many reasons for his choice. During these last years Schumann was principally occupied with plans for large works. Only sporadically did he grow enthusiastic about song composition, and when he did his choice was influenced by fashions and preoccupations of the day. Additionally, Kulmann's personal fate, particularly her death at the age of 17, probably fascinated the composer more than her poetry.

It is hard for us today to understand the esteem in which the verses of the young woman were held—rhymes that were published in large printings. They appealed in an age when tearful sentiment was much in vogue. Schumann called these poetic effusions "noble masterworks; a refuge in our chaotic times." He had always had a soft spot for orphaned children as is evidenced by the earlier *Armes Waisenkind* and *Die Waise,* which may have added to his excessive fondness for Kulmann's poetry. The child-like musical style with which he responded to the words of the "wonderfully gifted creature" contrasts sharply with the style of other late works. With these songs Schumann published a eulogy to which he added biographical information and other brief comments. These additions were included in the first edition published by Kistner and also in Dörffel's edition. Schumann ends with the following remarks: "Among her last poems is the *Traumgesicht nach meinem Tode* (Visionary Dream after My Death) in which she describes her own death. This may be one of the noblest poems of all time. Thus she left us, like an angel who crosses over lightly to the realm of the dead, leaving behind a brightly shining, heavenly apparition." Indeed, Kulmann's portrait graced the wall of Robert's study until the end.

It must be added that Schumann was not totally unaware of the poems' weaknesses. He omitted many verses: the fourth in *Mailied,* the last in *An die Nachtigall,* and the last four stanzas of *An den Abendstern.* Really imaginative music might have saved such lyrics, but Schumann was unable to rise to such a challenge. There is something distinctive about *Reich mir die Hand, O Wolke* (Reach down, O Cloud, Opus 104, No. 5), perhaps due to its likeness to Eichendorff's style. In the Kulmann songs (and in the last works in general) calmness reigns, the lack of concern for tempo coming dangerously close to a dissolution of musical contours. It is as though the composer's physical deterioration left traces in his music.

Schumann, tall and impressive in appearance, came to cherish silence and solitude above all. His walk was hesitant, dragging, his footsteps almost inaudible.   At home he moved on tiptoe most of the time. Due to his nearsightedness he constantly used a *lorgnette,* though none of the extant pictures portray it. He mumbled in a voice that lacked inflection. In all he conveyed the impression of a complete introvert. From the time he had formed a family and developed problems with alcohol he became silent and shunned social life. Friends no longer provided links to the outside world—links that he secretly desired. At the end he desperately sought such contacts, but such attempts were so inimical to his current state that he quickly regretted having made them. Being wrapped up in himself, and suffering frequent depressions, and reacting to these by drinking, to which he had become increasingly addicted, sapped his strength and will to live. The premonitions of Kulmann, the poet, and Schumann, the composer, seemed to converge.

Their most successful song was *Der Zeisig* (The Finch, Opus 104, No. 4) with its two competing canonic lines. The songs had been intended as an homage, but perhaps Schumann merely wrote them "in memory of the poet," as is indicated in the heading.

"A little family excursion on the Rhine" in July turned into a longer journey to Mont Blanc. These were happy weeks, full of new impressions, and on his return Schumann soon began to write more songs. *Die Spinnerin* (In the Spinning Room, Opus 107, No. 4; text by Heyse) was composed in August but was later included in the collection dedicated to the singer Sophie Schloss. Brahms was inspired to write a better song based on the same poem. Wolfgang Müller-von Königswinter furnished the lyrics for *Im Wald* (In the Forest, Opus 107, No. 5). Since the poem was not published during Schumann's lifetime it must have been made available to him through private channels.

The texts for three other songs composed in September were taken from the *Waldlieder* of Gustav Pfarrius (1800–1884). *Die Hütte* (The Hut, Opus 119, No. 1) is lively and attractive; not suffering from mannerisms such as suspensions to express languishing sentiment. The dark mood of *Warnung* (Warning, Opus 119, No. 2) is already established in the two opening measures; they shape the entire song in a rather stereotyped manner. Descending phrases with falling thirds in every first measure proceed without the voice; an original way to invite silence, as though singing might lead to death. Was Schumann thinking of himself? Modern singers might wish that the reference to the "dark owl" had been omitted. Voice and piano parts seem to be completely independent of each other, even unrelated.

Opus 136 once more points to an opera project that was never realized. A beautiful copy of the *Overture to Goethe's Hermann and Dorothea* carries the inscription "to my dear Clara, Christmas 1851." The orchestral overture, written December 19–23, 1851, is all that remains of a plan to compose Goethe's tale in verse as a *Singspiel*. In October, 1851 Schumann had written to the librettist of his *Rose* that "*Hermann and Dorothea* for a long time has been my pet project; let us not lose sight of it!" And a year later: "I should like to write a concert oratorio *Hermann and Dorothea*." But nothing beyond the overture ever was composed. It was not given until 1857 when Rietz performed it at the Gewandhaus, with moderate success. The critics were unhappy about the inclusion of the Marseillaise: 1848 was already ancient history!

The new year, which was to bring problems with his position and physical exhaustion brought on by conducting, began with Schumann's renewed interest in Uhland's poetry. *Provencalisches Lied* (Song of Provence, Opus 139, No. 4) and *Ballade,* Opus 139, No. 7, were composed early in the year. For the former, Schumann freely adapted the first and fourth stanzas of Uhland's long poem *Rudello,* and the last stanza of another, equally freely treated poem.

WOLFGANG
MÜLLER
(1816–1873)

He was known as von Königswinter, studied medicine in Bonn and settled in Düsseldorf as a general practitioner in 1842. From there he went as a delegate to the Frankfurt Parliament, but he soon withdrew from politics. Soon after having made Schumann's acquaintance in Düsseldorf he moved to Cologne, but he gave up his medical practice to devote himself entirely to writing. In 1869 he changed his residence to Wiesbaden. He wrote excellent poetry. Most of his writings, including some on art history, deal with the life and culture of the Rhineland.

A strange conglomerate resulted, resembling another work that was soon to follow. This is the "dramatic ballad" (really cantata) *Des Sängers Fluch* (The Singer's Curse) for soloists, chorus and orchestra, which Richard Pohl had assembled from various Uhland poems. Musically it is pompous and rather empty, especially where the stanzas are patched together. The postlude, however, possesses greater unity. The principal theme of *Provencalisches Lied* (Example 83) pervades the entire song; its simple beauty does honor to the composer who, at this late stage, was not "altogether lacking inspiration."

Uhland's *Ballade,* really "Three Songs," shows the poet's sovereign mastery of this genre. Schumann, with effort, does him justice, boldly changing to a distant key when direct speech occurs. When compared to Loewe's masterful setting of the same text, however, Schumann's work seems dry and colorless. The arpeggios of the accompaniment are meaningless and actually confuse the listener who hears the ballad by itself, not as part of Pohl's cantata version. Schumann was especially fond of the poem *Des Sängers Fluch;* years earlier he had praised his oldest daughter Marie who had memorized it for him. But it would have been better if Pohl had not been asked to "adapt" Uhland's gripping tale. At the story's climax, Pohl gives to the youth lines that Uhland had written in a different context. A dialogue ensues telling of the (newly invented) love of the young queen for the youth. Thus the story loses its focus, and the intended gripping effect is lost in an excess of words. In this ver-sion, *Provencalisches Lied* and *Ballade,* with harp accompaniment, serve merely as an interpolation. *Ballade* has one attractive feature: the impressive orchestral writing after the curse has been pronounced.

Schumann soon dedicated *Des Sängers Fluch* to his new young friend, Johannes Brahms; who according to his own testimony was pained by this attention.

In his setting of the ballad *Der Königssohn* (The King's Young Son, Opus 116) Schumann did not change Uhland's text save for the last lines. It, too, is scored for solo voices, chorus, and orchestra. A loud conclusion, striving for a broad effect, and unusually obvious tone painting were not at all in keeping with Schumann's style, nor did they succeed. More impressive are the sustained beginning and the Allegro section, "Im Walde läuft ein wildes Pferd." Generally speaking, Schumann missed the ballad's point, but that he was painfully unaware of this is obvious from his letter to Whistling, dated May 25, 1852: "[*Der Königssohn*] was recently given here. I think it is the most strikingly effective of all my compositions."

Much more impressive is the ballad *Vom Pagen und der Königstochter* (The Page Boy and the King's Daughter, Opus 140; text by Geibel). Here Schumann's creative powers are clearly in evidence, even though he committed it to paper in the greatest heat of summer and while suffering "convulsive spells," as he remembered later while in the Endenich asylum. Four contrasting parts are held together by the subject matter and common motifs. Colorful

Example 83

orchestration contributes to the total effect, to a degree that Schumann was rarely able to achieve. To revive this work would be a rewarding task!

Both the summer vacation and a last visit to Leipzig to perform the *Rose* were happy occasions, but they interrupted his creative work. He found resuming writing difficult, so that the pace and scope of his composing declined noticeably. On the morning of August 3, before a conducting obligation, he writes in the diary: "My energy is sadly diminishing," and, a few days later, "a time of much suffering." The changes in his condition were discouraging. As soon as he put manuscript paper on the table all activity came to a standstill. His mind remained clear—an idea was there, suspended in air. It spawned other ideas, each demanding precedence, but the connection between the idea and its execution was broken. Was it due to untreated diabetes or alcoholism? At times he could not lift a finger. Unable to tackle the task at hand he was oblivious to the passage of time. Before he knew it, evening had set in. He spent entire weeks, half asleep, in a state of confused drowsiness. Feelings of futility slowed him down, causing pain whenever he wanted to make plans. He imagined hearing things, suffered from dizziness, and his awareness of these conditions frightened him. He had no control over them; they must have made him aware of his incipient mental deterioration.

A trip to Scheveningen resulted in some slight improvement: by Christmas he was able to present Clara with his *Gedichte der Maria Stuart* (Poems of Mary Stuart, Opus 135). In his diary Schumann merely records that setting these old English poems (translated by Baron Gisbert Vincke) "gave me pleasure."

These poems, attributed to the unfortunate queen, assume a key position in Schumann's life, constituting a terminal point: they are the composer's last solo songs. The music, closely observing the text, seems to be modeled on the simple melodies of Elizabethan songs. Schumann describes the sorrows of the condemned woman in a consistent manner (four times in E minor and once in A minor), each song dealing with the inevitable fate. In the first song Mary looks back, and the music also evokes the past. A sad melody over a sixteenth-note accompaniment once more conjures up Romantic song. After this the style changes to spare monody, accompanied by

MARY,
QUEEN OF SCOTS

The daughter of James V of Scotland and Marie de Guise, she was educated at the court of France. In 1558 she was married to the Dauphin, the later King Francis II of France. As a granddaughter of Margaret Tudor, a daughter of Henry VII of England, she assumed the English title and coat-of-arms, disputing Queen Elizabeth's claim (whom she called the illegitimate daughter of Henry VIII) to the throne. Thus began the enmity of the two women and the power struggle for the English crown. It ended with Mary first accused of having murdered her husband and then with her execution, after 19 years of inprisonment in English castles. After much hesitation Elizabeth signed the death warrant on February 1, 1587. Mary was not granted the ministrations of a Catholic priest; she refused those of a Protestant minister. On the morning of her execution she received a host consecrated by the Pope, calmly entered the hall of execution, put her head on the block and loudly exclaimed: "Lord, into Thy hands I commend my spirit." Thus she died in her 47th year.

chords that suggest the sound of a harmonium.

The style of this small cycle does not allow for melodies in the manner that Schumann had initiated 13 years before. Language and its rhythm now govern form, including the manner of accompaniment. A style distantly related to what Wagner had fashioned now appears in the *Lied*. Relinquishing all oratory and emphasis, Schumann presents the spiritual condition of a woman under the shadow of death. She is reconciled to her fate when in No. 2, *Nach der Geburt ihres Sohnes* (After the Birth of Her Son), she prays to her Savior that He may protect her child—a prayer uttered in motionless declamation, as in psalmody. Four phrases, each more intense than the previous one and each on a higher scale step, express the urgency of her prayer, always to a descending fifth in the melody. *An die Königin Elisabeth* (To Queen Elizabeth) also is governed by the accents of speech, resulting in a kind of accompanied recitative. An angular rhythmic pattern supports the melody which provides no rests for breathing. There is a hint of courtly ceremonial. In *Abschied von der Welt* (Farewell to the World; No. 4) the initial six notes (Example 84) contain the only truly melodic element. Dark resignation prevails, repeatedly accentuated by "sighs" in the piano part. We are far removed from the Schumann of 1840, full of creative energy, who exclaimed "I want to keep singing like a nightingale until I die." Now the poet asks: "For these few hours of life, what use have I? My heart is dead to ev'ry mortal yearning," words that provide a key to the music and to Schumann's condition.

Example 84

In *Gebet* (Prayer, No. 5) Schumann succeeds in characterizing a moment of resignation, to a degree that Wagner, even with the greatest restraint, could not have accomplished. Still, it is fascinating that at this moment in history two composers, holding diametrically opposed positions, came close to each other through their declamatory styles. From their respective positions they were able to define a new kind of diction in German song. The Stuart songs mark the limit to which Schumann was able to restrict his vocal means of expression, reducing his musical language to a minimum. They stand at the end of a long, consistent development, from the fullness of unbridled fantasy to a soft, barely audible protest against the noisy music of his time.

Two choral works, also written in 1852, belong here. Through choral conducting in Düsseldorf Schumann came into contact with the Roman Catholic liturgy. It kindled his desire to "devote energy to sacred music," a goal that he had declared earlier to be the loftiest purpose of an artist. Out of this desire the works resulted which, according to their opus numbers, were his last ones: the *Mass in C Minor*, Opus 147, for four-part choir and orchestra, and the *Requiem*, Opus 148. These two works to a remarkable degree are expressions of Catholic mysticism. Alfred Einstein considered them to be "successors to Beethoven's *C Major Mass* and Mozart's *Requiem* in more than purely artistic ways."

In the Mass Schumann pays tribute to the Romantic veneration of the Virgin in such a fulsome way that he chose as text for the *oratorium* the "Tota pulchra es," scoring it for soprano solo accompanied by cello and organ. He also included the words "O Salutaris Hostia" in the Benedictus. The work appears to be more than the mere result of a commission. Nor can we consider Schumann's mysticism at this late stage to be only the manifestation of pathological introversion. It is related to the exaggerated desire of the German Romantics to escape from reality.

According to his own catalogue of works, Schumann sketched the Mass between February 13 and 22, 1852. First rehearsals of Kyrie and Gloria took place soon after they had been written; the first performance (only of the first movements) was on March 3, 1853 in the Geissler Auditorium in Düsseldorf, Schumann conducting. He never performed the entire work, nor did he ever hear it. Whoever has had the privilege of hearing the Mass will confirm that it is a moving experience, right to the concluding low D♭ of the cellos. The first performance of the complete work was given in Aachen in 1861, with Franz Wüllner conducting from the manuscript. Very few performances followed; among them we should specially mention that by Wolfgang Sawallisch in our own time.

The *Requiem* was begun on April 26. Once Schumann undertook to complete the original draft he decided on major cuts, especially in the Kyrie. As one of his last works it enjoys a certain esteem and is heard occasionally today. Schumann did not live to hear a performance; it was not published until eight years after his death. A diary entry on May 9, 1852, notes that he "played the *Requiem* for Clara." When he finally was committed to the Endenich clinic he requested the autograph. Though his imagination readily supplied new musical ideas their execution now became arduous. Numerous separate sketches for the *Requiem* exist; none of them contain any twelve successive measures without changes. Schumann undertook mysterious calculations: he counted the number of measures in each part of a movement, working out mathematical schemes and proportions. Composing, he once said proudly, was for him like a game of chess.

Nevertheless, Schumann's attitude toward church music was that of a poet: he was largely concerned with the emotional aspects of the sacred rite. According to reliable sources he repeatedly said that one composes a Requiem "for oneself," a remark that seems credible, for it is certain that he had decided to take his life. "I must leave:" these are the first words of the Mary Stuart translations; they end with "Save me!" His own attempted "execution," by drowning in the Rhine, was to occur shortly.

One thought appears to have helped him for the moment, a thought that earlier he did not wish to be true: the Europe in which he lived seemed hopelessly degenerate. In such times of decline, in the absence of new directions and ideas, a course of remedial action ought to become clear. But in such periods there also is such a confused mixture of wisdom and folly, of the beautiful and the common, that most people find it simpler to continue in accustomed ways and to believe in some mysterious reason for the inevitable decline.

Should he once more come out of the shell of his introverted seclusion? Schumann, no longer capable of making that decision, took refuge in evasive actions which only on the surface seem senseless or confused. There is a connection between the economy and verbal restraint of Schumann's last works and the cultural liquida-

Clara Schumann

tion of our own age—a kind of symbolic anticipation.

Schumann was annoyed by the lack of discipline and effort among those with whom he worked, especially the chorus. He was angered by those who urged him to relinquish his position to Tausch who substituted for him during Schumann's periodic illnesses, but he felt unable to deal with these matters. His physical strength clearly was deteriorating. His hearing and sense of rhythm, having become unreliable, interfered with performing and composing, rendering all work difficult. In May 1853, during rehearsals for the Music Festival of the Lower Rhine *(Niederrheinsches Musikfest)*, Schumann suffered a collapse. Düsseldorf's city council now requested that henceforth he conduct only his own works. It was only half a decision, apparently intended to demonstrate publicly that he continued to be associated with the city. But he considered such an arrangement an imposition. Instead he asked that his contract be terminated as of October 1, 1854. This was granted, but as it turned out, the date was too far in the future.

Not until shortly before the catastrophe did Clara give any indication of being aware of how serious the situation was. Friends visiting them in their home were troubled by the changes they noticed, especially Robert's impaired speech. This impairment had already developed during the early days in Düsseldorf, but Clara felt that Robert's bouts with depression and anxiety now were less apparent than before. She never completely understood the emotional world in which he lived. She could be tough and obstinate, at other times full of enthusiasm and burning ambition, and she had an uncanny influence over him. He felt this especially when they were making music together, or talked about music. She possessed the energy he lacked. As a young man he had already experienced her persistence which gave him no rest; apparently he would not have it otherwise. This behavior was one of the hidden aspects of his life.

Clara had resumed her own composing. "There is nothing like being productive myself, if only to have those hours when I can forget my own troubles, living and breathing only music."—One thinks of these words when listening to her *Six Songs from Jucunde by H. Rollet,* Opus 23.

Robert's own creative activity during the early months in Düsseldorf also increased. Any criticism of his struggles to achieve a new mode of expression was energetically rejected by Clara, thus also avoiding any potential disagreement with her husband. She unconditionally accepted his infatuation with Elisabeth Kulmann's poetry. On the other hand he eroded her self-confidence by brusquely criticizing her piano playing. "I hardly know any more how I should play," she complained on one occasion, after Robert's angry comments. "While I try my best to accompany a singer as delicately and flexibly as I can, Robert tells me that my playing is awful. If I didn't need the income from my playing I would never play another note in public. What good is the listeners' applause if I cannot satisfy him?" Nor did the trip to England, long in the planning, materialize: her duties as a mother kept her at home.

Chapter 25

Schumann quietly made plans for his departure—for ending the constant conflict between his obligations and his compulsion to compose. These plans included the completion, at long last, of the *Szenen aus Goethes Faust* (Scenes from Goethe's *Faust*) which still lacked a prelude. It seemed unsatisfactory to begin with the lyrical Scene in the Garden. In his will, made in 1851, he had stipulated that Gade should be in charge of editing his unpublished works. In the event that Gade was unavailable, Dietz was to make these decisions, "based on a thorough examination of the material. I particularly wish *Faust* and *Manfred* to be edited."

This Manfred, "doing good and evil to excess." a character of superhuman stature, has only one true counterpart in literature: Faust. It is therefore quite understandable that during his last ten active years Schumann was fascinated by the subject. Goethe's magic had attracted Schumann since childhood. As a mature composer he was even more under the spell of the poet's vision and restraint. "I owe everything to Goethe," he would confess, and the year 1849, "the most fruitful year of his life," stood entirely under Goethe's sign. *Genoveva* was attractive and picturesque; *Manfred,* the romantic hero, and his curse—these paled before *Faust,* both more profound and more detached.

Even as a young man Schumann saw himself as a reflection of Faust. Throughout his life he pondered the way of treating the subject in music, as an opera or a dramatic cantata based on excerpts from the play. Unlike Berlioz he never considered altering Goethe's text save in some insignificant details. In 1844, Schumann had considered Faust among various opera projects, which were turning over in his mind, but out of these plans for an oratorio soon developed instead—"a beautiful, daring" project with which, he hoped, Krüger would agree.

The third section of Schumann's score was completed first. It may have been intended to be used during the Goethe celebrations in Dresden, Weimar and Leipzig in 1849, at a time when few people were well acquainted with Part II of *Faust.* Even in our own time we should not assume that many people really know the entire *Faust,* no matter how much they praise it. Certain quotations and some memorable scenes have become famous, and it is to Schumann's credit that his use of popular snippets had no adverse effect on his work as a whole. He went far beyond them, and he was not afraid to set to music lines such as "Nur der verdient sich Freiheit wie das Leben, der täglich sie erobern muss." (To deserve a life of freedom, one must fight for it every day.)

We learned earlier that during the trip to Russia Schumann studied Part II of *Faust* thoroughly. As a result, Nos. 1,2,3, and 7 of the third section were written in 1844. Goethe's play offers a great deal to a composer's imagination. Schumann not only selected those parts which call for music; but mostly focused on scenes which one would not expect could be enhanced by musical treatment. These scenes, freely chosen, were effectively arranged to form three connected sections, preceded by an overture.

Nevertheless, these 13 scenes do not constitute a dramatic or musical whole. Their writing occupied Schumann for a considerable period of time and therefore reflect the ups and downs of his life, including periods of exhaustion, lack of concentration, and spiritual crises.

Schumann first tackled the thought-provoking last part; and he struggled tirelessly with this material. He arranged it in an order that is clear and logical, concentrating on the guilt, striving, struggles and salvation of Faustian man. Relatively few scenes are included that contain the well known, effective incidents: there is no poodle, no scene in Faust's study, no *Walpurgisnacht* (May Day Eve) which had served Mendelssohn's special purposes and had inspired a Loewe song; no Helen of Troy and, most surprisingly, very little of Mephistopheles.

The fact that Schumann approached the work from the perspective of the final chorus might explain his choices. In 1845, during one of the many interruptions in his work, he wrote to Mendelssohn: "The scene from *Faust* lies in my desk drawer; I am really anxious to take another look at it. What gave me the courage to tackle the subject in the first place was the moving, sublime poetry of the conclusion. I don't know whether I'll ever publish it."

It may seem strange that Schumann, the composer of secular oratorios, was specially fascinated by those scenes in *Faust* that are religious in character: the scene in the cathedral, Gretchen before the image of *Mater Dolorosa,* and the "Catholic" ending of Part II. In his *Geschichte der Musik in Italien, Deutschland und Frankreich,* Franz Brendel considers the third section of the *Scenes from Faust* to be religious music: "New ideas do not always find expression in music written specifically for the church, for liturgical purposes. Aspects of modern church music can also be found in the third section of Schumann's music for *Faust.*"

Certainly, Schumann's *Faust* focuses on the inner action. As in *Peri,* "salvation" is a central theme. "The subject matter and also the music recall *Peri* in that both characters, after intense striving and many errors, finally reach heaven." (Letter to Whistling, 1848.) Faust, the individual, is governed by an unknown fate. The final section moves on, beyond him, to transfiguration, to salvation which extends to Gretchen also. Her love is raised to a religious level. A reported theme in literature of the time was the image of the loving woman fused with the image of the Mother of God. Much earlier, in *Dichterliebe,* Schumann had included a Heine poem with the lines

Es schweben die Blumen und Englein
um unsre liebe Frau,
die Augen, die Lippen, die Wänglein,
die gleichen der Liebsten genau.

Our Lady sits mid the flowers,
and angels hover near;
her eyes, her lips and her cheeks
are those of my own dearest dear.

Schumann made it a point to omit those portions of *Faust* that were most popular, including most of the tragedy involving Gretchen, or the pact with the devil. He lifted the tragedy out of its historical context. To avoid the broad, epic proportions of the drama he turned to an appropriate medium: the symphonic oratorio. According to Heuberger, Schumann once remarked that a performance in one evening of all the scenes he had composed would be "an oddity," a statement that is hard to believe. Schumann finally gave up his original plan to compose an opera on the Faust theme, but as early as 1844 he wrote to Krüger: "What would you think of treating the entire play as an oratorio?"

Respect for Goethe did not keep Schumann from making some minor changes. If he adhered to the original text more closely than he had done elsewhere this need not, however, be seen as lack of self-confidence. An adaptation of the drama in the manner of Gounod's opera *Faust* would have seemed blasphemous to Schumann. Instead he set Goethe's text literally. True enough: his setting also amounts to a Romantic interpretation, emphasizing the religious aspects and reducing Mephistopheles to a marginal figure. But this recasting of Goethe's masterpiece does not represent a "failure," as some have rashly asserted. Backed by Goethe's text, Schumann was able to break the conventions of both opera and oratorio.

Above all, he disproved a common prejudice: that a text of high literary quality could not be set as an opera or oratorio. By choosing a literary masterwork he broke down the barriers between the genres and went some way in reducing the isolation of individual art forms. That the text in this case in part determined the shape of the music was an important contributing factor. Schumann's treatment

Autograph page from Schumann's Szenen aus Goethes Faust *(Scene in the Garden)* of the Faust subject transcends conventional musical genres.

The work was published without opus number as *Szenen aus Goethes Faust* for solo voices, chorus and orchestra. In spite of its clear formal design the overture (the last part of the score, written in August, 1853) lacks the intensity of the *Manfred* introduction. It is too insistently heroic, without relief, and the string writing offers formidable difficulties. Yet despite its weaknesses it is a work that moves the listener with its mixture, not easily achieved by Schumann, of emotion and skilfully crafted writing. A typical 19th Century overture, it is constructed in accord with the formula "through adversity and darkness to light," amounting to an orchestral condensation of the plot. Beginning with a sombre D minor it builds to the stretto of the final section in D major.

The ingratiating duet of the scene in the garden follows immediately, with the dialogue between Gretchen and Faust "Du kanntest mich, o kleiner Engel, wieder" (You recognized me, little angel). It reaches a high point, as a result of cuts in the text, in the "daisy-chain game:"—"He loves me, loves me not." Warmth and tenderness of melody do full justice to the text. A light orchestral texture with suspensions and woodwind chords, allows the *parlando* of the voices to be clearly heard. Mephistopheles, one of the moving dramatic forces in Goethe's treatment, is reduced by Schumann, if not to insignificance to at least a peripheral figure. A mood of helplessness characterizes Gretchen before the statue of the Virgin. She prays while decorating the statue with fresh flowers. Schumann's music closely reflects the dramatic situation: a figure in the violas represents her shaking hands. (Example 85) Gentle sounds

Example 85

describe her recollection of the rays of the morning sun in her bed-chamber; then her despair gains the upper hand. From its song-like beginning the music presses on to Gretchen's exclamation "Hilf,

rette mich von Schmach und Not!" (Example 86: Help! save me from disgrace and pain!) The sombre scene in the cathedral follows: Gretchen is subjected to the unrelenting accusations of the Evil Spirit. A choral setting of the *Dies Irae*, stern and threatening, expresses the inexorable, unforgiving attitude of the church. Schumann consistently contrasts Gretchen's helplessness, expressed in free declamation, with the stern, liturgical chant. This approach is entirely different from that of Berlioz in the "Dies Irae" of his *Fantastic Symphony*, of which Schumann wrote in a review: "Poetry, for a few moments, has put on the mask of irony to hide her sorrow. Perhaps the hand of a kind spirit will some day remove it."

Example 86

Schumann's interpretation of this scene is effective in a theatrical sense. He does not quote liturgical music but rather imitates its monophonic texture. It seems absurd that he should have been accused of having written music that was overly secular. An effective climax is reached with the choir's chordal *Judex ergo* which sweeps away both Gretchen's lament and the laughter of the Evil Spirit. All her anguished outcries are overshadowed by the *Dies Irae*, symbolizing the power of the church. Goethe's text provided the dramatic impact for the first three scenes, revolving around Gretchen's fate. Schumann had no trouble finding the right music for them. Her tragic love is treated in a subtle, psychological manner.

Greater obstacles to composition were offered by the opening scene of Part II. Here the text has musical implications. The restless

Example 87

Faust hopes to find sleep at dawn, in the "pleasant landscape." He is calmed by the singing of spirits, a transparent texture of six solo voices and chorus. One of Schumann's most languorous melodies, the pastoral tenor song in B♭ major, is accompanied by violins and harp (Example 87). Resplendent music then denotes the sunrise, in a manner which recalls the transition to the last movement of the Symphony in D Minor. Faust begins to sing, accompanied by quiet, low strings following which the music turns into a moving aria. Poetic sentiments and ideas are presented in a highly condensed manner. Schumann allows little room for the text's descriptions of nature; he subjects them to the formal disposition of an aria. It is a challenge for the singer to imbue the rather conventional melodic line with life and color. It seems as though the composer capitulated, faced with the multitude of ideas expressed in the text. Giving musical expression to the radiant light requires a sensitive, imaginative singer. The notes by themselves do not clearly indicate at this point what poet and composer intended to express.

In the following self-contained scene, "Midnight," Schumann demonstrates his skill in finding a musical equivalent for the expression of demonic energy. Want, Guilt, Care and Need, the four "Gray Hags," take turns casting their shadows on this sinister scene. Musical speech, recitative, forms a ghostly contrast to the timbres of woodwinds and low strings. An atmosphere of loneliness is fully established with greatest economy of means.

A fascinating scene immediately follows as Faust is stricken with blindness. In but a few lines darkness is depicted in a manner that compares favorably with what Wagner accomplished in *Lohengrin* or *Tristan*. At once, and indeed too quickly, darkness is dispelled. This conventional ending unfortunately does not sustain the brilliance of the preceding scene.

"Faust's Death" dwells on mortality. Mephisto leads the chorus of lemurs, sung by squeaking boys' voices. Their singing should not be as beautiful as it sometimes is. In "Courtyard of the Palace, Torches," Schumann writes a grotesque march such as Mahler would compose later. Faust's wish, that the beautiful moment may linger, cannot be fulfilled. He has failed to reach life's crowning achievement; instead, the lemurs are digging his grave. They take his body away to the tune of a distinctive funeral march that gradually fades away, its chordal leaps anticipating those of Strauss's *Zarathustra*. (Example 88)

Faust's solemn music dealt with words and their musical expression in a new and definitive manner, with greatest simplicity while maintaining melodic continuity. It is a language that can hold its own with that of Wagner who traveled along similar paths to a different goal.

Schumann manages to present some of the "profound," very German statements in *Faust* in a new light, free of any pathos, quietly communicating.

> Zum Augenblicke dürft' ich sagen:
> Verweile doch, du bist so schön!
> Es kann die Spur von meinen Erdentagen
> nicht in Äonen untergehn.
>
> (To the moment I could say:
> Linger, you are so fair!
> The record of my earthly days
> cannot disappear in the flight of time.)

Example 88

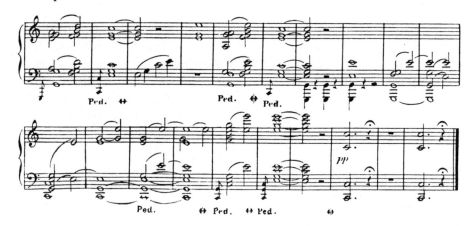

After the bitter, deadly struggle Mephisto's sarcastic postscript is sure to make its disillusioning point.

Schumann at one time gave the name "Faust's Transfiguration" to the last seven numbers of the work which make up the long, third section. This final scene is of special importance; it expresses Goethe's conviction that man's development, in spite of everything, will lead to a better future. Schumann's attempt to give greater intensity to Goethe's text through music is most successful here. That he should single out this allegorical ending reveals something of his infallible instinct. To the composer it represented the rise and transfiguration of striving man who is received into the realm of those who have found fulfillment. Faust partakes of the grace of the blessed by the intercession of atoning love.

Initially Schumann resisted any concern over providing a musical foundation for the ideas expressed. The Gretchen tragedy was not added until later. Faust's awakening and death were also late additions. In this way a more or less complete dramatic plot was achieved, interwoven with several atmospheric scenes. Yet there was the danger that Schumann's music might not be capable of doing justice to the cosmic dimensions of the tragedy. And so the composer sought to provide a substantial ending that would unify the work. Would he succeed?

As late as 1848 he voiced his concerns to Brendel: "I'm afraid people will ask: why add music to poetry that is perfect by itself?" To deal with this poetic language, musical in itself, he fell back on a genre which he had created: the lyric oratorio, with roots in the *Lied* transferred to the secular choral idiom. Goethe's disposition of the text suggested seven musical sections to Schumann. He did not think of each as a separate, elaborate piece but rather thought that together they had the character of a cohesive finale. From the opening *Pastorale* of the holy Anchorites to the emotional recital of the *Pater ecstaticus* with solo cello, to the hymn of the *Pater profundus,* accompanied by trombones, the music proceeds (through the tonalities of F major, D minor and B♭ major) to the response of the *Pater seraphicus,* accompanied by a three-part chorus of women's voices. Faust's "immortal remains" are carried upward by a choir of angels; solo and choral singing alternate. Their powerful "gerettet" (he is saved) is set off from the lyrical effusions of the Blessed, as Gretchen's voice once more emerges.

"I had thought that I'd never be able to finish the work, especially the concluding chorus," Schumann admitted, after hearing an intimate performance in 1848. While the second version of the final chorus was recommended for performance, it actually is less successful (due to its conventional *forte* ending and the reduced place of the four soloists) than the rejected first version which, without appearing to be a finale, makes a far stronger impression. After the buildup to the climax, "Das Unbeschreibliche, hier ist's getan" ("That which defies description, is here fulfilled"), the end fades away in an ethereal *pianissimo*. A feature that detracts from the finale's impact is the oratorio-like wordiness that invades the music, after the impressive beginning, to the words "Zieht uns hinan . . . zieht uns hinan" ("lifts us upward").

In spite of this shortcoming we can conclude that Schumann's *Scenes from Faust* is the most valid setting of this famous and often-composed text. Some of its visionary aspects caused him great pain, such as the lemurs' songs and the angelic choirs, but he succeeded in interpreting them in ways that express their inner meaning more convincingly than the settings by other composers, Liszt, Berlioz, Mahler and Busoni, who tried their hands at setting the drama. Liszt performed Schumann's as yet incomplete *Scenes* in 1 8 4 9, at the time of the Goethe celebrations in Dresden and Leipzig. He was able to report to his friend that "this beautiful, grandiose work made the most beautiful and most grandiose impression." Schumann accomplished this without resorting to sure-fire effects and without dazzling staging. His *Faust* concentrated on the essential at a time when the prevailing objective was to "bowl over" an audience.

This Dr. Faust was for Schumann the incarnation of insatiable modern man. As he worked on his score he came to terms with this new psyche—the person (including the artist) who rushes from experience to experience, from one desire to another, making the most of every moment which is so beautiful that he wants to sustain it forever.

Chapter 26

When, on September 30, 1853, Schumann recorded in his diary: "Mr. Brahms from Hamburg," he had, in many ways, reached the end of the road. His position as music director in Düsseldorf had come to an end and no other comparable post was in sight. Only a few of his recent compositions had proved successful. He was aging visibly, in marked contrast to Brahms who had in abundance all that Schumann seemed to no longer possess. The *Davids-bündler,* silent for some months, now mustered his remaining strength and with great enthusiasm and imagination he wrote an article, *Neue Bahnen* (New Paths), to enlighten musical Germany about the budding genius, Johannes Brahms.

Strenuous preparations for the *Niederrheinisches Musikfest* were concluded to everyone's satisfaction. Schumann conducted the revised version of his Symphony in D Minor after which he was presented with a well-deserved laurel wreath. Then, in November, the Schumanns departed for Holland, leaving behind all the unpleasantness and intrigues swirling in Düsseldorf. His spirits had been lifted through several stimulating contacts with Joseph Joachim, the young violinist. For a period he even lost interest in the occult, having recently become fascinated by such things as table-lifting seances.

Once more poetry by Uhland inspired Schumann to write a choral work: *Das Glück von Edenhall* (The Good Fortune of Edenhall, Opus 143). He continued to feel the need to write dramatic music, but now turned to genres that did not require staging. Litzmann was right when he observed that "Schumann knew that with these works he was creating a new genre. During his last years

they took the place of opera." Unfortunately the text arrangement of Schumann's last Uhland ballad, involving several protagonists, was not his own, for the composer had turned it over to Dr. Hasenclever, his physician in Düsseldorf. If the finished composition reflects Schumann's illness rather clearly, Hasenclever's liberties with the text, resulting in an awkward libretto, must also bear some responsibility. The music, however, is genuine Schumann, which alone should be sufficient reason to revive the work. Schumann never published this "Ballad with Orchestra;" that matter fell to Clara after his death, who first solicited Brahms's opinion. Brahms had serious reservations, as he did in the case of all works Schumann himself had not readied for print. Nevertheless Clara decided to go ahead. In the end, Brahms edited only the Supplement volume to the Complete Edition.

In the four choral ballads Schumann was anxious—too anxious—to write in an impressive and effecting manner; all of them differing from his oratorios in this way. Painting with loud colors and striving for obvious effects were not his style, and these ballads show it. Their stature is far below that of the ballads with piano accompaniment.

In September Robert had given Clara a grand piano. The present was accompanied by a vocal quartet, *Orange und Myrthe* (Orange and Myrtle), on a text that probably was his own, which to the present writing has not been published. (Translator's note: according to Grove's *Dictionary,* 6th ed., it was published in 1942.) Once before, in July, 1840, a poem had served to accompany the gift of a new grand piano. The closing lines of the 1853 poem

Johannes Brahms, ca. 1854

He also advised that for the winter of 1854–55 he intended to free himself of obligations in Düsseldorf and would spend some time in Vienna. "We are fed up with the small-town atmosphere in Düsseldorf. Everything seems to be in a rut here; the same things continue to be done by the same people. We are anxious to break out of this and breathe a different air."

The air in Holland was good for Schumann. The Dutch gave his music a reception quite different from that which it had received in Germany. Later, Mahler was to experience the same thing. Schumann found well-trained orchestras; conducting them once more gave him pleasure. His symphonies, choral works, chamber music and piano music, as well as many songs and duets delighted the public. Full of favorable impressions and deeply satisfied, the couple returned to Düsseldorf on December 23. For the last time they decorated their children's Christmas tree together.

It seems as though shortly before the catastrophe Schumann once more was in high spirits. There is no evidence to the contrary in the delightful, humorous *Romanze vom Gänsebuben* (Tale of the Gooseherd, Opus 145, No. 5; text, from the Spanish, by O. van der Malsburg), for soloists and mixed voices. The four solo voices relate the story; the chorus chimes in with the humorous refrain, "Helf mir Gott, wie fliegen die Gänse!" (Heaven help me the geese are flying away!). The entire piece is well conceived and executed, with its Spanish flavor suggested by bits of imitation here and there, sudden changes from *piano* to *forte,* coloraturas and trills. Schumann may have had in mind agile voices from southern lands.

With the second number of Opus 146 Schumann returned to his favorite poet, Burns. He now completed the ballad *Bänkelsänger* (Rattlin', Roarin' Willie), begun in 1849. It, too, sounds like Schumann at his best. The setting of Uhland's *Der Traum* (The Dream, Opus 146, No. 3) although simple is convincing and is followed by one of the jewels of German choral song: *Das Schifflein* (The Little Boat, Opus 146, No. 5) by Uhland, a poem that was warmly received at the time. A setting by Loewe, with guitar accompaniment, had been published shortly before and was widely performed. In his setting Schumann demonstrated his concept of what a ballad should be. In the first stanza the chorus is heard; after

admonish the recipient: "Und kann ich nicht immer bei Dir sein,/eil' dann zum Freund und denke mein!" (And if I cannot always be near you, seek the friend's company, and think of me!")

Before he left for Holland, Schumann sent the *Ballade vom Haideknaben* to its dedicatee, van Bruyck, who shortly before had dedicated his own piano sonata to Schumann. He requested van Bruyck to pass on the second copy to Hebbel, the author of the text.

Example 8 9

the opening of the second stanza a French horn, mournfully played by one of the passengers, a woodsman who had taken out his hunting horn, chimes in (Example 8 9). Its melody develops easily into the soprano melody but does not interfere with the telling of the story, and soon another passenger joins in, this time a flute player. After a brief prelude, he plays a similar tune, in a higher register. Charmed by their playing, the "dumb" girl miraculously begins to sing, her phrases are brief and simple (Example 9 0), and ending with "adieu", with the chorus silent and the instruments finishing on a long fermata. The river crossing is over; the little boat has reached the other shore. The passengers all go their separate ways, and the poet asks: "Wann treffen wir uns, Brüder, auf einem Schifflein wieder?" (Brothers, when shall we meet again on another crossing?) Horn and flute answer from a distance to the thrice-repeated question. The charming poem was ennobled, indeed, fulfilled, by the masterly musical setting. An illustration in Ludwig Richter's family album, *Beschauliches und Erbauliches*, entitled *Überfahrt* might well have served as an illustration for Schumann's ballad.

Example 9 0

With the *Three Songs for Women's Voices and Piano,* Opus 114, we bid farewell to Schumann as a writer of vocal music. They can hardly be surpassed in their simplicity. Save for a hint of canon in the concluding *Spruch* (Motto; text by Rückert), they consist chiefly of harmonized melody. For his setting of Bechstein's *Nänie* (Elegy; Opus 114, No. 1) he merely indicates the tempo ("slow") and general dynamic levels ("The first verse *piano;* the second, *pianissimo.*")

In *Triolett* (Opus 114, No. 2; text by L'Egru) the piano accompaniment rises to importance only during the interlude. Schumann no longer writes atmospheric music, nor did the text inspire a specific formal concept. Further, Schumann's reflections on Wagner may be involved. Schumann viewed Wagner as the victim of destructive forces, building but at the same time demolishing, creating intensity but also, alas, superficiality.

Schumann's trip to Hannover in January, 1854 was probably the last pleasurable event in his life. Brahms and Joachim had arranged a small Schumann festival which turned out to be an unqualified success, blotting out all the accumulated feelings of bitterness. On his return Schumann once more settled down to work, composing the Concert-Allegro for Piano and Orchestra, the Violin Concerto

Ludwig Richter: The river crossing at Schreckenstein

for Joachim, and finally two movements for the Sonata F-A-E ("Frei aber einsam"—free but lonely: Joachim's motto).

The voice is silent in Schumann's swan song. *Gesänge der Frühe* (Songs of Youth) represents a return to the piano, though, in a sense, they seem like a last vocal message. Schumann wrote to the publisher: "These pieces describe morning—my feelings about it, and its gradual change. They are more an expression of feeling than painting." Their moods seem to capture the feelings of what is inevitable—even perhaps longing for death. The work is dedicated to "the august poetess, Bettina;" she visited Schumann in the asylum and reported that to her great amazement his mind was entirely clear. Following the dedication is another heading: "To Diotima," referring to his sense of closeness to Hölderlin. Schumann's farewell to music is tantamount to forsaking all those hopes which had sustained him through his life.

A love of poetry had animated him since his early days; in time it became the focus of his creative work. Now, at the end of the road, words once more occupied all his time and energy, save when alcohol intervened. Tension between him and Clara increased, brought on in part by her pregnancy with their last son. He made a survey of poetry which and poets who displayed an affinity to music. Among these were some whose lyrics he already had set to music: Byron and Hebbel.

We are close to the time when reliable accounts of Schumann cease to exist and where we fall back on conjecture. There are a few letters, written from the asylum, and reports by an occasional visitor. But just before this time Schumann once more returned to the three figures who are ever-present in his music and yet existed only in his imagination: Florestan, Eusebius, and Raro. Schumann now returned to some of the aphorisms he had written 20 years earlier, adding to and collecting them in a *Denk-und Dichtbüchlein* (Little Book of Thoughts and Poems). He revised the earlier ones, rendering them more precise and to the point. Each thought was assigned to one of the three imaginary figures. If it seems incredible that Schumann could, at this point, carry out these revisions with such sureness and precision, we must keep in mind that our view of his mental disease or confusion is distorted. His alcoholism was almost invariably overlooked or glossed over in reports by psycho-

LUDWIG
BECHSTEIN
(1801–1860)

Bechstein was orphaned as a boy. He became a
pharmacist, then studied philosophy, history, and literature in Leipzig and Munich. Later he held positions as
librarian and archivist in several towns in Thuringia. He
wrote poetry as well as flat, heavy novels. As a writer he
is virtually forgotten today, save for one of his undertakings: his collection of German fairy tales and legends,
widely known under the title *Bechsteins Märchen.*

logists and physicians. One did not speak of these things, and yet it
was an obvious consequence of his earlier depressions and phobias.
Following his famous article on Brahms in the *Neue Zeitschrift für
Musik,* his *Dichtergarten,* published in May, 1854, was his last literary
effort. It was one of the last great satisfactions given a man whose
health was sadly but rapidly deteriorating. His attempt to assess the
musical situation of the day really dealt with the more general
problem of the meaning of art in contemporary society. His personal views were reflected in his withdrawal from the busy-ness of
the art world, from the company of other artists whose messages he
considered increasingly coarse and persistent. He had opened his
arms to humanity but, in the end, felt rejected. In doubting the
value and significance of what music and musicians around him
proclaimed he isolated himself, thus sealing his own fate.
Frightened by his illness he became incapable of further develop-

ment as an artist, indeed, of living. Wasielewski helped him with
editing and copying the two volumes of aphorisms which were
rejected by the publishers Breitkopf & Härtel.

A last letter to Joachim, written while still working on the
Dichtergarten, contains passages that hint at what was about to
happen: "I often wrote to you with sympathetic ink, and in this
letter, too, there are messages between the lines written in secret
ink; they will become legible later . . . My music now has become
silent, at least to the ear . . . I must close now. Darkness is setting
in."

On February 9, 1854, for the first time he heard tones that
would not stop. He wrote down a theme that had been dictated to
him by "angels," and began to write variations. But one morning
later the angelic sounds turned into demonic noises that caused him
to cry out in pain. Bedrest was prescribed, to no avail. He refused to
see Clara and would not allow her to be near him at night. Working
on the proofs for the cello concerto provided no relief from his
suffering.

It seems as though he was withdrawing from a state of acute
anxiety, aggravated by the infatuation of their house guest,
Johannes Brahms, for Clara.

After the decision to enter an asylum (in part to protect his
family from potentially aggressive behavior), he had a change of
mind: it now seemed best to seek a quick death. On the Monday
before Lent at noon, during a heavy rain storm, he quietly left his
bedroom, partly dressed and in bedroom slippers, and walked to the
center of the bridge over the nearby Rhine. He attracted the toll
keepers' attention when he asked to pay the then still required toll
with a silk handkerchief, having no money with him. He was seen
by fishermen as he jumped in the river who immediately rescued
him. But he was no longer wearing his wedding ring. The story
which Clara two years later recounted to her children is ambiguous:
"We were unable to find his wedding band. I suppose he threw it in
the river before he jumped, imagining that there it would be united
with my ring." She spoke of documents that confirm the story but
never produced them.

The obscure aspects of this crisis, involving three remarkable
people, are not likely to be cleared up. Who could know, even

The Endenich Asylum—place of Schumann's death

among their friends, what secrets there were among three loving people? In such cases diaries lose their value. As we endeavored to point out earlier, Schumann was able to express in his songs many thoughts and feelings which he would or could not express in other ways.

During the following months Clara received many expressions of friendship and encouragement but increasingly took refuge in music to find relief from the oppressive situation in which she now found herself. On March, 23 she took turns playing with Brahms and Grimm, four-hand, the *Spanisches Liederspiel.* After Schumann had entered the asylum Brahms, to the dismay of friends and relatives, assumed the position of head of the family and the godfather of Felix, born in June, 1854. Several months passed before Robert inquired after Clara; a year later he requested her picture. His condition improved rapidly; he was allowed to walk in the garden and soon resumed composing, setting the chorale *Wenn mein Stündlein vorhanden ist, aus dieser Welt zu scheiden* (When my

Hour Comes to Depart from this World). Together with some sheet music, Clara sent him a copy of *Des Knaben Wunderhorn* which pleased him greatly for he recalled having "composed much of it." His letters to Clara, however, contain few expressions of emotion nor do they make mention of the future, let alone of a future together. His focus was largely confined to his work, writing to Clara: "I should like to know how things are with the thematic catalogue that Breitkopf & Härtel were going to issue; there are some mistakes on it. Also: what about the *Concertstück in D Major,* for piano and orchestra, that you played in Holland; the *Gesänge der Frühe* for piano, the second *Spanisches Liederspiel, Neujahrslied, Requiem,* and *Faustszenen*—have any of these been published?" He also requested that a copy of Elisabeth Kulmann's poems be sent to him.

Information about Schumann's days in Endenich is more than scanty. Notes by Dr. Richarz who treated him are lost; only the results of the post-mortem examination are preserved in Zwickau.

On August 19, 1854 Brahms visited the asylum and was allowed to observe Schumann but not speak to him. His report to Clara sounded optimistic: improved condition, better appetite and sleep, no more hallucinations. Dr. Peters, the assistant physician, noted that the patient was extraordinarily silent. Accompanied by a male nurse he often walked to some of his favorite spots in Bonn. The day after Christmas, Joachim visited and even talked with Schumann. He, too, expressed hope of a cure. On January 11, 1855 Brahms played for the sick man. Another visit by Brahms, and Schumann's letters to him and to Joachim, reinforced the impression of continuing improvement.

In April, Schumann's interest in work took an upswing: music journals were ordered, he continued with some composing, and he corresponded with the publisher Simrock about publishing his last song cycle. At Brahm's instigation Simrock had written, inquiring about compositions to which Schumann replied that he "would be pleased if such a prestigious publisher would issue any of my compositions. I can offer Five Poems by Queen Mary Stuart, for mezzo soprano and piano. The translation by Baron Gisbert Vincke, from a collection of old English poems, is excellent. I have set them, respecting the simple, national quality of the poems in both the voice and piano parts." But Simrock had reservations and refused to publish them.

Das Glück von Edenhall was performed at the Leipzig Gewandhaus on October 23. This was the first occasion upon which the name Johannes Brahms appeared on a Gewandhaus program: Clara played the Andante and Scherzo of his Sonata in F Minor, Opus 4.

During his university vacation, Dr. Richarz's young nephew stayed at Endenich, where he occupied the room adjoining Schumann's. He played the piano regularly and the patient next door persistently knocked on the wall to correct every wrong note.

In his last letter to Clara, written in a stiff, awkward hand on May 5, 1855, Schumann declared that he wished to leave Endenich and move to a place nearer Düsseldorf. He indicated that restlessness and insomnia overcame him again, together with hearing imaginary voices and hallucinations involving his senses of smell and taste. Joachim immediately went to Endenich. The physicians with whom he talked considered Schumann's decline to be temporary. But the "terrible depression" deepened as reported by Wasielewski who found him sitting at the piano, "a man whose spiritual and mental capacities were completely shattered." Brahms continued occasional visits, and in the fall of 1855 planned to have him transferred to a sanatorium where he would be given cold water treatments. Conversation with Schumann now was no longer possible so Brahms brought a large atlas, from which Schumann made lists of cities and countries in alphabetical order.

Soon after, Schumann would no longer receive any visitors nor write anything. On July 23, 1856 he was near death, refusing nourishment, with edema in both legs. Clara was now requested, at long last, to visit him. Clara and Brahms travelled to Endenich, but on Brahms's urging she avoided the shock of seeing Robert. Four days later she felt she must return to the asylum, and on that Sunday she saw him, for the first time after 2½years of separation. She construed his smile as a sign of recognition for he was no longer able to speak. On the following day she and Brahms sat with him for several hours and he took a few drops of wine from her finger. His suffering ended on July 29.

The post-mortem, published in 1872, refers to "congestion of blood vessels in the brain" and "bone growths at the base of the skull," as well as "thickening of the meninges" and atrophy of the brain. It is worth noting that Schumann's physician considered his consciousness impaired but not destroyed—that he never lost clear awareness of his identity. Excessive depression, but never a complete disintegration of personality, as may happen during the last stages of paralysis marked his last weeks. An unassailable diagnosis has not been made to this day.

Schumann's friend Ferdinand Hiller in his funeral oration was the first to interpret Schumann's work in relation to his illness—a dubious construction which unfortunately became the accepted view. Clara notes: "Johannes and Joachim walked in front of the coffin. I had not published an announcement as I did not wish strangers to come. His dearest friends walked ahead of him; I, unnoticed, behind. Undoubtedly this was how he would have wished it." To this day there is no proof that Clara attended the funeral.

Chapter 27

It has appeared to many, and not only to those who observed from the periphery, that during his last decade Schumann failed to find the musical equivalents for the ideas he espoused. However, he had in point of fact reached a new starting point, a new stage of musical expression which, due to his illness, was never fully explored and developed.

Wasielewski's metaphor is apropos and to the point: an ore subjected to all the purification processes will yield a smaller quantity of pure metal. If Schumann moved away from that which was immediately comprehensible and readily performed to a vision of a simpler mode, the reason may lie in his silent but firm rebellion against an age that sought only magnificence and exaggeration. His music developed in the direction of silence, to a degree that seems unhealthy. He was prepared to bear the consequences of such an essentially uncreative attitude. From the chaos on the horizon there was, he felt, no escape, and the contradictions within his own existence, between purpose and reality, seemed insurmountable.

Schumann refused to lower himself to become an anti-Wagnerian, to adopt a hostile attitude toward that "mad fellow" whom he must have felt to be a rival and who, even much later, was not above spiteful remarks about the "family members" of the hated Mendelssohn. Schumann, experimenting with speech-related song, came close to the declamatory style of the giant of Bayreuth—but this was not intentional, but rather the result of Schumann's rigorous pursuit of a new and simple vision of music. Nietzsche branded as "neighbors," i.e., fellow travelers, those who were so influenced by Wagner that they lost their critical capacities

and taste. This charge cannot be levelled at Schumann.

Schumann could not and would not subscribe to a division between existence and purpose which typifies the modern mind. He turned to silence, to formulating plans for action that led to no action; to composing without tones; to benevolent support of the young while renouncing his own future. In his last ten years he composed fitfully yet feverishly. Had he been assigned to review his own works, as he did the music of others, he might have been at a loss to find words sufficiently harsh.

In the *Aphorisms* Schumann expressed his belief that the artist's mission was to "send light to the depth of the human heart." His vocal music reached this objective, even that of the darkest days. His outstanding songs soon made their way, affecting the genre far into the future. Their influence on later song writing may have been greater than that of Schubert. Richard Strauss, Hans Pfitzner, Othmar Schoeck are indebted to Schumann above all, whether they were prepared to admit it or not.

His art also affected French song, more slowly but just as surely. For example, note Gabriel Fauré's *Après un rêve,* where chord sequences in the accompaniment, harmonic progressions in descending fifths, and an abundance of dissonances treated as passing notes over a simple bass line were all clearly adopted from Schumann's song *Mein schöner Stern* (Example 91). Such affinities can also be found in songs by César Franck, Edouard Lalo and Henri Duparc. Once more, as in the case of Schubert, Franz Liszt prepared the way for Schumann with the publication in France of an arrangement of *Widmung,* for piano alone, in 1849. Six songs from the repertory of Jenny Lind were published there in 1855, and, in the following year, the Twelve Songs, Opus 39.

Hardly more than 40 of the more than 150 solo songs by Schumann are heard in recital today—a fact that does not reflect poorly on the rest. Blame for this narrow selection must be attributed to singers who prefer to stay with what they know, and to the public which always demands the "old favorites." Important as those favorites may be, they ought not to stand in the way of discovering the rest. Only familiarity with his entire oeuvre can lead to appreciation of a different Schumann speaking from each one of his songs.

Hermann Rosenwald's analysis of the *Lieder* repertory from Schubert's death to Schumann's beginnings, in which he clarifies the significance of Schumann's achievement, surely deserves mention here.

From the routine formulae of epigones, satisfied with their accomplishments, Schumann raised the art song to a new, and distinctive plane. He neither overlooked nor spurned the fine qualities of Romantic student songs of southwest Germany, despite the influence of formal aspects of music derived from Mendelssohn and his circle.

Schumann's successors may have traveled along different roads, but virtually all of them adopted or expanded his technique of fusing voice and accompaniment, and in particular the style revealed in his "Year of Songs."

The *Lied* was and remains an isolated and unique genre; Schumann was unable to change this. He had formulated a hypothesis for song independence with his statement that "political freedom may be the true nourishment of poetry." Today's song writers returned to this thought.

Schumann had set out on the road to simple, clear writing, without frills, but soon collided with the obstacles presented by a new *Zeitgeist* which favored pathos and heavy, florid writing. He was clearly aware that he lived in a time of transition. Like Agnes Carus and Henriette Voigt, the friends of his youth, he was always conscious of the shadow of death. He shared their belief that music must be elevated beyond the comfortable milieu of the Biedermeyer to purity and clarity. A note in Henriette Voigt's diary of 1836 which

Example 91

was not intended for others but was discovered after her death among her household books, speaks to this; "I see the hustle and bustle of today's music as a passing phase (granted that there are exceptions) which is bound to lead to better and clearer works. The struggle may be on now, but victory is not yet in sight."

But victory no longer was possible: the stream of music had burst the dam. In 1845, after ten years, Schumann had relinquished the editorship of his *Zeitschrift,* one reason being that much of what he had wished for in 1834 had been accomplished. But a sense of resignation relative to the course of history was also involved. Events were moving in directions that Schumann could not accept. Schumann the writer had warned: "The sky is strangely red: is it morning, is it evening? I do not know—but we must work to achieve light!"

We can obtain some idea about his own goals when we realize that he now distanced himself from his earlier, poetic piano compositions, considering them the product of a tumultuous, earlier phase of his life. In most of his later works, melodies are derived from contrapuntal elements, even if they are not developed contrapuntally. During his years of composition his melodies became shorter, tauter, and more muscular. He deleted final measures first written with soft endings; excised passages that he found supple or ingratiating. The individual voice lines had to mesh; legato lines had to be interrupted. Anything that sounded easy and full was suspect; the final form of a work had to be angular, precise. He was working toward a new stylistic goal that he was not allowed to reach; during this period of experimentation his efforts consisted largely of condensing and paring.

Throughout music history the relation between words and music has swung from one pole to the other. In his early life, Schumann's strong literary convictions clearly defined his position. Though he later distanced himself from the controversies, his music was invariably oriented to illuminating the text, clarifying what was being said, or not said, with words. Upon completion of *Kreisleriana,* he noted with deep satisfaction that he had succeeded in creating music which sounded *"sprachvoll aus dem Herzen"* (like eloquent speech, coming from the heart). Schumann indeed gave to his music a language all its own and by doing so contributed immeasurably to a richer and more varied expression of human spirituality.

Bibliography

Note: The reader may also wish to examine the extensive bibliography given in *The New Grove Dictionary of Music and Musicians,* S. Sadie, ed., London, 1980, vol. 16, pp. 867ff., especially p. 869 (vocal music).

Abbreviations

AfMW – Archiv für Musikwissenschaft
BzMw – Beiträge zur Musikwissenschaft
Diss. – Dissertation
DMZ – Deutsche Musikerzeitung
DR – Deutsche Revue
Fs. – Festschrift
Gb. – Die Grenzboten
JbP – Jahrbuch der Musikbibliothek Peters
Kgr.-Ber. – Kongress-Bericht
KW – Der Kunstwart
Mf – Die Musikforschung
MidS – Musik in der Schule
MiU – Musik im Unterricht
Mk – Die Musik
MuG – Musik und Gesellschaft
MWBl – Musikalisches Wochenblatt
NMZ – Neue Musik-Zeitung
NZfM – Neue Zeitschrift für Musik
RMTz – Rheinische Musik- und Theaterzeitung
SbRSG – Sammelbände der Robert Schumann-Gesellschaft

StMw – Studien zur Musikwissenschaft
VfMw – Vierteljahrsschrift für Musikwissenschaft
ZfMw – Zeitschrift für Musikwissenschaft

Abert, H.: Robert Schumann, Berlin 1903
Abert, H.: Wort und Ton in der Musik des 18. Jahrhunderts. In: AfMw V. 1923
Adorno, Th. W.: Coda: Schumanns Lieder-Kreis nach Eichendorff-Gedichten op. 39. In: Akzente. Zeitschrift f. Dichtung (München) 5, 1958

Batka, R.: Schumann. Leipzig n.d. [1891]
Bauer, M.: Die Lieder Franz Schuberts. Leipzig 1915
Beaufils, M.: Mythos und Maske bei Robert Schumann. In: SbRSG 2, 1966
Bie, O.: Robert Schumann. In: Das deutsche Lied. Berlin 1926
Boettcher, H.: Beethoven als Liederkomponist. Augsburg 1928
Boetticher, W.: Robert Schumann. Einführung in Persönlichkeit und Werk. Berlin 1941
Boetticher, W.: Robert Schumann in seinen Schriften und Briefen. Berlin 1942
Boucourechliev, A.: Robert Schumann in Selbstzeugnissen und Bilddokumenten. Hamburg 1965
Bücken, E.: Das deutsche Lied. Hamburg 1939
Bücken, E.: Die Lieder Beethovens. In: Beethoven-Jahrbuch II, 1925
Bücken, E.: Franz Schubert und Robert Schumann als Naturmaler.

In: Musikalische Charakterköpfe. Leipzig n.d. [1925]
Bücken, E.: Robert Schumann. Köln 1940
Busch, G.: C. Ph. E. Bach und seine Lieder. Regensburg 1956

Conrad, D.: Schumanns Liedkompositionen – von Schubert her gesehen. In: Mf XXIV, 1971
Creuzberg, E.: Robert Schumann. Leipzig 1955

Dahms, W.: Schumann. Berlin and Leipzig 1916
Degen, M.: Die Lieder von C. M. v. Weber. Freiburg 1923
Dohn, J.: Robert Schumann. Das Paradies und die Peri. Record album notes. Lüdenscheid 1974
Dräger, H. H.: Zur Frage des Wort-Tonverhältnisses im Hinblick auf Schuberts Strophenlied. In: AfMw XI, 1954

Eckhoff, A. (Ed.): Dichterliebe. Heine im Lied. Hamburg 1972
Edelmann, W.: Über Text und Musik in Robert Schumanns Sololiedern. Diss. Münster 1950
Eggebrecht, H. H.: Prinzipien des Schubertliedes. In: AfMw XXVII, 1970
Egger, R.: Die Deklamationsrhythmik Hugo Wolfs in historischer Sicht. Tutzing 1963
Eismann, G.: Robert Schumann. Ein Quellenwerk über sein Leben. Leipzig 1956
Eismann, G.: Robert Schumann. Eine Biographie in Wort und Bild. Leipzig 1956
Eismann, G.: Robert Schumanns Ehetagebücher entsiegelt. In: MuG I, 1951
Eismann, G.: Robert und Clara Schumanns Reise nach Russland. In: MuG 4, 1954
Erler, H.: Robert Schumanns Leben. Aus seinen Briefen geschildert. Berlin 1886

Feil, A.: Studien zu Schuberts Rhythmik. München 1966
Feldmann, F.: Zur Frage des »Liederjahres« bei Robert Schumann. In: AfMw 9, 1952
Friedlaender, M.: Balladen – Fragmente von Robert Schumann. In: JbP 4, 1897

Friedmann, A.: Robert Schumann und Friedrich Hebbel. In: NMZ 17, 1896

Geck, M.: Sentiment und Sentimentalität im volkstümlichen Liede Felix Mendelssohn-Bartholdys. In: In memoriam Hans Albrecht. Kassel 1962
Georgiades, T.: Schubert. Musik und Lyrik. Göttingen 1967
Gerber, R.: Formprobleme im Brahmsschen Lied. In: JbP 1932
Gerstenberg, W.: Schubertiade. Anmerkungen zu einigen Liedern. In: Fs. O. E. Deutsch. Kassel 1963

Haas, H.: Über die Bedeutung der Harmonik in den Liedern Franz Schuberts. Bonn 1957
Hanslick, E.: Schumann als Opernkomponist. In: Die moderne Oper. Berlin 1875
Höcker, K.: Clara Schumann. Regensburg 1938
Hoffmann, E. T. A.: Schriften zur Musik Ed. F. Schnapp. München 1963
Hueffer, F.: Robert Schumanns Briefe an A. W. von Zuccalmaglio. In: Die Poesie in der Musik Leipzig n.d. [1875]

Jansen, F. G.: Schumann und Vesque von Püttlingen. In: Gb 53/3, 1894
Jansen, F. G.: Die Davidsbündler. Aus Robert Schumann's Sturm- und Drangperiode. Leipzig 1883
Jansen, F. G.: Ungedruckte Briefe Robert Schumanns. In: Gb 57/3, 1898
Jansen, F. G.: Robert Schumanns Briefe. Neue Folge: Leipzig 1886

Kerner, D.: Robert Schumann. In: Kerner, D.: Krankheiten grosser Musiker. Stuttgart 1963
Kleemann, H.: Beiträge zur Ästhetik und Geschichte der Loeweschen Ballade. Halle 1913
Knaus, H.: Musiksprache und Werkstruktur in Schumanns »Liederkreis« München-Salzburg 1954
Kohut, A.: Robert Schumann und Richard Wagner. In: RMTz, 1906
Kreisig, M.: Robert Schumann und Heinrich Heine. Zum Todestag Robert Schumanns am 29. Juli. In: Zwickauer Tageblatt. 30. 7. 1925

Kretzschmer, H.: Geschichte des neuen deutschen Liedes I = Kleine Handbücher der Musikgeschichte nach Gattungen IV. Leipzig 1911

Lange-Eichbaum, W.: Robert Schumann. In: Genie, Irrsinn und Ruhm. München/Basel 1967

Lindner, O.: Geschichte des deutschen Liedes im 18. Jahrhundert. Leipzig 1871

Linke, N. and G. Kneip: Robert Schumann. Zur Aktualität moderner Musik. Wiesbaden 1978

Liszt, F.: Robert Schumann. In: Gesammelte Schriften Vol. 4. Leipzig 1882

Litzmann, B.: Clara Schumann. Ein Künstlerleben nach Tagebüchern und Briefen. Leipzig 1902–1908

Michaeli, O.: Robert Schumann und Richard Wagner. In: NMZ 14, 1893

Mies, P.: Stilmomente und Ausdrucksformen im Brahmsschen Lied. Leipzig 1923

Morik, W.: J. Brahms und sein Verhältnis zum deutschen Volkslied. Tutzing 1965

Moser, H. J.: Das deutsche Lied seit Mozart. Berlin and Zürich 1937

Moser, H. J.: Robert Schumanns Liederreihe (Kerner) und Liederkreis (Eichendorff). In: Das deutsche Lied seit Mozart. Berlin and Zürich 1937

Moser, H. J.: Robert Schumanns Liedschaffen. In: Das deutsche Lied seit Mozart. Berlin and Zürich 1937

Müller, G.: Geschichte des deutschen Liedes. Vom Zeitalter des Barock bis zur Gegenwart. = Geschichte der deutschen Literatur nach Gattungen, Vol. 3. München 1925

Müller-Blattau, J.: Das Verhältnis von Wort und Ton in der Geschichte der Musik. Stuttgart 1952

Müller-Reuter, T.: Aus Robert Schumanns Leben. Beiträge zur Schumann-Biographie. Nach Aufzeichnungen des Komponisten veröffentlicht. In: RMTz 11, 1910, Nr. 18

Nef, A.: Das Lied in der deutschen Schweiz im letzten Drittel des 18. und im Anfang des 19. Jahrhunderts. Zürich 1909

Ninck, M.: Schumann und die Romantik in der Musik. Heidelberg 1929

Oehlmann, W.: Robert Schumann. In: Liedführer, Leipzig 1973

Oehlmann, W.: Liszt, Schumann und George Sand über Chopin. In: Das Fünfminutenlexikon. Frankfurt a. M. 1950

Oehm, F.: Das Stimmungslied Schumanns. Diss. Leipzig 1919

Payk, T. R.: R. Schumann als Patient in Endenich. In: Confinia psychiatrica 1977

Penner, E.: Didaktische Prinzipien in Schumanns musikalischen Haus-und Lebensregeln. In: MidS 7, 1956

Pfordten, H. v. d.: Franz Schubert und das deutsche Lied. Leipzig 1928

Pfordten, H. v. d.: Robert Schumann. Leipzig 1920

Pfordten, H. v. d.: Robert Schumann. In: KW 23, 1910, Nr. 17

Pohl, R.: Erinnerungen an Robert Schumann. In: DR 2/4, 1878

Pohl, R.: Schumanns Genoveva. In: NZfM Vol. 51, 1859

Pollak-Schlaffenberg, J.: Die Wiener Liedmusik von 1770–1800. = StMw V. 1918

Porter, E. G.: Schubert's Song Technique. London 1961

Probst, G.: Robert Schumanns Oratorien. Wiesbaden 1975

Rehberg, P. and W.: Robert Schumann. Sein Leben und sein Werk. Zürich 1954

Reinecke, C.: Erinnerungen an Robert Schumann. In: DR 21/3 Septemberheft 1896

Reinecke, C.: Schumann. In: Meister der Tonkunst. Berlin and Stuttgart 1903

Reissmann, A.: Robert Schumann. Sein Leben und seine Werke. Berlin 1865

Rosenwald, H. H.: Geschichte des deutschen Liedes zwischen Schubert und Schumann. Berlin 1930

Rosenwald, H. H.: Die geschichtliche Bedeutung des Schumannschen Liedes. In: Mk 24/2, 1931/32

Sams, E.: Hat Schumann in seinen Werken Chiffren benützt? In: NZfM 127, 1966

Sams, E.: The Songs of Hugo Wolf. London 1962

Sams, E.: The Songs of Robert Schumann. London 1956

Schmidt, H. G.: Das Männerchorlied Franz Schuberts. Ein historisch-stilkritischer Beitrang zur Geschichte des deutschen Männerchorliedes im 19. Jahrhundert. Hildburghausen 1931

Schmitz, A.: Die ästhetischen Anschauungen R. Schumanns in ihren Beziehungen zur romantischen Literatur. In: ZfMw 3, 1920/21

Schnapper, E.: Die Gesänge des jungen Schubert vor dem Durchbruch des romantischen Liedprinzips. Bern 1937

Schneider, H.: R. Schumann. Manuskripte, Briefe, Schumanniana (Catalogue). Tutzing 1979

Schumann, A.: Der junge Schumann. Dichtungen und Briefe. Leipzig 1910

Schumann, C.: Jugendbriefe an Robert Schumann. Nach den Originalen mitgeteilt. Leipzig 1885

Schumann, E.: Robert Schumann. Ein Lebensbild meines Vaters. Leipzig 1931

Schumann, R.: Erinnerungen an Felix Mendelssohn-Bartholdy. In Facsimile, ed. by G. Eismann. Zwickau 1947

Schumann, R.: Gesammelte Schriften über Musik und Musiker. Leipzig 1854

Schumann, R.: Moskauer Gedichte. ed. by G. Eismann. In: BzMw I, 1959

Schuncke, M.: Die Künstlerfreundschaft zwischen Robert Schumann und Ludwig Schuncke. In: SbRSG 1, 1961

Schwab, H. W.: Sangbarkeit, Popularität und Kunstlied. Studien zu Lied und Liedästhetik der mittleren Goethezeit 1770–1814 = Studien zur Musikgeschichte des 19. Jahrhunderts Vol. 3. Regensburg 1965

Schwarmath, E.: Musikalischer Bau und Sprachvertonung in Schuberts Liedern. Tutzing 1969

Schwarz, W.: Robert Schumann als Musikerzieher. In: MiU (B) 51, 1960

Schweisheimer, W.: War Robert Schumann geisteskrank? In: DMZ 20, 1938

Seidlin, O.: Versuch über Eichendorff. Göttingen 1965

Seyfert, B.: Das musikalisch-volksthümliche Lied von 1770–1800. In: VfMw X, 1894

Siegfried, E.: Robert Schumanns Liedercyclus »Frauenliebe und-leben«. In: NZfM 70, 1903

Siegmund-Schultze, W.: Wort und Ton bei Robert Schumann. In: Kgr.Ber. der Gesellschaft für Musikforschung Hamburg 1956. Kassel and Basel 1956

Spitta, P.: Ein Lebensbild Robert Schumanns. Leipzig 1882

Stein, F.: Robert Schumann als Student in Heidelberg. In: NMZ 27, 1906

Stein, S.: Poem and Music in Hugo Wolf's Mörike Songs. In: Musical Quarterly LIII, 1967

Stolz, H.: Heine und Schumann. In: Das Tor, Düsseldorf 1956

Storck, K.: Robert Schumann, der Romantiker. In: Der Türmer (Stuttgart) July 1906

Sutermeister, H. M.: Das Rätsel um Robert Schumanns Krankheit. Bern 1959

Sutermeister, P.: Robert Schumann. Sein Leben nach Briefen, Tagebüchern und Erinnerungen des Meisters nach seiner Gattin. Zürich 1949

Thürmer, H.: Die Melodik in den Liedern von Hugo Wolf. Giebing üb. Prien (Chiemsee) 1970

Wasielewski, W. J. v.: Aus siebzig Jahren. Lebenserinnerungen. Stuttgart and Leipzig 1897

Wasielewski, W. J. v.: Robert Schumann. Dresden 1858

Wasielewski, W. J. v.: Schumanniana. Bonn 1883

Wörner, K. H.: Robert Schumann. Zürich 1949

Wolff, E.: Robert Schumann, Berlin 1906

Wolff, V. E.: Lieder Robert Schumanns in ersten und späteren Fassungen. Leipzig 1914

Index to the Vocal Compositions

(according to titles and first lines)

Index of Names

List of Illustrations

Sources for the illustrations are indicated by the following abbreviations: AK: Archiv für Kunst und Geschichte, Berlin BP: Bildarchiv Preussischer Kulturbesitz, Berlin BH: Bild-Archiv Kultur & Geschichte G. E. Habermann, Gräfelfing DS: Deutsche Staatsbibliothek (DDR), Berlin HP: Historia-Photo, Hamburg KH: Kurt Hoffmann, *Die Erstdrucke der Werke Robert Schumanns*, Hans Schneider, Tutzing, 1979 NO: Nasjonalgalleriet, Oslo PB: Private collection RS: Robert-Schumann-Haus, Zwickau

Portraits for the short biographical sketches were taken from the following sources:
AK: 52, 53, 63, 66, 72, 93, 98, 186
BP: 24, 46, 55, 65, 113, 117, 135, 160, 178, 179, 187, 196, 213
BH: 131, 139, 153, 157, 194
HP: 55, 58, 96, 102, 138, 170, 178, 183, 198